Towards a Mental Health System that Works

Research has established that there are efficacious psychological therapies for most common mental disorders. In *Towards a Mental Health System that Works,* psychologist Michael J Scott details the reforms necessary to ensure that consumers of services receive an evidence-based treatment.

This book examines:

- the social significance of interventions that target mental well-being and psychological disorder
- why treatments are 'lost in translation' from research to routine practice
- steps that can be taken towards a translation that better recognises the complexity of research and ensures fidelity to an evidence-based treatment protocol
- the deleterious effects of current provision on clients and therapists.

Towards a Mental Health System that Works is a valuable resource for therapists, mental health practitioners, Clinical Commissioning Groups and politicians, enabling them to critically evaluate service provision, distil what constitutes cost-effective evidence-based mental health practice across the whole spectrum of disorders and client populations, and chart a new direction. It also serves as a guide to consumers of mental health services, as well as their friends and family, allowing them to understand what they are likely to experience and what they can demand.

Michael J Scott is a Chartered Psychologist and Chartered Scientist, and has been consultant to a number of organisations. He specialises in the assessment and treatment of patients following trauma and regularly provides workshops on the cognitive behavioural treatment of psychological disorders. Michael is the editor of a published, four-volume work on traumatic stress and the author of twelve books and numerous chapters and papers.

Towards a Mental Health System that Works

A Professional Guide to Getting Psychological Help

Michael J Scott

LONDON AND NEW YORK

First published 2017
by Routledge
2 Park Square, Milton Park, Abingdon, Oxon OX14 4RN

and by Routledge
711 Third Avenue, New York, NY 10017

Routledge is an imprint of the Taylor & Francis Group, an informa business

© 2017 Michael J Scott

The right of Michael J Scott to be identified as author of this work has
been asserted by him in accordance with sections 77 and 78 of the
Copyright, Designs and Patents Act 1988.

All rights reserved. No part of this book may be reprinted or reproduced or
utilised in any form or by any electronic, mechanical, or other means, now
known or hereafter invented, including photocopying and recording, or in
any information storage or retrieval system, without permission in writing
from the publishers.

Trademark notice: Product or corporate names may be trademarks or
registered trademarks, and are used only for identification and explanation
without intent to infringe.

British Library Cataloguing in Publication Data
A catalogue record for this book is available from the British Library

Library of Congress Cataloging in Publication Data
Names: Scott, Michael J., 1948 – author.
Title: Towards a mental health system that works : a professional guide
    to getting psychological help / Michael J Scott.
Description: Abingdon, Oxon ; New York, NY : Routledge, 2017. |
    Includes bibliographical references.
Identifiers: LCCN 2016027271 | ISBN 9781138932951 (hbk) |
    ISBN 9781138932968 (pbk) | ISBN 9781315677699 (ebk)
Subjects: | MESH: Mental Health Services—standards | Mental Health
    Services—supply & distribution | Quality of Health Care—standards |
    Health Services Accessibility | Mental Health | Great Britain
Classification: LCC RA790.6 | NLM WM 30 FA1 | DDC 616.8900941—dc23
LC record available at https://lccn.loc.gov/2016027271

ISBN: 978-1-138-93295-1 (hbk)
ISBN: 978-1-138-93296-8 (pbk)
ISBN: 978-1-315-67769-9 (ebk)

Typeset in Times New Roman
by Apex CoVantage, LLC

Contents

List of tables	vii
List of figures	viii
Towards a mental health system that works	1

PART I
A public health approach to mental health — 3

1	Mental well-being and stress	5
2	Positive psychology	13
3	Overstating preventative capacity and diagnostic creep	17

PART II
Crystallising mental health problems — 21

4	Difficulties in deciding whether something is wrong	23
5	Social support, psychological disorders and psychoeducation	39

PART III
The quantity and quality of psychological help available — 67

6	Availability of psychological therapy services	69
7	Quality of psychological therapy services	81

vi *Contents*

PART IV
Realising the potential of psychological therapies 103

8 Creating a mental health system fit for purpose 105

9 Maintaining the social significance of psychological therapy 117

10 Wounded healers 127

Postscript 133

Appendix A   Warwick-Edinburgh Mental Well-being Scale 135
Appendix B   First step questionnaire/interview 136
Appendix C   Standardised assessment of personality –
abbreviated scale 139
Appendix D   Depression survival manual 140
Appendix E   Summary of criteria for empirically supported
psychological therapies – Chambless and Hollon (1998) 155
References 156
Index 168

Tables

1.1	NHS advice for improving mental well-being	6
5.1	Interrater reliability of diagnoses from the initial DSM-5 field trials	47
5.2	Screen for PTSD	56
5.3	Screen for substance abuse/dependence	56
7.1	Attrition and recovery in an IAPT programme for anxiety and depression in routine practice from Richards and Borglin (2011)	82
7.2	Anonymised example from IAPT documentation	94
7.3	IAPT outcome	98
7.4	Little variation in recovery rate by disorder	98
9.1	Treatment fidelity scales for depression	123

Figures

1.1	Distribution of mental health	7
5.1	Stages of change based on Prochaska and Di Clemente (1992)	40
5.2	Intrapsychic and interpersonal determinants of emotion	42
5.3	The mechanics of recovery	53
8.1	A model of evidence-based practice	112
9.1	The competence engine	124
10.1	Stress – when demands exceed resources	130

Towards a mental health system that works

Michael J Scott

Mental health difficulties are ubiquitous, but the laudable pursuit of mental well-being has produced uncertain outcomes. The good news is that evidence-based treatments (EBTs) for many psychological disorders exist. The bad news is that in routine practice psychological therapy is a scarce resource. Even with the planned expansion of current services, three quarters of those affected will not receive help for the foreseeable future. The even worse news is that psychological therapies delivered in practice more often than not fail a 'Trading Standards Test'. This volume addresses the question of how to improve the quality and quantity of psychological therapy, by conducting reliable assessments of need, ensuring fidelity to EBTs, utilising a multi-dimensional model of competence, making greater use of groups, reducing reliance on surrogate outcome measures and utilising supervision for quality control. But such improvements can only take place when the mental health workforce is no longer demoralised and Clinical Commissioning Groups, professional bodies, service providers and politicians have a clear understanding of and commitment to socially significant psychological therapies. This volume seeks to raise the consciousness of professionals, politicians, consumers of mental health services and their friends and family of ideal provision and the gap between it and current provision, acting as a motivational force to bridge that gap.

Introduction

> I look at the data and I'm concerned. I don't see a reduction in the rate of suicide or prevalence of mental illness or any measure of morbidity. I see it in other areas of medicine and I don't see it for mental illness. That was the basis for my comment that people with mental illness deserve better.

> Dr. Thomas Insel, Director of the US National Institute on Mental Health (2013)

The first section of this volume explores whether shifting the focus from psychological disorder to a broader concept of mental well-being and targeting the latter might be a better way forward. Unfortunately, evidence for the effectiveness of

2 *Towards a mental health system that works*

preventative mental health interventions is not compelling. The second section of this volume looks at problem solving of mental health difficulties/disorders with first a clear crystallisation of the problem, a locking on to those problems, and the need to by-pass stigma and utilise evidence-based treatments. [The term *evidence-based treatments* (EBTs) is used interchangeably with *evidence-supported treatments* (ESTs) in this volume.] In the third section the focus is on how current services facilitate or impede the problem-solving process. It is suggested that the main player in the provision of psychological therapies, Improving Access to Psychological Therapy (IAPT), is falling far short of the UK Government target of 50% of affected individuals fully recovering from their disorder with treatment. In the final section there is a critical examination of what has gone wrong with provision of psychological therapy in routine practice: exaggerating the reach and power of guided self-help, unreliable assessment, failure to track fidelity to an evidence-based treatment protocol, inadequate supervision and a demoralised workforce. This is followed by the delineation of new pathways to mental health involving the following: reliable triage, direction of clients to interventions that are needs led and not short-term cost led, ensuring that therapists adhere to protocols and deliver them skilfully, greater use of group interventions and supervision that is primarily a catalyst for evidence-based treatment. It is suggested that such changes can only be maintained by an organisational climate that is not overly involved and critical. Further service providers can themselves only flourish when Clinical Commissioning Groups, general practitioners (GPs) and the Care Quality Commission are as concerned about the quality of provision as the quantity and are not duped by the use of surrogate measures of outcome.

Part I

A public health approach to mental health

1 Mental well-being and stress

The World Health Organisation [WHO (2004)] defines mental health as 'a state of well-being in which every individual realizes his or her own potential, can cope with the normal stresses of life, can work productively and fruitfully, and is able to make a contribution to her or his community' and adds, 'Health is a state of complete physical, mental and social well-being and not merely the absence of disease or infirmity'. Thus not having a recognised psychiatric disorder might be a necessary condition for mental health, but may not be sufficient. WHO offers criteria for psychiatric disorders [ICD-10 (2010)] but highlights the need to also address mental well-being, which appears to be an operational approximation to 'happiness'. Whether addressing mental well-being (MWB) will prevent the development of mental 'disorders' remains to be demonstrated, but there may be benefits in addressing MWB for its own sake. MWB is the 'new kid on the block' and there is little research on how it can be effectively targeted by comparison with the evaluations of treatments for psychiatric disorders.

The NHS website (www.nhs.uk) invites visitors to complete a 'wellbeing self-assessment tool' [it is actually the Warwick-Edinburgh Mental Well-being Scale (WEMWBS) developed by Tennant et al. (2007), reproduced by permission in Appendix A]. The items include 'I've been feeling optimistic about the future', 'I've been feeling close to other people' and 'I've been interested in new things', and respondents answer on a five-point scale, from 'none of the time' to 'all of the time', how frequently they would agree with the item. Completing this two-minute test online today (September 2015) I was told I scored 59 out of a possible 70 and that most people score between 41 and 59. Further I was advised to 'get active, keep learning and connect with others'. 'Hmm', I thought, and mused whether this instrument was just for the 'worried well' and whether it would actually reach those who were low on the WEMWBS; if it does it might be useful. But given that it is so readily available and entirely private, even if a tiny proportion of those low on the WEMWBS access it this may be a step forward but it remains to be seen how many of them would actually act on the advice proffered. Perhaps more might do so if those with low WEMWBS could avail themselves of guided help say via e-mail.

6   *Part I*

The NHS website advises the following steps which 'we can all take to improve our wellbeing':

Table 1.1 NHS advice for improving mental well-being

- Connect – connect with the people around you: your family, friends, colleagues and neighbours. Spend time developing these relationships.
- Be active – you don't have to go the gym. Take a walk, go cycling or play a game of football. Find the activity you enjoy and make it part of your life.
- Keep learning – learning new skills can give you a sense of achievement and a new confidence. So why not sign up for that cooking course, start learning to play a musical instrument or figure out how to fix your bike.
- Give to others – even the smallest act can count, whether it's a smile, a thank you or a kind word. Larger acts, such as volunteering at your local community centre, can improve your mental well-being and help you build new social networks.
- Be mindful – be more aware of the present moment, including your feelings and thoughts, your body and the world around you. Some people call this awareness 'mindfulness', and it can positively change the way you feel about life and how you approach challenges.

It is extremely difficult to give across-the-board advice to anyone. It is easy to see how the advice in Table 1.1 might be useful to an anxious student starting university, but an elderly person might have few if any people to connect with because of bereavements, be physically (and/or financially) unable to utilise public transport, never have been a reader or great mixer and their nearest approach to being 'mindful' might be prayer at school assemblies many years ago. The general advice may go unheeded unless tailored to the individual.

Mental well-being value for money?

Though the WEMWBS is a measure of mental well-being, it is not clear whether it would measure changes following an intervention, for example, whether elderly people in receipt of a weekly telephone call from a volunteer would change significantly on this measure compared to a person not receiving a call service. Changes of score of three on the WEMWBS have been hailed as important and eight or more as definitely important [Maheswaran et al. (2012)] in a variety of populations, including parents attending a group parent-training programme and users of a computerised CBT skill training course. But caution is needed in extrapolating from these findings, as there is no indication of how the results on the WEMWBS correlate with other psychometric tests. For example Maheswaran et al. (2012) cite evaluation with a group parent-training programme, but there is no data furnished on whether this intervention was effective using an established measure such as the Eyberg Child Behavior Inventory [Eyberg and Ross (1978)] and its correlation with that measure. In this context it is not clear that the WEMWBS is a valid measure representing changes that are socially significant, i.e. make a real-world difference.

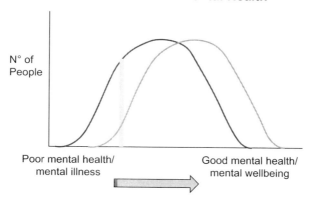

Figure 1.1 Distribution of mental health

The Rose Hypothesis. Shifting the mean of a population distribution reduces the proportion of people with a diagnosis

Given that well-being interventions are far less costly than individual psychological interventions and can be made widely available, they offer the enticing prospect of making a difference to the nation's mental health in an affordable way. But it does depend on the size of the shift (if any) that it makes. Stewart-Brown's (2015) public health perspective on mental health can be summarised using Figure 1.1 [Stewart-Brown (2015)].

Figure 1.1 shows that people's mental health follows a bell-shaped curve (normal distribution) with most people in the middle and a few at either extreme. If it is possible to shift the bell to the right as in Figure 1.1, many fewer people will have serious mental health problems needing professional attention.

This public health perspective on mental health can be applied to bullying. Approximately one half of those experiencing bullying at school experience mental health problems as an adult, with 8% of thirteen-year-olds experiencing bullying on a daily basis and 40% of children having been bullied in the last twelve months [Anti-bullying Alliance (2015)]. A third of those bullied avoid school or college as a way of coping. It may be that efforts to use fellow students to mentor children who are bullied may create just the sort of societal shift envisioned in Figure 1.1, but it remains to be demonstrated.

Sociotherapy

In societies where the social fabric has been destroyed, it may be possible to make the public health shift shown in Figure 1.1 by using sociotherapy. Jansen et al. (2015) have described the sociotherapy programme that operates in

8 *Part I*

Rwanda. In 1994 genocide against the Tutsi erupted in Rwanda; within a population of 7 million, an estimated 800,000 people were killed in 100 days. It was not just a matter of killings but a social violation, in that victims and aggressors lived side by side in the same communities. The aim of sociotherapy is to build safe, trustful and supportive group environments to facilitate the alleviation of both individual and social distress. Sociotherapy participants meet weekly in a group of 10–15 people in a place of safety in their community, for 3 hours over 15 sessions; these groups address safety, trust, care, respect, new life orientations and memory. The primary aim is for participants to regain their capacity to relate and connect with others. Participants are not diagnosed and may self-refer. It is hypothesised that improved mental health outcomes are a consequence of this process. Jansen et al. (2015) observe that whilst there is no hard evidence to substantiate this claim, a study by Scholte et al. (2011) using the Self-Reporting Questionnaire did show participants reporting significantly fewer mental health symptoms than those in a control group, and this improvement persisted at an eight-month follow up. It may be that such an approach would also be helpful in refugee populations in high-income countries.

I have just picked up a booklet announcing Liverpool's 6th Annual World Mental Health Day Festival, to take place on October 10, 2015. It tells me that in my home town:

> one in three appointments with GPs are about things such as depression, anxiety, stress, panic and other so-called mental health problems. These are higher in Liverpool than in most other parts of the country and can be linked to causes such as low income, unemployment, poor housing and loneliness. It's estimated that 26% of the Liverpool population experience these sorts of difficulties in any given year.

The scale of the problem is clearly vast, and the festival is a response by local organisations to 'raise awareness, challenge stigma and promote wellbeing'. The range of events is extensive, including 'mental health first aid lite training', 'volunteer drop in sessions', 'art workshops' and an assembly of choirs. But do such collective organisational endeavours actually shift the well-being distribution, the bell curve? Whilst it is a consummation devoutly to be wished, their effects are simply unknown. The National Institute for Health and Care Excellence have a raft of documents relating to mental health and well-being, including 'Mental wellbeing and older people' (2015), which suggests the benefits of walking and exercise, and 'Promoting mental wellbeing at work overview' (2015). This latter offers a definition of well-being at work:

> Mental wellbeing is a dynamic state in which the individual is able to develop their potential, work productively and creatively, build strong and positive relationships with others and contribute to their community. It is enhanced when an individual is able to fulfil their personal and social goals and achieve

Mental well-being and stress 9

a sense of purpose in society. Mental wellbeing at work is determined by the interaction between the working environment, the nature of the work and the individual.

Thus, beyond the organisations with an explicit mental health focus, others such as employers and churches have a commitment to building community, lessening isolation and helping those troubled; in a similar way schools are encouraged to become part of the community with fun runs, etc. Helping us 'put our own inner house in order' [Schumacher (2011)] is such a mammoth task that it requires all to 'put their hands to the pump', but with some uncertainty as to whether 'well-being' efforts are making any difference, this task is also a necessary act of faith.

The task of putting 'our own inner house in order' [Schumacher (2011)] is a concern of a plethora of agencies, and Schumacher (2011) claims that 'traditional wisdom' is the power house for this refurbishment. But traditional wisdom does not advocate the direct pursuit of happiness (or arguably its update/operationalisation mental well-being); rather, the focus is on virtue and a life of great meaning as the ultimate reference point, pursued even when what we commonly take to be happiness may not be present. Thus a life of great meaning/virtue is not necessarily a life of great happiness at every point. In this perspective it is not the roles we perform that confer worth, but worth is intrinsic to the metaphysical narrative; such a narrative can be religious, e.g. a Christian believing, 'And even the very hairs of your head are all numbered. So don't be afraid; you are worth more than many sparrows' [Mathew 10:30–31], and involving pursuit of the seven virtues (faith, hope, charity, fortitude, justice, prudence and temperance). But equally the narrative can be non-religious, e.g. a Marxist whose actions and worth are dependent on his or her involvement in the class struggle. It may be that happiness is a much shallower concept than meaning and it could be that it is the loss of meaning and virtue that leads to mental health difficulties.

Values and science

A few days ago I donated to a food bank. I don't know that this will improve anyone's mental (or for that matter physical) well-being; I can't prove it. Though I think the action is justified, its foundation lies only partly in a scientific paradigm (I know that a significant number of the population find it extremely difficult to manage on benefits or tax credits) but also in a complementary but separate ethical paradigm of what is 'good' (one ought not to walk by on the other side of the road when people are in need). As McGrath (2015) has persuasively argued, there is a need to interweave a scientific paradigm with a separate ethical paradigm to move forward. Further, science describes what 'is'; it is not possible to derive an 'ought' from an 'is', i.e. prescription does not follow from description. The scientific and ethical strands, far from being antagonistic, reinforce each other, making a rope that can be climbed. To give an example of this, as I am writing (with Radio 4 on in the background, October 14, 2015) I have just overheard a news

10 *Part I*

item featuring researchers from Edinburgh University describing pressures academics are under to publish papers in prestigious journals and to secure research grants. These researchers found that in only one in five studies reviewed in the biological sciences were adequate steps being taken to ensure that bias was not present in the assessment of outcome, for example, where a medication was involved ensuring that the research assessor did not know who had taken what medication, i.e. was 'blind' (The same point has been made by Holman et al. [2015]). The science clearly needs reinforcing by an ethical paradigm about a need for honesty. But following McGrath's (2015) argument, science itself cannot declare that honesty is necessary; no experiment would reveal this, rather it is a matter for philosophy/theology. Thus the 'good' and 'faith' are located in a complementary framework to science. The Edinburgh researchers opined that the failure to counteract bias in research was not confined to the biological sciences. In later chapters I will make the point that it also applies to the evaluation of psychological interventions.

Anything less than flourishing is a problem

Those without a psychological disorder are not a homogenous group, functioning about the same and markedly different to those who have a psychological disorder. Keyes (2005), found that only about two in ten of the adults free of mental disorder could be classified as flourishing or completely mentally healthy. Almost as many adults were mentally unhealthy (i.e. languishing) as were mentally healthy (i.e. flourishing) and most adults were moderately mentally healthy. Those not flourishing had greater levels of dysfunction in terms of work reductions, health limitations and psychosocial functioning. Moreover, pure languishing was as dysfunctional as psychological disorder. Psychological disorder when combined with languishing was worse than psychological disorder alone. These findings led Keyes (2005) to conclude that there is not a simple continuum of mental well-being with psychological disorder at one pole and mental health at the other pole (represented by a horizontal line), but a dual continuum with a flourishing-languishing axis (represented by a vertical line) bisecting it, forming a cross. Thus each person's functioning could be located by their score on the horizontal axis and their score on the vertical axis (coordinates), and these in turn predicted risk of developing cardiovascular disease [Keyes (2004)]. There is therefore reason to focus on the needs of those without a psychological disorder as with those with a psychological disorder.

Stress

The term *mental well-being* has been in vogue for the past decade; prior to that the main focus was on stress, which was defined by the Health and Safety Executive (2016) as 'the process that arises where work demands of various types and combinations exceed the person's capacity and capability to cope'. More generally stress was an imbalance between environmental demands, e.g. marital, occupational and personal resources. Thus the term *stress* has been located in a particular context. Implicit in the notion of stress was the idea that dis-stress might be as much a product of a toxic environment, e.g. a bullying boss, as it is of the individual, e.g. the particular way that they perceive the job tasks. By contrast the term *mental well-being* shifts the focus away from environmental concerns to ensuring that the individual can handle normal hassles.

In 2014–2015 a diagnosis of stress accounted for 35% of all work-related ill health and 43% of all working days lost due to illness [Health and Safety Executive website February 14th 2016]. Further the condition was much more prevalent in public services, particularly education, health and social care. (Outside of the work context over-demanding relationships are equally likely to exert a toll, but their effect has been less documented save for the extremes of spouse abuse.) The most stressed occupation was social worker, followed in order by teacher, fire brigade, paramedic, vet, clerical and administration, management (private sector), prison officer, researcher (academic) and police officer. Amongst those in managerial roles more than three quarters considered creating a work-life balance as the employee's responsibility, not theirs. Service providers liaising with employers in promoting mental well-being is likely to be less threatening than talking about stress but may do a disservice to individuals. Employers can within a mental well-being umbrella refer for counselling, a demonstration of care without any acknowledgement that they may be part of the problem. The main work factors cited as causing work-related stress, depression or anxiety were workload pressures, including tight deadlines and too much responsibility and a lack of managerial support [Health and Safety Executive (2016)]. Arguably the term *stress* has more utility than *mental well-being* and avoids an unnecessary individualising of problems. Indeed stress appears to be a major problem for NHS psychological therapists; in February 2016 the British Psychological Society published the results of a survey of over 1,300 therapists and found that 'the overall picture is one of burnout, low morale and worrying levels of stress'. It is difficult to see how the needs of consumers can be meaningfully met by such wounded healers, a point to which I will return in the final chapter of this volume.

Stressor related disorders

DSM-5 [American Psychiatric Association (2013)] has distilled a category of 'Trauma and Stressor Related Disorders' to indicate that distress is often a transaction between the environment and the individual; this is a move away from seeing the majority of disorders as predominantly a product of intrapsychic difficulties. In creating a category of stressor related disorders, the diagnosis of adjustment disorder has been removed from its dustbin status as a diagnosis of last resort to be used when no other label seems to apply, and given credence as a response to an identifiable stressor, but it is not suggested that this is necessarily treated with medication or psychotherapy, i.e. it is not intrinsically abnormal. The following example illustrates how usage of this category can result in more

12 *Part I*

realistic help being proffered than with vague usage of terms like *stress, anxiety* and *depression*:

> *Sonya was descending the stairs of her rented property; as she leant on the banister it gave way and she fell down the stairs, injuring her lower back. She was particularly distressed at this as she was a single parent with a two-year-old daughter to care for. Sonya managed to ring her mother for help and attended her GP the next day. Her records showed that before the baby's birth she had suffered from what was variably termed anxiety, depression or stress, as she was unsure whether the baby's father was going to be supportive. Sonya was prescribed diazepam to manage her back pain. Her landlord had promised a repair that had not materialized, and although she was too fearful to sleep upstairs, she would negotiate them taking her daughter to bed (her daughter was not yet potty trained). She was having difficulty sleeping because of her back pain and she returned to her GP two weeks later in a distressed state, saying that the repair had still not been carried out. The GP wanted to prescribe Zopiclone (a hypnotic) but she would not take it because she felt she would miss hearing the baby cry in the night. The GP decided to refer for physiotherapy and to the local IAPT (Improving Access to Psychological Therapy Services). Sonya attended twelve therapy sessions and said she found them 'a bit helpful'. She was also given thought records, encouraged to be active and asked to complete questionnaires weekly. She said that she found it 'a bit helpful' but could not specify in what way it was helpful and was given no diagnosis. Sonya said that her mood did not improve until she was rehoused by a housing association eleven months later. An independent diagnostic interview revealed that she had suffered from a DSM-5 defined adjustment disorder following the incident that lasted until she was rehoused. Sonya did not need psychological therapy following this fall; she needed an advocate so that she could be rehoused as soon as possible. The adjustment disorder diagnostic label focuses as much attention on the stressor as the individual and the latter can be the most appropriate foci, rather than wasting scarce psychological therapy resources.*

2 Positive psychology

Positive psychology's focus is on the non-psychological disorder end of the mental well-being spectrum. In the preface to his book *Flourish* (2011), Martin Seligman expresses his fatigue and frustration at working as a psychologist for many years at the psychological disorders end of the well-being spectrum. Seligman (2011) has become a leading advocate of focusing on well-being—as the title of his book suggests, helping all to flourish. On this side of the Atlantic, Layard and Clark (2014), in their book *Thrive*, have espoused a similar message, albeit that they are more positive than Seligman about the benefits of disorder-based psychological interventions. At www.authentichappiness.org, which is under the auspices of the University of Pennsylvania, Seligman provides scales for measuring inter alia flourishing and depression.

Building on sand?

Despite his advocacy of Positive psychology Seligman (2011) sounds a cautionary note: 'It is certainly not that the evidence is irresistible. The science is quite new, and the evidence, if not scanty, is far from irresistible'. He extols the virtues of Positive psychology programmes in a wide range of contexts, including schools, the army (to prevent PTSD) and businesses, contending that a happy workforce is more productive. Seligman (2011) also quotes a conversation with Lord Layard (a House of Lords Peer) in which the latter told him that in order for an enterprise to get government backing it was not necessary to prove unequivocally that something worked (in this instance Positive psychology) for it to be adopted, as this watermark was almost never achieved, but that a combination of sufficient evidence and political will was enough. Seligman reports that he was much encouraged by this advice. However, I will argue later that this lowering of the bar of the burden of proof has led to the UK Government's continuing endorsement of the Improving Access to Psychological Therapies Programme fuelled by the prime movers behind the inception of IAPT, Layard and Clark (2014).

14 *Part I*

Does Positive psychology make a socially significant difference?

But how much of a difference does Positive psychology make? Its justification lies in a public health framework, in which efforts to stop people smoking or provide clean running water have paid huge dividends and are an acknowledged complementary measure to the treatment of diseases such as cancer. Bolier et al. (2013) have performed a meta-analysis of randomised controlled trials of Positive psychology and found that the effect sizes are small, i.e. the shift in the position of the bell curve in Figure 1.1 (Chapter One) is small. Effect size is a measure of the difference in the scores at the end of treatment/waiting list between those who have undergone a Positive psychology intervention and those in another group who had not, divided by the spread of the initial scores in each group (technically the pooled standard deviation). An effect size of 1.0 would mean that the average person in the treated group would score 1 standard deviation less than the average person in the comparison group. Amongst the fourteen studies considered by Bolier et al. (2013) for preventing depression the effect size (ES) was just 0.23. The effect size for subjective well-being (appraisal of one's own life as a whole) was 0.34, and the ES for subjective well-being was 0.20. Further all the studies, except for two, were confined to only those who completed treatment; there was no intention to treat analysis for twelve of the studies. An intention to treat analysis enables a statement to be made about the real-world effects of an intervention, as it can be the case that those who complete a treatment are atypical in some way. The two studies that did perform an intention to treat analyses had insignificant effect sizes. In addition most studies involved people who had volunteered to enter a programme. No studies have been conducted of any anxiety disorder and Positive psychology.

Positive psychology – achieving a balance with psychological therapy

The well-being focus can be a distraction from focussing on the treatment of recognised psychological disorders; Seligman (2011) says that he surprised the military by wanting to talk about the prevention of PTSD rather than its treatment:

> Focusing on the pathologies of depression, anxiety, suicide, and PTSD was the tail wagging the dog. What the army could do was to move the entire distribution of the reaction to adversity in the direction of resilience and growth. This would not only help prevent PTSD but also increase the number of soldiers who bounce back readily from adversity.

Seligman justified this focus by saying that half of soldiers with PTSD were in the bottom 15% of those with mental and physical health problems [Leard et al. (2009)], implying that energies would be better spent targeting this population, notwithstanding that there are no evidence-based strategies for preventing PTSD! Whilst it may be the case that people with a pre-existing history of anxiety or depression catastrophise more, there is no evidence that teaching the most vulnerable military personnel to de-catastrophise would prevent the onset of PTSD post-trauma. Further, the Leard et al. (2009) study that Seligman relied upon used only self-report measures to assess PTSD symptoms; there were no standardised reliable diagnostic interviews conducted, and the authors admitted that they had used a surrogate for a diagnostic interview.

The focus on post-traumatic growth can also distract from the very real needs of those with diagnosable PTSD. Whilst the latter do on occasion mention some positive benefit post-trauma, a change of priorities, e.g. 'I spend more time now with the kids than at work', the overwhelming effect of the condition is negative. Those not suffering any psychological disorder post-trauma may feel they have 'grown' in some way, and whilst it might be useful to understand how they have managed this feat of resilience, there is no evidence that this has been identified in a manner that could be used to prevent PTSD. This PTSD exemplar does raise questions about the balance to be struck in funding well-being promotion and evidence-based psychological treatments.

The current enthusiasm for Positive psychology should be tempered by the possibility that 'Positive Psychology Is Mainly for Rich White People', as suggested by the title of Professor James Coyne's August 21, 2013 blog post. He cites Fredrickson's [Fredrickson and Losada (2005)] claim that a balance of 2.9 of positive to negative feelings was necessary to flourish. This was based on the use of the Short Flourishing Scale, which asked respondents how often in the past week they would have endorsed 'that you had something important to contribute to society', 'that you belonged to a community', 'that our society is a good place, or is becoming a better place, for all people', 'that people are basically good', and 'that the way our society works made sense to you'. The claims for this positivity ratio were found to be unfounded following rigorous statistical analysis [Brown et al. (2013)].

Values and mental health

Power (2015) has performed a valuable critique of Positive psychology and argues that happiness is a somewhat illusory goal and that resilience, adaptability in the face of adversity, psychological flexibility, and a sense of generativity and creativity are far more achievable as life goals. He questions the Positive psychology theme that 'blissful happiness is ten easy steps away'. However, he takes it as self-evident that one should pursue close relationships and engage in valued roles. But if these are not a means to happiness, on what basis should they be pursued? He suggests that happiness cannot be directly sought but is a by-product of close relationships and valued roles. Interestingly, Power (2015) cites the American Declaration of Independence as a trigger for this 'pursuit of happiness': 'We hold these truths to be self-evident – that all men are created equal; that they are endowed by their Creator with certain inalienable rights, that among these are life, liberty, and

16   *Part I*

the pursuit of happiness'. However the American Declaration of Independence, with the exception of the phrase 'the pursuit of happiness', is a reflection of the Judeo-Christian tradition. Within this tradition there is no focus on the pursuit of happiness per se; rather, happiness is conceived as a by-product of the good life, by which is meant a virtuous/moral life, and curiously there are echoes of this in Power's (2015) thesis, though the latter is avowedly atheistic. But this tradition would provide the basis for seeking the close relationships and performing the valued roles that Power (2015) espouses.

3 Overstating preventative capacity and diagnostic creep

It is obviously much better to prevent a disorder developing than to treat a disorder, but the success to date of traditional medicine in preventing disorder is limited. Frances (2015) has observed:

> With few exceptions (e.g. screening for lung cancer in smokers or colon cancer in everyone), the testing is often not good for the patients – not really improving outcomes, while further burdening them with aggressive, expensive, and unnecessary treatments. And the waste to society runs to hundreds of billions of dollars a year that could be better used treating really sick people. . . . Preventative medicine is a terrific goal gone badly astray because it became industrialized and enslaved by profit and hype.

He then goes on to point out how in the development of DSM-5 [American Psychiatric Association (2013)] there was a proposal to introduce a new diagnosis called 'psychosis risk syndrome' that would encourage the early identification and preventive treatment of youngsters who might otherwise eventually become schizophrenic. Frances (2015) then gave five compelling arguments against such a category: 1. Most people getting the scary-sounding diagnosis 'psychosis risk' would in fact be mislabelled – in the normal course of events, only a very small proportion would ever become psychotic; 2. There is no proven way to prevent psychosis, even in those really at risk; 3. Many people would suffer collateral damage, receiving unnecessary antipsychotic drugs that can cause obesity, diabetes, heart diseases, and likely a shortened life expectancy; 4. There would be a stigma associated with such a diagnostic label and unnecessary worry that psychosis is just around the corner; 5 having a 'risk' is not commensurate with having a 'disease'. Fortunately this new category was not included in DSM-5, but the discussions surrounding it provide a salutary lesson in overemphasising the benefits of prevention.

No matter how one refines diagnostic criteria for a disorder, there will always be a fuzzy boundary between normality and disorder. Disagreements are likely to be particularly common in considering the differences between 'mild disorder' and 'some distress'. But the use of diagnosis has proven a very useful common language in medicine and has arguably proven useful also in the mental health sphere.

18   *Part I*

It can quite reasonably be objected that as there are, at least as yet, no biological markers of any psychological disorder, the medical model is inappropriate. But borrowing the language of *diagnosis* does not mean that one is compelled to believe in 'real diseases'; rather, as Frances (2013) puts it, these are simply temporary constructs of some utility. Since Aaron Beck's seminal work on cognitive behaviour therapy for depression, there have been a raft of other disorder-specific protocols for depression, the anxiety disorders and PTSD of demonstrated efficacy, underlying the utility of this pragmatic approach to the concept of diagnosis. Interestingly, Beck's first work (1962) was on the impossibility of research without clear diagnostic criteria.

Unfortunately DSM-5 has encouraged diagnostic creep, with the introduction of 'disruptive mood dysregulation disorder', 'mild neurocognitive disorder' and 'adult attention deficit hyperactivity disorder'. The public needs to be extremely wary if these diagnostic labels are used. Temper tantrums are part of normal development; to label such disruptions to a parent's tranquillity as a product of the child's 'disruptive mood dysregulation disorder' is an unnecessary stigmatisation of the child. This label ignores the fact that usually child management difficulties are a result of the dynamic interaction of parent and child, rather than the problem residing in either one. Parents can have varying numbers of problems managing their children, and those with many problems may benefit from professional help, but medicalising the matter is no help to caregiver or child. At the other end of the age spectrum, the elderly can undergo a similar stigmatisation. Some cognitive decline is part of the ageing process: forgetting names more, being a bit more disorganised. These slight frustrations could qualify for 'mild neurocognitive disorder', but there is no lab test for this and no evidence that it is predictive of dementia. Usage of this label would result in many, many false positives with attendant stigmatisation. Further, there is no drug or treatment for 'mild neurocognitive disorder'. This diagnosis has no utility and the label appears to have been driven by a belief that at some future date it will become a marker for dementia.

Even before DSM-5 there had been an epidemic of attention deficit hyperactivity disorder in children, partly because in routine practice the DSM-IV criteria had not been properly applied. In routine practice it was found that boys were six to nine times more likely to be diagnosed with ADHD than girls, but in carefully designed research studies this ratio was only 3:1. Bruchmuller et al. (2011, p. 137) concluded:

> One way to reduce the influence of diagnostic biases would be to establish more compulsory and thorough diagnostic training of prospective therapists. Only if therapists recognise how easily diagnostic decisions can be biased can they avoid such pitfalls. In addition, our results indicate how important it is to use structured interviews and other standardized tools as accepted instruments in clinical practice.

This highlights a more general problem with DSM: almost no attention has been paid to how it should be used in routine practice. It has, however unintentionally, catered solely for the needs of researchers. There is a stricture in DSM-IV-TR (2000, p. xxxii) that states that proper use of DSM involves directly asking questions about each of the symptoms that comprise a diagnostic set, but even this is absent in DSM-5. The result is that by and large non-researchers pay lip service to diagnostic criteria. The advent of 'adult hyperactivity disorder' in DSM-5 further compounds misgivings about the usage of the ADHD label. It suggests that adult ADHD may develop in adults, albeit one of the symptoms that can count to the diagnosis of ADHD in children is the presence of inattention and restlessness hyperactivity before the age of twelve, and this not a necessary condition for adult ADHD. Yet these symptoms in adults can be most plausibly be explained by a wide range of other conditions, like depression and generalised anxiety disorder. The danger is that the focus is taken away from these well-established disorders with proven treatments and turned to adult ADHD, the utility of which has not been tested.

When DSM-IV was in preparation the diagnostic criteria were first tested in the field and the results reviewed before distilling the final diagnostic criteria. Unfortunately no such field testing has occurred with DSM-5, resulting in major flaws such as adult ADHD.

The deleterious effects of unbridled clinical judgement

Ignoring the diagnostic context of efficacy studies results in the application of psychotherapeutic techniques beyond their evidence base. The usage of Eye Movement Desensitisation Reprocessing (EMDR) [Shapiro (2001)] provides an illustration of this. EMDR is a recognised treatment for post-traumatic stress disorder [NICE (2011)], but in the author's experience it is commonplace for it to be applied to anyone who has had a trauma. Many road traffic accident victims suffer not from PTSD but from a simple phobia about driving and travelling as a passenger in a car; EMDR is applied nevertheless and the client is re-victimised by a forced re-living of the trauma. Usage of EMDR beyond the confines of PTSD is not evidence-based, but powerful marketing by the originators of the strategy has ensured its dissemination. It is not just drug companies who have a vested interest in marketing their wares. The consequences of this are illustrated by the following example:

> *Petrov was riding his scooter when a 'boy racer' went through traffic lights on red. Petrov was thrown off his scooter and tried to get up but was unable to do so. Petrov was hospitalised and long afterward still remembered the horrible smell from his right foot; he and his wife both decided that amputation was their best option. He was unable to return to work in his role as a courier but was found a managerial role. Petrov was briefly upset when he heard ambulance sirens with their blue lights on. He occasionally felt angry at the young man but thought 'we have all been young', and he would be briefly upset by reminders such as drains that triggered a memory of his foot putrefying in hospital. Petrov was referred to a CBT counsellor by his*

20 *Part I*

occupational health department and was treated with EMDR. Petrov understood that the procedure was to get rid of the memory but was perplexed when the CBT counsellor wished then to discuss the trauma in the session. After a few sessions he dropped out of treatment, and he then saw another counsellor who at least 'did not try to change the world'. But a standardised diagnostic interview revealed that he had never suffered from post-traumatic stress disorder or any recognised psychiatric disorder. When asked why he had gone through the counseling, he said that he did so just in the way he went through physio – because he assumed others knew better.

The pragmatic use of diagnosis has a fault line in that it is not anchored to a specific biological malfunction; there is an ever-present danger that it can be hijacked to serve the interests of a drug company or some researcher or research group with a pet interest. If the normal can be transmuted as far as possible into the abnormal, then the market for psychotropic drugs or the peddling of a particular psychological intervention is increased. There is also the danger that a mental health diagnosis is used to give credibility to a particular course of action with scant regard to methodological rigour in assessing an individual, in some instances with benign intent, for example legitimating extra resources for a child with 'autism'.

Jettisoning reliable diagnosis in favour of clinical judgement

In our society stigma is a cost of diagnosis, and diagnostic inflation amplifies stigma. There is a pressing need to go carefully and cautiously with regards to diagnosis, with watchful waiting as the modal response to expressions of distress. In a bid to increase access to psychological therapies, the UK government funded IAPT Service, which welcomes self-referrers, and in the year 2014–2015 self-servers comprised 39% of the one million people seen by the Service [IAPT Annual Report (2014–2015)]. Without watchful waiting first and then a definitive diagnosis, many people could be unnecessarily stigmatised. If the clinicians who first see those referred have little more knowledge of diagnosis and treatment than what a suffering intelligent member of the public may have gleaned from the Internet and daily papers, there cannot be a carefully considered watchful waiting. The public do self-refer to a GP, but most would accept that there is a clear differential between the knowledge base of the GP and of an ordinary member of the public. Thus, I might attend concerned about the appearance of my stomach – 'Perhaps I am putting on weight' – but the GP might reassure me that it is not a weight problem but just that my stomach is bloated; one can be much less certain that there is such a differential between the first-line mental health contact and a member of the public. Unfortunately, CBT training courses pay scant attention to diagnosis and treatment fidelity.

Part II

Crystallising mental health problems

4 Difficulties in deciding whether something is wrong

It is not possible to begin to categorise a problem without the insight that a problem exists. To solve a problem a person has to ultimately acknowledge that they have a problem, and sometimes the problem is more apparent to those close to the person, even if they don't know how to quite label it. People with acquired mild cognitive impairments may not see themselves as any different from before their trauma or stroke, but those close may see a difference. Similarly those with a severe mental illness may not, at least at certain times, see their delusion or hallucination as in any way misguided. Sometimes those with obsessive-compulsive disorder see, for example, their repeated checking/cleaning/ritual as absolutely necessary. The absence of insight makes it particularly challenging for relatives, friends and clinicians to make the therapeutic alliance necessary for problem solving.

Problem solving is an attempt to close the gap between a current and desired state. This chapter looks at effective problem solving by a) tightly defining the problem; b) brainstorming as many solutions as possible; c) choosing a solution; d) planning implementation of the solution; e) reviewing how the solution is working out, and if necessary trying out another solution. The process is illustrated by examining the difficulties of a parent in deciding on the normality of their child's behaviour and how a cognitive processing bias, in this instance automatically blaming self or others, can sabotage problem solving.

Different problems have different solutions. If I mistakenly believe I have a problem with my printer when my computer is at fault, I may go to the unnecessary expense of buying a new printer. In this chapter the utility of using diagnosis as a way of categorising problems is explored. It is acknowledged that though there are disadvantages to using diagnosis, it is the least-worst system currently available. An example is given of the consequences of two clinicians using assessment protocols of different reliability. It is argued that a cognitive assessment should be an integral part of an initial assessment.

Ambivalence to treatment is commonplace

I recently went to the doctor after many months (perhaps a year, if I am honest!) of suffering indigestion; for a long time I thought I was just 'fussing', and this was compounded by a general dislike of medical doctors going back to childhood. In

24   *Part II*

many ways I was not orientated to solving the problem despite brief conversations with the medics in my family. Discussions of problem solving usually focus on the stages a) 'tightly defining the problem' to e) 'reviewing how the solution is working out' described above, but actually there is an important stage of problem orientation before all these. Problem orientation refers to the process of locking on to a problem. But a further discussion with one of my medic daughters crystallised my resolve, and I finally made an appointment with my GP. The GP then collaboratively involved me in defining the problem with probes such as 'what sort of pain is it, a sharp pain, burning sensation?'; the GP also came up with a two-pronged solution: take 30mg of lansoprazole daily and go for a gastroscopy. Historically I am not enamoured of taking medication, but in line with the problem-solving process outlined above I decided to try it out; contrary to my prejudice, it worked instantly. I do not know whether I was pleased or disappointed. On the one hand I was free of indigestion, but I then had to admit to my daughters and son-in-law medic that they might have a role after all, and I was pretty stupid to delay so long before problem solving. Reluctantly I went for the gastroscopy, with my mental schema of 'they are just fussing' now reinforced because the medication had already sorted the problem, only to discover that I had a hiatus hernia (part of stomach in chest). The menu of options in the problem-solving process was then revisited by the suggestion of doubling the daily medication and a further gastroscopy in six weeks to review whether the problem had been resolved. Thus, whilst the problem-solving process is in principle quite simple, it is bedevilled by ambivalence and the person's mental schemas (templates for processing information). Ambivalence is likely to also characterise those contemplating seeking psychological help and is unlikely to cease to be an issue once they enter the consulting room. As such both therapist and would-be client will need to acknowledge ambivalence; it is often the elephant in the room.

Problem orientation and mental health

The door to getting psychological help may be likened to turning a nut with a spanner (problem solving), but it may take considerable effort to get the spanner on the nut in the first place, i.e. to become problem orientated. The longer the delay the more difficult it is to treat problems; the duration of untreated illness is associated with worse outcomes in psychosis, bipolar disorder and major depressive and anxiety disorders [Boonstra et al. (2012) and Dell'Osso et al. (2013)]. Stigma can result in a failure to address a problem, and this issue is a focus at the end of this chapter. There may need to be several contacts with a mental health professional before a person is fully orientated to solving their mental health problem, but the quality of the professional's interaction is likely to shorten the time for which the disorder/difficulty goes untreated.

Problem orientation can be sabotaged by overuse of the adage 'time is a great healer'. This adage is often used when people experience a bereavement or trauma, and indeed the majority of those affected return to their normal functioning within a couple of months. Too precipitous an intervention can cause problems, for example;

Deciding whether something is wrong   25

Bisson et al. (1997) examined the effects of one session psychological debriefing (PD) on burn victims and found that at follow-up 26% of the PD group had PTSD compared to 9% in a control group. However, the PD group had higher initial questionnaire scores and more severe dimensions of burn trauma than the control group. Nevertheless the effects of single-session PD appears to be at best neutral and sometimes negative [see Rose et al. (2001)]. It is therefore not unreasonable to have a period of watchful waiting in the aftermath of negative life events, but beyond this there is a need for active intervention.

'Am I just fussing?'

The following example illustrates this uncertainty:

> *Jane was concerned about the behaviour of her seven-year-old son, Jake; he did the opposite of whatever she said but was a perfect angel in school. His temper tantrums were wearing her out. She found putting Jake to bed a particular trauma when her partner, who did shift work, was not present. Jane felt fed up, was sleeping poorly, irritable and couldn't concentrate on TV. She also felt confused. Friends told her Jake was just going through a phase, whilst her own mother confidently asserted that there was something wrong with him.*

A fit case for psychological treatment? But which, if any, of the participants in the above scenario needs treatment? Unfortunately there are no biological tests that can be given to the individuals to decide whether they have a psychological disorder. Diagnosis is an intended aid to resolving these difficulties, and evidence-based treatments for psychological disorders are for the most part diagnosis specific, i.e. there is a different treatment protocol for a person suffering from, say, depression than for another person with panic disorder. An evidence-based treatment is one that has been tested in a randomised controlled trial in which one group of subjects is given treatment A, for example cognitive therapy for depression, and another group of subjects given treatment B, for example usual treatment whilst on a waiting list, and the results compared. For a treatment to be considered evidence based, the treatment must have shown demonstrated superiority in at least two controlled trials conducted by researchers not involved in the original development of the treatment [see Chambless and Hollon (1998), Appendix E] and the preponderance of studies must support the evidence-supported treatment.

Diagnosis – an aid to defining the problem

Following problem orientation, the next step in problem solving is to precisely define the problem. Often problems are not resolved because they are vaguely defined. To return to the example above, Jane's mother often opined that 'Jake is a pain just like his father', but this was not of any assistance to Jane and it did not highlight any course of action; in terms of problem solving it was a 'fuzzy'.

26 *Part II*

Diagnosis is a means of bringing a 'fuzzy' into focus; thus when Jane is fed up, has difficulties in concentration and insomnia, her problems seem to resemble a prototype for depression. But though prototypes are a useful starting point they are based on what people deem to be the key or cardinal symptoms of a disorder, and other symptoms can be no less important. For example in deciding whether a person is suffering from post-traumatic stress disorder (PTSD), the symptom most people would probably have in mind is nightmares of an extreme trauma. However, the post-trauma development of an exaggerated startle response is as much a symptom, and it is possible to suffer from the disorder without disturbing dreams or indeed without any one of the twenty-symptom criteria in DSM-5 [American Psychiatric Association (2013)]. Diagnosis is based on the presence of a specified number of symptoms causing a significant impairment in functioning. Thus, the DSM-5 criteria for depression require the presence of five or more symptoms from a set of nine, at least one of which has to be either a) depressed and down most of the day more days than not or b) loss in interest or pleasure in usual activities.

Applying the lens of diagnosis to Jane, to bring her problems better into focus, there would be a need to refine what was meant by her being 'fed up' and determine whether this reached a threshold of being 'depressed and down most of the day, more days than not'. There would also be a need to enquire whether she has lost interest in hobbies or pastimes to determine whether she met the symptom criteria of 'loss of interest or pleasure in usual activities'. Diagnosis is not just a symptom count; for a symptom to be endorsed as present it has to be more than uncomfortable and impair functioning, i.e. to make a real-world difference. The advantage of diagnostic criteria is that it ensures all are speaking the same language, that my case of depression is not your case of psychosis. Before the advent of diagnostic criteria, research was impossible [see Beck et al. (1962)], but symptom counts are somewhat arbitrary. For example, with regards to depression, a person with just four symptoms may be clinically as functionally impaired as the person with the required minimum of five symptoms. In clinical practice it seems reasonable to treat them the same. Diagnoses for diagnoses' sake is pointless and likely to be harmful, but diagnoses should rather be used as a springboard for treatment.

Psychometric tests as an aid to defining the problem

Jane met the DSM criteria for depression, but is this the appropriate focus? What about her difficulties with Jake? Jane completed the Eyberg Child Behaviour Inventory [ECBI Eyberg and Ross (1978) – reproduced in Scott (2015a)] and identified 16 of the 36 possible child behaviours as being currently present, as well as indicating how often these problems happened. Items that are scored 'often' or 'always' helps to identify treatment goals. If a child's score is 15 or above on the problem scale, then the child is displaying a significant number of behaviour problems. On this basis Jane would probably be regarded as a suitable candidate for a group parent-training programme [Scott and Stradling (1987)]. Jane underwent cognitive behaviour therapy for depression, without any focus on her child-management skills, and the perceived number of problems with Jake reduced by half by the end of treatment.

Deciding whether something is wrong   27

This example illustrates how a psychometric test can readily suggest treatment targets and can be used as a measure of the effectiveness of an intervention. But there is a certain arbitrariness in deciding that those who score above a certain level are suitable candidates for treatment. It is not dissimilar to, within a diagnostic framework, pronouncing that those with x or more symptoms are 'cases' of the disorder and thereby suitable candidates for treatment.

Diagnosis or psychometric tests?

If diagnosis and psychometric tests are both about refining the definition of the problem, then they ought to be complementary. But psychometric tests should play a subsidiary role, as their context often needs elaborating. For example, the ECBI [Eyberg and Ross (1978)] asks the caregiver to specify current child behaviour problems, but children do go through phases and it is questionable use of clinical resources if the problems have not been enduring. Thus in the DSM-5, criteria for oppositional defiant disorder require a pattern of negativistic, hostile, and defiant behaviour lasting at least six months and then specifies eight behaviours, at least four of which have to be present. It is not clear whether depression causes a perception of oppositional defiance or whether such behaviour causes depression in the caregiver. There are thus two equally credible interventions in the above example: cognitive behaviour therapy for depression or an evidence-based psychosocial treatment for oppositional defiant disorder [Eyberg et al. (2008)]. But it is evidence-based treatment options that should appear on the problem-solving treatment menu. Which option is taken up first may depend on the local availability of services; in some instances it may be possible to address more than one disorder simultaneously. For example, many sufferers with PTSD abuse alcohol; both may be concurrent treatment foci.

The dangers of diagnosis

Diagnosis is dangerous if it is not located in a problem-solving process; for example, historically if a person was given a diagnosis of personality disorder it was a recipe for therapeutic despair. If a diagnosis does not lead to the distillation of series of treatment options it becomes a meaningless exercise in labelling, which in turn can become a pejorative labelling in which the sufferer is blamed for their disorder. Further the label may be used against the person if medical records have to be accessed for a job application.

Diagnosis is particularly problematic when it comes to children. Whilst Jake in the example above may meet DSM-5 criteria for Oppositional Defiant Disorder, such a term would be taken by most to indicate a mental illness, and this label could well disadvantage him as he grows up. The aura of mental illness is particularly problematic as there are no clear biological tests for any DSM disorder. But in physical health there are often disorders for which there is no compelling evidence for the biological mechanisms involved. For example, Parkinson's disease was initially simply a description of a particular constellation of symptoms that James

28   *Part II*

Parkinson called collectively 'shaking palsy'; he provided no conclusions as to its aetiology. In a similar fashion the United States Institute of Medicine has recently identified chronic fatigue syndrome as a bona fide disease, re-labelled 'Systemic Exertion Intolerance Disease', without identifying causation.

Formulation

The proper use of diagnosis not only involves locating it in a problem-solving framework, but taking care that when it is communicated to fellow professionals, the sufferer themselves or their family, they are given a context in which the label is explained. Elaboration of this context has been termed a 'case formulation' or 'formulation'. Thus in the example above the formulation might run:

> *Sometimes Jake does things like not obeying Mum that go beyond her toler-ance threshold. Mum then sometimes overreacts to this, and then Jake over-reacts and a vicious circle is set up. Who first goes over the top on any one day will probably depend on what sort of day each have had. If Jane has had an argument with her partner or her mum she is more likely to overreact, and if Jake is bored or has been bullied he is likely to overreact. Mum gets depressed because she feels she is not performing the role of being a 'good mum' and has a longstanding tendency to automatically blame herself when anything goes wrong. Jake gets stressed by the repeated conflicts.*

Diagnosis can become a label left hanging around the neck of an individual. It needs explaining that such labels are often not so much properties of individuals, but the results of interpersonal transactions and the wider environment. This is not to say that there might not also be individual genetic vulnerabilities. Diagnoses are simply convenient ports of entry for resolving problems, but they do need handling with great care to ensure that the benefits outweigh the costs. As I write (March 2016) the TV drama *Not the A Word* highlights these issues as a little boy is diag-nosed with autism, and he and his family struggle to cope. At times an intended refinement of diagnostic criteria makes matters worse, e.g. DSM-5 recently made things much worse when it turned normal temper tantrums into 'Disruptive Mood Dysregulation Disorder'.

Problem lists as a modus operandi

One way of circumventing the difficulties posed by diagnosis is to simply create a problem list. The task of a clinician is then to help resolve those problems. Most contact with professionals rightly begins with an open-ended interview in which clients are given the opportunity to tell their story. This in turn usually suggests a list of problems, not all of which the client may be aware of.

The recent history of social work provides a worrying example of what can happen when problem lists are made a sole focus. Task-centred social work addressed such problem lists. Gradually task-centred social work was pushed to

Deciding whether something is wrong 29

the margins, the therapeutic role of social workers declined and a protective function came to dominate. The author made a shift from social work to psychology in part because of the inadequacy of the therapeutic aspects of the role. I remember an older colleague telling me that in the 1960s, when area social work departments were set up they leafleted the local neighbourhood about all manner of problems they would tackle; they were soon totally overwhelmed by demands! The difficulty was that task-centred social work was not an evidence-based treatment for anything. There are no quality randomised controlled trials (RCTs) of task-centred social work. Instead reliance is placed on evidence-based practice but without any acknowledgement that the results of RCTs have to be the foundation for practice. In their work *The Task-Centred Book* Marsh and Doel (2005) assert, 'The book's main reference point is the voice of practitioner, service users and carers'; whilst this can be applauded for being inclusive, it masks the inadequate evidence base for the interventions. But this does not stop these authors extolling at great length what should be considered evidence-based practice but in fact is eminence-based practice.

In practice, problem lists are often too fuzzy, too non-specific for action. It is unclear which problems are more important than others and how much energy should be expended on what, using what strategy. Government funding has just been announced (March 2016) to fund the training of mental health social workers whose role will be to provide support for those with severe and enduring mental health problems. This sounds like a re-launching of psychiatric social work, without any therapeutic role. The problem for social work is that it does not have any unique knowledge base and tends to use a 'pick and mix' from other areas such as psychology and law. It seems likely that the new mental health social workers will be more concerned with monitoring clients with severe and enduring mental health problems, (akin to how social workers already operate with adults with learning difficulties), than with a therapeutic input. This is not to say mental health social workers could not in principle play an important therapeutic role. For example many adults suffering from a psychotic disorder are cared for and live with elderly parents who may become seriously physically ill; a 'stress' group for these adults might be very useful to help them manage transitions. But it seems unlikely that a therapeutic role for mental health social workers will come to pass.

The DSM venture into problems

Problem lists are useful but only when they are sheltered under the umbrella of an identified disorder or general problem. Thus the ECBI [Eyberg and Ross (1978)] detailed above constituted a reasonable list only when Jane reported that child management problems were affecting her functioning. The DSM-5 recognises this with a category of 'Other Conditions That May Be a Focus of Clinical Attention', and it expressly states that the categories listed in this chapter are *not* mental disorders but are a legitimate focus for a clinician, adding that this focus may be legitimised because these conditions may affect 'the diagnosis, course, prognosis, or treatment of a patient's mental disorder' (p715). One of the categories listed in

30 *Part II*

this DSM-5 chapter is 'Relationship Distress With Spouse or Intimate Partner'. To return to the example of Jane, it could be that her depression and child-management difficulties were adversely affecting her relationship with her partner or that the relationship itself, e.g. the partner's shift work, was creating these problems. If both partners saw their relationship as being a problem and wanted to work on it, relationship therapy would become another option on the treatment menu. In such a scenario a problem list could be generated using the Areas of Change Questionnaire (ACQ) [Weiss and Margolin (1977) and reproduced in Scott (2015a)]. Completion of the ACQ involves each partner specifying what changes they want in their partner. The first phase of evidence-based treatment involves behavioural exchange, both partners agreeing to make specific changes beginning with the least problematic, progressing to cognitive restructuring and the use of communication guidelines [Scott (2015a)]. Interestingly Beach and O'Leary found that depressed women who received cognitive behavioural relationship therapy fared better than depressed women who received CBT. Women in both treatments showed reductions in depression, but women who received CBT relationship therapy showed both reduction in depression and increases in relationship satisfaction.

In terms of the problem-solving process, in relation to Jane above there are at least three possible evidence-based treatment programmes: CBT, group parent-training programme and CBT relationship therapy. The problem-solving guidelines outlined at the start of this chapter suggest experimenting with an option, reviewing how well this option worked out and, if unsuccessful or only partially successful, returning to the menu and trying out another option. In practice the first option to be tried will depend on availability of the intervention locally; generally CBT for depression is much more available than either a group parent-training programme or CBT relationship therapy. But motivation to take up one of the interventions may vary with modality, and motivation is the subject of the next chapter.

Stigma

On November 24, 2014, then-Deputy Prime Minister Nick Clegg declared:

> For far too long mental health has been in the shadows and many people have suffered in silence as a result. It is time to turn a corner on outdated attitudes and bring mental health issues out into the open. It is time that the whole of society started providing the care and support to those with mental health conditions in the same way that they would to those with a physical condition.

Clegg announced the formation of a Mental Health Taskforce, thus providing a much-needed impetus to the expansion and refinement of psychological services. But the task is daunting; if you can't make it to a social engagement or to work the last reason most people want to give is a mental health problem – images of disapproval or of a deleterious effect on your career readily spring to mind. The

Deciding whether something is wrong 31

stigma of mental illness is still alive and kicking in the twenty-first century despite respected public figures such as Stephen Fry declaring their difficulties. Approximately one in four people have a mental health problem, but up to 75% of those affected do not receive treatment and those who do receive treatment are given mostly medication. The stigma associated with mental disorder is an important factor preventing or delaying people seeking help with a resultant worse outcome.

Stigma is not confined to mental health problems; historically, there has been a stigma surrounding leprosy, cancer and more recently AIDS. In July 1991, Princess Diana gave hugs to AIDS sufferers at an English Hospital. This visit made headline news, helping change people's perception about the disease. Stigma is an unnecessary extra burden for the sufferer, and whilst public figures and mental health professionals can seek to minimise it, they are unlikely to eradicate it. In some instances the mental health professional may consider that the need for treatment is so important, e.g. the treatment of a thirteen-year-old with anorexia, that it outweighs any possible stigmatisation that may arise as a consequence of this treatment being detailed in the GP records. The various forms of stigmatisation and their clinical implications are discussed in the rest of this chapter.

Internalized stigma

Internalized stigma refers to holding a stigmatizing view about oneself; the following case illustrates its operation:

> *Luke was riding a motorcycle when without warning a car pulled out across his path. He knew a collision was inevitable and was thrown over the top of the car. He was paralysed from the neck down and after hospitalisation went to live at a spinal unit. A counsellor attached to the unit found him very grumpy and suspected that he might have post-traumatic stress disorder from the incident. Luke refused any psychological therapy. He said that he had always despised anyone with disability as being 'weak' and since his accident despised himself. He denied being affected by the accident, as he had had lots of accidents before; they were part and parcel of being a biker, and he was a 'coper'. Friends that he had been riding with on the day of the incident still kept in touch, but Luke rarely interacted with any other residents of the unit.*

In instances of internalized stigma such as the above, the most that can be hoped for is that those in contact with the person will counter the implicit stereotypes, and the individual will move forward towards treatment. But this can be a complex process. In the above example some of Luke's friends, whilst being supportive, shared the same stereotype as him. On the other hand the counsellor and the staff at the unit felt that his stereotypes were clearly unhelpful. The counsellor endeavoured to create a therapeutic milieu within the unit, so that Luke's stereotypes could be tackled experientially by his contact with other residents and staff

32   *Part II*

modelling reverence for residents. But managing Luke's beliefs about being a 'coper' was likely to be problematic.

Perceived stigmatisation

Perceived stigmatization refers to the extent to which the sufferer from mental health problems anticipates others having stigmatizing attitudes or behaviours towards them. To return to the example above:

> *Two of Luke's friends visited him weekly in the unit, and weather permitting they would take him out for a walk in his wheelchair. Luke tried to keep the conversation on biking matters, but conversation became strained as there were no longer common biking experiences, and little was happening in his life. He noted however that one of his friends felt very guilty over the accident as he had just let Luke take over the lead position in the group of bikers and had tucked in behind him to avoid the wind. The friend who felt guilty said 'I am so sorry' at each visit, Luke was both irritated by and concerned for this friend. Luke began to wonder if others would be as put out by his saying how fed up he was as he thought.*

Thus, whilst perceived stigmatization is a barrier to seeking help, it is not immutable to change. In the above example, with regard to his guilty friend, Luke has hung back from stigma endorsement. A first step in overcoming perceived stigmatisation is an appreciation that people's responses to mental health problems are very varied. Nevertheless some diagnostic labels do carry more stigma than others; at one end of the spectrum is schizophrenia and at the other would be a specific phobia. Bipolar disorder is probably less threatening in the public imagination than schizophrenia, whereas the diagnostic label of depression will likely attract more opprobrium than a specific phobia. This raises the issue of whether the diagnostic labels of schizophrenia and bipolar disorder are really necessary – are there meaningful distinctions between them? Bentall (2009) has cogently argued that they are inappropriate, confusing labels. He suggests that the fear factor in these labels arises from seeing them as prototypical of 'mental illness', with the implication that the person is totally at the mercy of the illness and the effects on others are thereby entirely unpredictable.

There is an initial comfort for an individual and their relatives in having their difficulties described as an illness, whether it be schizophrenia, bipolar disorder or an addiction, but for the most part this is short lived because rightly or wrongly the public perceives that the individual can make choices, and failure to make the 'right' choices evokes anger and criticism. Mental health practitioners, perhaps because they do not have to live with the affected person, even though they may not ascribe to an illness model, tend to play down the client's ability to choose, and they seek to minimise the expressed emotion (high levels of criticism and over-involvement) of family, not least because high EE is predictive of relapse. It is difficult for the mental health practitioner to make the case that there is a limited

Deciding whether something is wrong 33

range of actions open to the affected individual. Philosophically it is not an easy position to justify, as the polar opposite positions that either behaviour is biologically determined or that the individual is a free agent, have a more attractive simplicity, i.e. 'he/she is either bad or mad'.

Treatment stigmatisation

In seeking psychological help there is an explicit acknowledgement of a problem; when mental health concerns are kept private it is easier to pretend that they are not real. Whilst disclosure of a problem is a necessary first step towards effective treatment, it does oftentimes come with a price tag – a sinking feeling in that acknowledgement. The following example illustrates the withering away of treatment stigmatisation:

> *In one of his visits Luke's guilty friend disclosed that he had been referred for CBT and been diagnosed as having PTSD with regards to flashbacks of seeing Luke lying in the road apparently dead and feeling helpless. Luke learnt that his friend had also talked about his guilt feelings. Luke was relieved by this as his own 'don't be stupid' increase spacing response did not seem to cut any ice. Hearing this made Luke ponder whether he should seek treatment. Though he wasn't disturbed by memories of the incident, they were just an irritation; he did, however, feel low all the time and often could not be bothered with anything.*

What is interesting in the above example is that Luke's move towards treatment is prompted by a perceived credible source, his friend and fellow biker, and not directly by the counsellor. In terms of the Elaboration Likelihood Model of Persuasion [Petty and Cacioppo (1986)], central messages that require effortful processing such as NICE's claims about the most appropriate treatment, conveyed by say a GP or mental health practitioner, are likely to be dismissed in favour of a less-demanding message (peripheral processing) conveyed by a peer or fellow member of an in-group. It is not surprising therefore that treatment stigma is likely to be more prominent in disadvantaged and minority groups. To the extent that the mental health practitioners are unlike the clients they hope to serve, services are likely to be underutilised.

Efforts to reduce stigma

It is possible to reduce stigma by inviting would-be clients to a group session in which they are given a taster of what treatment would involve. Such a session would be devoted to increasing the psychological-mindedness of the client, a socialisation for treatment. As such it is an opportunity to dispel therapy misconceptions and create a vision of what can be achieved in treatment. White et al. (1992) implicitly did this by running a stress control evening class in which no personal problems were to be addressed. Drawing on this it may be feasible to run, for example, Managing Panic, Managing Trauma, etc. evenings with direct access

34   Part II

from the public and referral. By including a coffee break there is the opportunity for sufferers to learn that they are not that unusual and that other sufferers are likeable. White et al. (1992) also approached local religious leaders to get them to promote the classes in their congregations.

It is possible to by-pass stigma by the use of Mobile Mental Health (m-Health) or self-help materials; the former are as yet largely untested, and the latter appear useful but not as a stand-alone intervention. However even in these contexts stigma has a way of rearing its ugly head:

> *John was undergoing CBT treatment for PTSD. As part of his psychoeducation the therapist had suggested he read the introductory chapters of* Moving On After Trauma *[Scott (2008)]. He was sitting at his coffee table reading it when he heard a car pull up on the driveway; he anticipated it was his son. Hurriedly he concealed the book under a newspaper on the coffee table. His son entered the living room, and John went to make him a coffee. During this process there was a cry of 'What's this?' from his son and John was mortified when he saw him holding the book.*

Societal creation of stigma

Mental health clinicians are not exempt from stigmatising people, and the worst example of this occurred in Nazi Germany. Germany's leading professors of psychiatry planned, without coercion, the destruction of at least 275,000 people whose lives they considered not worth living [Wertham (1968)]. The first gas chambers were installed in psychiatric hospitals before export to concentration camps. It is chastening to reflect that this slaughter took place at the instigation of mental health clinicians; the role of the Nazi regime was only permissive. It appears there is an evolutionary impetus to protect only those 'just like us'. This constitutes a grave danger to civilisation unless offset by a belief in the intrinsic value of each individual.

Societal belief systems and social conditions set the context for stigma to operate – the recent recession which followed the near collapse of the banking system has led to the emergence of food banks. Many are highly embarrassed at having to utilise such services, fearful that they may be discovered. This emotional and financial impoverishment can very easily lead to symptoms of depression.

Associated stigma

The effects of stigma are not confined to the mental health sufferer; 'associated stigma' [Ricci and Dixon (2015)] may affect family members or close friends. They may feel a degree of blame and contamination, and this in turn may interfere with their family relationships and ability to pursue support. One consequence can be that there is a delay in helping their relative seek treatment. There is a program called I Will Listen (www.IWILLListen.org) which encourages people to listen to their friends, family members and colleagues with an open mind and without judgement when it comes to mental health.

Deciding whether something is wrong   35

If a person believes they are mentally ill, they are likely to seek pills rather than the skills that may be on offer via psychological treatment. Similarly a person who is extremely self-reliant is likely to be very reluctant to seek psychological treatment.

At first glance a belief that one has to sort out one's own problems is diametrically opposed to a belief that one is ill and needs the ministrations of others, medications etc. But there is an extreme of self-reliance that results in brief recourse to an illness script when the task is manifestly unmanageable, and the person oscillates between the two poles:

> *Tom was a police sergeant. He liked to drink after a shift to unwind, feeling it helped him get to sleep. But he began missing a few shifts because he was hungover. His boss referred him to the force welfare officer in the occupational health department, but he was very reluctant to disclose anything at the interview, fearing what might go on his records and the effect on his promotion prospects. At the interview he stressed that he was the 'piggy in the middle', between the excessive demands of management and the scarce resource of officers at the coalface'. His wife was getting annoyed with him about his drinking; it was causing rows between them, and his constant retort was 'I'll sort it'. He and his wife finally saw the force psychiatrist, who declared that he was alcohol dependent. She was irritated at this, but the psychiatrist pacified her by telling her it was an illness. Tom did not challenge the description of his being ill. In accepting it he was avoiding sanctions at work and criticism from his wife, whilst still being determined to sort out his problems himself. He agreed to medication to help his withdrawal from alcohol and to attend Alcoholics Anonymous, but within three months he had relapsed.*

There are doubtless biological correlates for all psychological disorders, but that does not mean that these disorders are caused by biology. Jeffrey Lieberman (2015) a former president of the American Psychiatric Association, has opined that if psychological disorders were taken by the public as being of biological origin, then the stigma of mental illness would be removed. However, whilst the public finds the initial declaration of 'illness' as attractive in that it may be a treatable illness, they soon feel that to a degree at least the person is an agent of their own misfortune:

> *Tom attended a review with the occupational health psychiatrist three months after his initial assessment; his absences had increased. He explained that he had been okay for a few weeks but then gone to the police club with colleagues to watch a European football game. He felt it would be unsociable not to have just one drink and ended up drinking much more than he intended. His wife was not amused at his drunken state when he got home. Over the ensuing weeks her high levels of criticism led to deterioration in his mood and a persistence of his drinking.*

36   *Part II*

Developmental origins of compulsive self-reliance and insecure attachment

Compulsive self-reliance can develop as a consequence of the non-availability of caregivers in childhood. The child does not expect help to become forthcoming from others and as an adult does not therefore seek intimacy. Further, as the child is given little or no help to label emotions (alexithymia), they may have little insight into the origins of their actions or their negative impact on others. Actions such as self-harm or a somatic disorder may bring them into contact with the mental health services, but engagement in a therapeutic relationship is very problematic because of the avoidant attachment style. The lack of understanding of their emotions can lead them to have no story to tell a therapist, and they may resort to a default option of 'I'm ill'. By contrast, clients who have had insecure attachments in childhood may make some therapeutic relationships drawing on the capital of one or more good childhood relationships even though the main caregivers proved unreliable. Nevertheless, they may be particularly prone to perceiving the therapist as abandoning them, for example if the therapist is unable to reschedule a missed appointment any time soon. But those with insecure attachments, unlike those with an avoidant attachment style, do have a narrative to give to a therapist. There is growing evidence that reducing the duration of untreated illness (DUI), defined as the interval between the onset of a person's disorder and the beginning of the first appropriate treatment [Dell'Osso and Altamura (2010)], correlates with improved clinical outcome and the course of disorders such as schizophrenia [Marshall et al. (2005)], bipolar disorder [Goldberg and Ernst (2002)], depression [Ghio et al. (2014)], panic disorder [Altamura et al. (2005)], generalized anxiety disorder [Altamura et al. (2006)] and obsessive-compulsive disorder [Dell'Osso et al. (2010)]. Thus increasing sufferers' motivation to seek treatment has to be a major target of mental health policy whether the proffered treatment is an enhancement of skills or pills.

Motivation for skill acquisition

Whilst problem recognition is a necessary step towards problem solving, problems will only be tackled if there is a belief that a) there is the capacity to solve the problem and b) what could be done would make a worthwhile difference, i.e. there is a sense of self-efficacy. Motivation may be sapped at the different fences of referral, assessment and treatment, such that those completing the 'race'/treatment are a significant minority. Those with severe mental illness/personality disorders often have low self-efficacy and often fail at the assessment and treatment fences, in part because of a lack of clarity of task within and between the treatment agencies.

Just Google it!

Confronted by a practical or emotional difficulty, it is increasingly common for people to do a Google search on the perceived problem. With regards to emotional problems, this has the added value of privacy. However, the person is likely to be

Deciding whether something is wrong 37

confronted by a bewildering array of information which has not been critically evaluated by any credible independent body. Nevertheless, the person may at least be able to contact support groups such as Mind and Young Mind, which may socialise a person for treatment. But most people will make the wrong diagnosis using the Internet, in part because it does not specify the range of information pertinent to making a diagnosis, i.e. it does not control for information variance, and partly because it does not specify the threshold over which a symptom can be considered present, i.e. it does not control for criterion variance. Thus they could join the wrong support group.

The motivation of an individual depends on a person's perception of the effectiveness of the services on offer, of whether contact (or ongoing contact) with them would make a worthwhile difference. This perception will in turn depend on the marketing of services by service providers to consumers of services and the experiences of sources of referral such as GPs. In the UK there is almost no direct-to-consumer marketing of services by government-funded agencies, save for some charities, although private clinicians may market their wares and some bodies operate via insurers. Motivation is, in many ways, a product of the interaction between the individual, agencies and sources of referral.

The appropriateness of psychotropic medication

Although NICE treatment guidelines for disorders such as depression and PTSD recommend psychological therapies as the first line of treatment, in practice medication is the most commonly offered treatment, largely because of its greater availability. Rates of remission from depression with antidepressants range from 35–45%, but 25% of those receiving a placebo also remit [Thase et al. (2001)]. (The definition of remission used in the studies reviewed by Thase et al. (2001) was achieving a score <8 on the clinician-administered Hamilton Rating Scale for Depression; in these studies the assessor was blind to the treatment condition.) These remission rates refer to recovery within six to eight weeks of treatment, but relapse following treatment is commonplace, with 61% relapsing within twelve to eighteen months [Vittengl et al. (2007)]. Cognitive therapy for depression fares slightly better than medication, with roughly two-thirds of those who complete no longer meeting criteria for a major depressive episode and about half of responders relapsing within two years [Craighead et al. (2007)]. For those with PTSD the remission rate with antidepressant treatment is 20–30% (differences in treatment effectiveness are quantified by a measure called 'effect size'. This is the difference between the mean of the treatment group at the end of treatment minus the mean end of treatment of the placebo group at the end of treatment divided by the pooled standard deviation). In comparisons of SSRIs with placebo for PTSD, the effect size is 0.5, which is very modest, An effect size of 1 means the treated person is one standard deviation better off after treatment than those in the control group.

Antidepressants are often prescribed as the only treatment, but combining them with psychotherapy appears to be better for depression, panic disorder and obsessive-compulsive disorder [Cuijpers et al. (2014)]. However Cuijpers et al. (2014) did

38   *Part II*

not distinguish between the different psychotherapies; only half the studies included were of CBT. In an earlier work Cuijpers et al. (2010) reviewed whether there is a publication bias in the psychotherapy studies of depression. She and her colleagues note that pharmaceutical companies have a vested interest in proclaiming the efficacy of their products and that editors of journals prefer positive results, with negative results not seeing the light of day – the 'file drawer' problem. Cuijpers et al. (2010) suggest that promoters of psychological therapies may also have vested interests such as promoting their career and that her and her colleagues' statistical analyses suggest that the effect size between CBT for depression and a control condition reduces from 0.69 to 0.49 when adjusting for publication bias.

The NICE Guidelines (2005) suggest that for children and adolescents, antidepressants should only be prescribed alongside psychological therapy and then only for moderate and severe cases. But in practice, because of the poor availability of psychological therapy antidepressants are often prescribed alone. Whilst the antidepressant fluoxetine is licensed for use in children under eighteen, other antidepressants are often prescribed. Antidepressants were developed with adults in mind, and their effect on the developing brain is unknown. A study by Sharma et al. (2016) of two classes of antidepressants, selective serotonin and serotonin-norepinephrine reuptake inhibitors, showed that taking these drugs (which include fluoxetine, paroxetine and sertraline) doubled the risk of suicidality (suicide, suicide attempt or preparatory behaviour, intentional self-harm and suicidal ideation) and aggression in children and adolescents.

Because of the possible adverse consequences of antidepressants, e.g. loss of libido or weight gain, appropriate withdrawal is a consideration. The Royal College of Psychiatrists has produced a very useful leaflet 'Coming Off Antidepressants', available on the college's website (rcpsych.ac.uk). The symptoms of withdrawal from antidepressant medication often look to the person like a return of their original symptoms but are often in fact more anxiety-based withdrawal symptoms, with symptoms often settling in a few weeks. Oftentimes people withdraw too abruptly with consequent deleterious effects, e.g. headaches. The period of withdrawal has to be determined by the length of time on the medication, with gradual reduction of antidepressants over four to six weeks for those who have been on the medication for a few years.

5 Social support, psychological disorders and psychoeducation

Patient.co.uk lists over 1,800 UK support organisations, self-help groups, and health and disease information providers. There are support groups for almost every disorder, e.g. Obsessive Compulsive Disorder, and difficulty, e.g. dental fear. Under the category 'mental health – stress/phobia/anxiety' there are fifty-two groups listed, with thirty-two listed under 'mental health depression', seventeen listed under 'mental health eating disorders', eleven listed under 'mental health psychosis/schizophrenia' and twenty-six listed under 'mental health children'. But the highest listing of eighty-five is for 'addictions alcohol/drugs'. The following example indicates how a support group can figure in an individual's journey to mental health:

> *John drank socially on weekends before his retirement; he found that afterwards his days lacked structure and he began drinking daily. By five years post-retirement he was drinking one to two bottles of wine a day. He loved his grandchildren, but over the past nine months he had repeatedly broken arrangements to go and see them. John had attended Alcoholics Anonymous on a number of occasions in this period, resolving each time to go regularly, but never had.*

Support groups as an umbrella for all stages of change

Popular support groups such as Alcoholics Anonymous have become part of our collective consciousness as a resource for helping with drinking problems. A particular strength of support groups is that they can be utilised by a person at whatever stage of change [Prochaska and Di Clemente (1992)] they are operating. In the above example John had been in a pre-contemplative (not ready) stage [see Figure 5.1] about his drinking for the first nine months post-retirement, but in recent months there had been some recognition that he had a problem, seeing advantages and disadvantages of tackling the problem (contemplative stage – getting ready – see Figure 5.1). With spasmodic attendances at AA he had been in Prochaska and Di Clemente's preparation stage. He had not entered Prochaska and Di Clemente's (1992) action phase of drinking reduction/abstinence and regular attendance at AA. The final phase of Prochaska and Di Clemente's (1992) model is maintenance, in

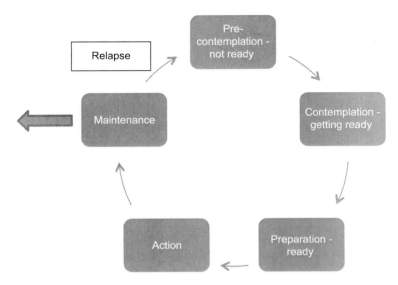

Figure 5.1 Stages of change based on Prochaska and Di Clemente (1992)

John's case a prolonged period without alcohol, but he had not been for more than twenty-four hours without alcohol; were he to do so he could have gone on to relapse, with AA being also available to those who have slipped. Recovery involves movement through the stages, sometimes in a cyclical fashion – for example, back to pre-contemplation after a slip – but a support group such as AA is there for the duration, perhaps unlike therapy, which is focussed primarily on the action phase. Whether the stages of change in Prochaska and di Clemente's (1992) model are as fixed as they suggest and whether individuals operate with the stable plans implicit in the model is debatable. Nevertheless the support group spans a spectrum of motivation greater than therapy. A support group can 'house' the stages of change, as seen in Figure 5.1.

AA epitomises the strengths of the support group: an open door, frequented by others who have had similar problems, able to model better coping. Those attending are likely to find others that they can easily identify with.

Support groups strengths and weaknesses

Attendance at support groups pre-supposes a self-labelling. Further, the self-labelling may be inaccurate/incomplete and may go unchallenged in a support group. Nevertheless, support groups can be a first step in socialisation for treatment. Many local groups have regular social outings. For example, Headway, a support group for those with acquired brain injury, invites not only the sufferer but also their carers to gatherings. Groups such as Carers UK offer online chat forums for carers

Social support 41

of people with variously dementia and multiple sclerosis. Oftentimes the carers have become very isolated, sometimes having given up their paid work with consequent financial problems, to look after the affected person. Some support groups such as OCD awareness groups also have a professional input, with annual conferences for professionals and sufferers. But not all areas of the country are served by local groups. Local support groups are usually highly dependent on the input of volunteers and can become inactive. Further, a local support group may have the blessing of some national charity, acting as a guarantor of the quality of service, but in other instances an umbrella body simply advertises the provisions of a local group.

The therapeutic neglect of social support

Social support is a major predictor of naturally occurring recovery from conditions as diverse as depression, post-traumatic stress disorder and psychosis. Meta-analytical studies of PTSD risk/protective factors placed perceived social support at the top of the list of predictive factors [Brewin et al. (2000) and Ozer et al. (2003)]. Yet social support is rarely a target in psychotherapeutic interventions. In this chapter consideration is given to providing a routine focus on engineering social support in therapy. But clinicians need to be mindful that it is the perception of social support that makes the difference rather than the absolute level of support. Evidence-based treatments such as CBT tend to be largely intra-psychic, and it is suggested that their potency may be enhanced by the inclusion of an interpersonal focus. If a person does not have the finances to heat their home, their very survival, in a long winter, is in question. So, too, our mental well-being is dependent on our climate. Whilst Alford and Beck (1997) have drawn attention to the reciprocal interactions of our cognition, emotion, behaviour and physiology in determining our functioning, our bodily and intrapsychic processes are also affected by the climate, as seen in Figure 5.2.

Cognition, emotion, physiology and behaviour can be regarded as constituting four ports of entry into the individual. For ease of illustration, in Figure 5.2 climate is shown as operating via the cognitive port, but the interpersonal climate may act via any port; thus a friend may pay a surprise visit, lifting my spirits (emotion) as I recall many happy exchanges (cognition) and suggest we go sit in the garden (behaviour), where I experience the pleasant warmth (physiology) of the sun and reflect (cognition) that it is good to feel the warmth after such a long winter.

Therapists do not routinely invite the partners of clients into a therapy session, though they may tolerate this at the initial face-to-face assessment, if the client feels in need of such support. The non-inclusion of significant others in assessment and treatment may be driven partly by understandable concerns that the client may be reluctant to divulge in the presence of others. But comprehensive assessment involves the distillation of information from as wide a range of sources as possible, including significant others, review of GP records and the findings of interview. Without an opportunity for the significant other to tell their story of the client's

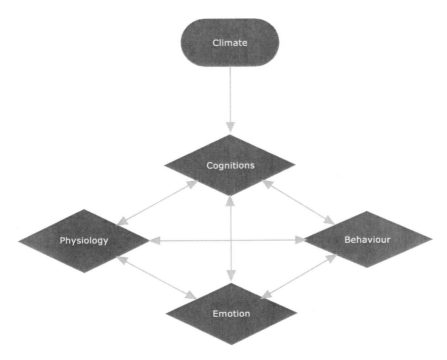

Figure 5.2 Intrapsychic and interpersonal determinants of emotion

functioning, not only is important data lost, but the family member or friend is excluded from contributing to the therapeutic process.

Friends and family are with the client twenty-four seven, so their potential therapeutic contribution should not be neglected. The evidence-based psychotherapies such as CBT place a strong emphasis on a client's practice of new skills outside of the therapy session. Mausbach et al. (2010) reviewed twenty-three studies looking at the effects of homework compliance on treatment outcome and found a small to moderate effect ($r = 0.26$), suggesting that greater compliance with homework is associated with better outcome. Encouragement by significant others can do much to ensure a client's compliance with therapy homework. But others need to be involved in the therapeutic process to fully appreciate the significance of homework assignments and to be recruited as a quasi-therapist in the community.

Friends/family as arbiters of socially significant change

Those involved in supporting the client might be the best judges of whether a treatment has meaningfully improved the client's functioning or returned them to their best functioning state, because they are on the receiving end of the client's functioning. But studies very rarely use these arguably more objective yardsticks. It appears that the friends and family of clients are largely excluded from assisting clients along the mental health pathway. Unsurprisingly, where clients arrive at as a result of treatment may not be recognisable to significant others, but the beauty of where they arrive at may lie only in the eye of the therapist or of the body responsible for employing the clinician. It is tempting for agencies and clinicians to rely solely on relatively opaque measures of improvement such as 'clinically significant improvement' on some psychometric test, completed by the client in the presence of the therapist. This can create a 'therapist delusion' in which the client's desire to please and/or extricate himself/herself from therapy is ignored and in which the change observed on the test is problematically connected to the desired socially significant outcome.

The beneficial and adverse effects of friends/family

'No man is an island, entire of itself' wrote John Donne, English clergyman and poet, 400 years ago [Meditation XVII], perhaps anticipating that a wholly intra-psychic focus on an individual's concerns was unlikely to prove particularly fruitful. Whilst significant others can help bring about positive 'climate' change in others, there is a negative toxic effect, and the reduction of this toxicity may be a prime therapeutic target. Veterans who return home from war to unsympathetic, judgemental and possibly hostile social environments show greater vulnerability to developing psychopathology. Negative responses of support providers ('negative support') have been implicated as a more powerful predictor of distress than 'positive social support' among victims of crime or abuse [Campbell et al. (2001)].

Enabling friends/family to question psychological treatment

Friends, family and society in general inevitably have a stake in evaluating whether the client has had appropriate treatment. But how might they judge this as non-experts? Parents are in a similar position with regards to their child's education; most would be concerned if there was no evidence that the child had been given any homework. It would be expected that the child's homework was written down, and most parents would regard it as unsatisfactory if the teacher simply told the child what to do with regard to homework. Given that the evidence-based psychotherapies are essentially psycho-educational, unless there is written evidence of homework and review of homework, it is doubtful that evidence-based practice (EBP) has taken place. Just as teachers and schools are accountable and must be seen to have addressed homework, so too clinicians and their service-providing agency need to demonstrate similar accountability. Regrettably, it is rare to find in records of mental health agencies the specifics of what the client was asked to do, much less how the assignment worked out in practice, making it near impossible to distil what learning has occurred. Friends and family members need empowering to challenge this poor service.

44 *Part II*

Friends, family members, sufferers themselves and therapists need to be aware that many mental health practices are not in fact evidence-based but are variously eminence-based (where status counts), vehemence-based (where stridency counts), eloquence-based (where smoothness of tongue counts) and confidence-based (based purely on bravado). [Isaac and Fitzgerald (1999)]. It takes courage to say, 'The Emperor has no clothes'.

Telephone assessments of clients preclude the involvement of significant others and sets the scene for the non-involvement of the latter in the therapeutic process. This stands in stark contrast to recent developments in physical medicine, where for example cancer patients are invited to attend with a relative and other sufferers whilst the surgeon explains what chemotherapy would involve, shows where it and any subsequent operation would take place and describes the aftercare involved.

When support is not enough

Therapists sometimes legitimate their activities by describing them as providing support for clients. Indeed clients may express satisfaction with a therapist's ministrations on the basis that they felt supported, but this does not necessarily mean that the problem/s that led them to seek help have been resolved. Thus a client's perception of having been supported by a therapist is essentially a surrogate outcome measure, necessary but not sufficient. Sometimes a service continues to be funded because nobody has questioned whether intended support is actually happening at the coalface:

> *Barbara was the twenty-six-year-old single parent of three children all under five. She was physically and sexually abused as a child and was placed with a foster parent. She moved out of the foster mother's home at age nineteen, but the latter continued to be funded to provide support. However, though Barbara continued to keep in contact with her foster mother, she did not regard this as 'support'. She had concerns about whether one of her children might be abused by his natural father and was distressed by the inappropriate photographs he sent her of both her and her child. Barbara related well to a social worker attached to the children's centre, and he addressed her safety concerns but did not have the resources or training to provide her with the therapy he believed she needed. She was aware that she used sex as a way of avoiding abandonment even though this led to abusive relationships. It was a solicitor who made her aware that monies ought to be following her for her to purchase the services she needed and not to reside automatically in the local authority.*

In this example the positive support the client had from her social worker, the children's centre and, to a lesser degree, her foster mother was outweighed by the negative support' from her children's father, and there was need for a therapeutic input to help redress the imbalance.

Support groups are oftentimes one-dimensional or lacking in any dimension

Despite the undoubted benefits of support groups, their identity tends to be wrapped up in a single disorder despite co-morbidity being the norm. Patients with co-morbidity have a poorer prognosis. The most consistent predictor of a poor treatment outcome for clients in treatment for substance misuse is the presence of psychopathology [McLellan et al. (1983) and Rounsaville et al. (1987)]. Similarly, substance misuse is a predictor of poor treatment outcome for mentally ill patients [Drake and Wallach (1989) and Carey et al. (1991)]. Research evidence suggests that drug treatment outcomes improve if mental disorders are treated [e.g. Woody et al. (1985)]. In this connection the effect of AA may be limited.

Local charities and national charities such as Mind often run time-limited as well as open support groups. Typically these groups invite all comers and have vaguely defined remits such as 'managing stress'. Those attending often report that they were valuable and may even recommend them to a friend or family member similarly affected. However, there is little empirical evidence that they change the diagnostic status of a person:

> *Sheila attended an eight-week stress support group run by a local charity. She said that she found it helpful to get things off her chest and to be with others who she felt understood her. Sheila was a support worker who was badly assaulted by a service user with learning difficulties as she was about to assist him crossing a busy road that he took fright at. She felt unsupported by her manager and employer, who she felt were simply concerned about her speedy return to work. Sheila was suffering from post-traumatic stress disorder and depression as a consequence of the assault; neither disorder had been systematically addressed in the support group and she had lost her job.*

Support groups are often run by charities, who employ paid professionals such as Sheila, mentioned above, as well as utilising volunteers.

There is a line of a Beatles song which says, 'I get by with a little help from my friend', summarising a major finding from research that perceived social support has often been found to be the biggest predictor of recovery from disorders such as depression and PTSD. Building on this, many charities offer support groups for those with mental health problems, but whilst such groups are an aid to recovery they are rarely sufficient. Whilst attendees often extol their virtues, fundamental difficulties often go unaddressed, as the following case illustrates:

> *Kieron was involved in the Hillsborough Football tragedy of 1988, in which he saw people being crushed at the gates. He suffered flashbacks, his mood deteriorated and he became increasingly irritable. At various times he had seen an assistant psychologist, a clinical psychologist and a consultant psychiatrist. Subsequent to Hillsborough he had made two suicide attempts and had a brief period of imprisonment. It was noted that he had become extremely*

46　*Part II*

anxious, but the records and correspondence revealed that there was no consideration that he might have post-traumatic stress disorder and no evidence-based treatment had been proferred. Thirty-seven years after the tragedy he was still having difficulties and his marriage was strained, but he did find solace in attending a weekly support group.

At a minimum he may have benefitted from some psychoeducation about his difficulties. This could have taken two different forms: a) unguided self-help; for example, the National Center for PTSD in the United States offers an app for the PTSD Coach to give an entirely personal and private way of dealing with difficulties, or he could have been encouraged by his GP to read *Moving On After Trauma* [Scott (2009)], in which the reader is invited to identify with one of twenty trauma victims and follow in their footsteps to recovery; or b) guided self-help, in which a mental health worker, say a low intensity IAPT worker, had up to four contact sessions (face to face, e-mail or over the phone) to guide him through the relevant text, e.g. a PTSD survival manual [Scott (2009)]. Such psychoeducation may have socialised him for psychological treatment. Given his preparedness to attend a support group, he may have been particularly open to engage in group CBT for PTSD; a protocol for this based around a PTSD survival manual is discussed in Scott (2009). Group CBT has been found to be as effective as individual CBT for depression and most anxiety disorders. Its particular virtue is that it capitalises on social support. However, despite its economic benefits, (Scott and Stradling [1991] estimate a 50% saving) it is not a major player in the provision of psychological therapy services in the UK. By contrast, in Denmark, group and individual CBT are given equal status with a subtle interweaving of the two modalities.

Psychological disorders

The case can be made that it is a better use of scarce psychotherapy services to focus them only on where there is a clear need, i.e. on those known to have a psychological disorder. But how reliably can it be known that a person has a psychological disorder?

Reliability

The levels of agreement for psychiatric disorders in DSM-5 are shown in Table 5.1. They are expressed in terms of a statistic called 'kappa' [Freedman et al. (2013)]. For illustration, if an illness appears in 10% of a clinic's patients and two clinicians agree on its diagnosis 85% of the time, the kappa statistic is 0.46, similar to the weighted composite statistic for schizophrenia in this DSM-5 field trial.

A kappa of 0.4 and above is regarded as good or very good agreement, 0.2 to 0.39 denotes questionable agreement and less than 0.2 indicates an unacceptable level of agreement. Whilst some disorders such as post-traumatic stress disorder had high reliability (kappa 0.67) others such as depression (kappa 0.28) had questionable agreement; so too did the personality disorders, with the notable exception

Table 5.1 Interrater reliability of diagnoses from the initial DSM-5 field trials

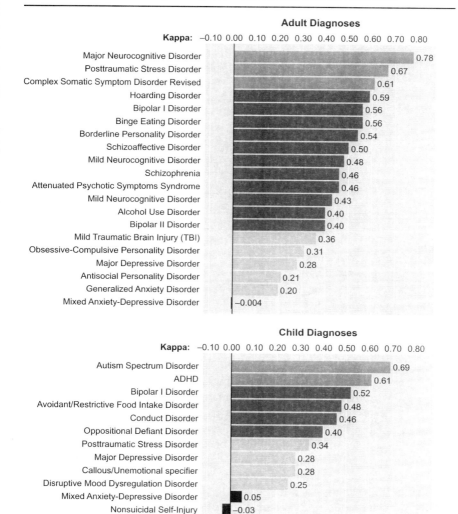

of borderline personality disorder with a kappa of 0.54. 'Mixed anxiety and depression' had a kappa of 0, making this diagnosis wholly unreliable. With regard to children, autism spectrum disorder and ADHD had very good agreement. Overall the field trial suggests that two-thirds of people could receive a reliable diagnosis at a first interview. The focus of the field trial was on a single assessment – whether or not a higher proportion of people would receive a reliable diagnosis after a few

48   *Part II*

visits to their clinician is unknown. But it seems likely that over the course of a few sessions a clinician is better able to make a definitive diagnosis. Arguably, accurate diagnosis involves an ongoing dialogue with the client, as the essence of their difficulties often emerges gradually.

It is apparent from Table 5.1 that use of diagnostic criteria does not guarantee a reliable assessment, but it is arguably a lot better than the alternative.

Unreliable routine assessments

In a study of 145 non-psychotic clients attending community clinics, Shear et al. (2000) found that 58 had been diagnosed as having an adjustment disorder using a routine open-ended psychiatric interview. By contrast when the gold-standard SCID [First et al. (1997)] interview was used, only five met criteria for an adjustment disorder. (The SCID asks one or more questions about each symptom that comprises a disorder and specifies criteria for judging whether that symptom is present at a clinically significant level.) In addition, the SCID identified twenty-two sufferers from PTSD whilst the routine interview identified only one. Rettew et al. (2009) aggregated thirty-eight studies reporting the agreement between clinician-generated diagnoses and those from structured diagnostic interviews and reported categorical agreement, kappa, of only 0.27 across all disorders.

Routine open-ended interviews tend to miss the presence of additional disorders (co-morbidity). In a study [Zimmerman and Mattia (1999)] comparing the prevalence of disorders in 500 clients given a traditional, open-ended diagnostic interview, with 500 patients given a structured interview [SCID First et al. (1997)], individuals interviewed with the SCID were assigned significantly more axis I diagnoses than individuals assessed with an unstructured interview. More than one-third of the clients interviewed with the SCID were diagnosed with three or more disorders, in contrast to fewer than ten per cent of the clients assessed with an unstructured interview. Fifteen disorders were more frequently diagnosed in the SCID sample, and these differences occurred across mood, anxiety, eating, somatoform, and impulse-control disorder categories. The results suggest that in routine clinical practice, clinicians under-recognize diagnostic comorbidity. Anxiety, somatoform, and not otherwise specified (NOS) disorders were the most frequently under-detected disorders. This research was subsequently independently replicated in other settings [Basco et al. (2000), Shear et al. (2000) and Miller et al. (2002)].

Further, there is evidence that using an open-ended interview, clinicians tend to stop at the first disorder identified [Zimmerman and Mattia (2000)]. This can have serious consequences. For example, [Panagioti et al. (2012)] found that the suicidality of PTSD clients was strongly mediated by the level of comorbid depression. Thus a clinician using an open-ended interview with a traumatised client might readily identify what the clinician takes to be cardinal symptoms of PTSD, e.g. nightmares/flashbacks, but then neglect to make sufficiently detailed enquiry about depression and thereby make a poor risk assessment. A structured interview ensures that no disorders are missed.

The poor agreement between routine open-ended interviews (i.e. those routinely used by clinicians) and semi-structured interviews is not confined to the emotional disorders but applies also to the recognition of personality disorders. Samuels (2015) reviewed the literature on the concordance between clinician's judgements of personality disorder and that established by a semi-structured interview and found a poor median level of agreement, kappa 0.26. Accurate identification of a personality disorder is important as it portends a poor prognosis for coexisting disorders, e.g. depression [Newton-Howes (2006)].

Increasing reliability

In the DSM-5 field trials two different clinicians would interview the same client, the second typically a week later, both armed with a DSM-5 checklist. Whilst a checklist is good for ensuring that questions are asked about all the symptoms of a disorder, i.e. it controls for information variance, they do not specify in any detail the threshold for determining whether a symptom should be regarded as present at a clinically significant level, i.e., it does not control for criterion variance. For example, following an extreme trauma a person may well have nightmares of the trauma that may have initially caused them to wake up distressed, but nine months later, though nightmares might still be happening, they are not being woken by them; the latter might be considered below a functional impairment threshold whilst the former would likely be above it. This approach is taken in the SCID [SCID DSM-5] standardised semi-structured interview, controlling not only for information variance but also for criterion variance. Thus, the reliabilities shown in Table 5.1 are likely to be enhanced if such an instrument is employed. The SCID [First et al. (2002)] has been the ultimate 'gold standard' in most controlled trials, along with other standardised semi-structured interviews such as the Anxiety Disorders Interview Schedule [ADIS DiNardo et al. (1994)] .

The reliability studies for DSM-5 have produced worse results than for DSM-IV, but this is likely to be due largely to a difference in methodology [Chmielewski et al. (2015)]. In the earlier versions of the DSM reliability was assessed by one clinician interviewing a client and another clinician watching/listening to a recording of the session and making his/her diagnosis. This is a different procedure than two clinicians interviewing the same person, typically a week apart. Chmielewski et al. (2015) produce data (using DSM-IV criteria) that the kappa for depression using the recording method was 0.92 whereas using the test-retest method it was 0.60, and for a specific phobia using a recording the kappa was 0.73 compared to 0.54. Thus even a week later a person is likely to give a somewhat different account of their functioning. This makes it imperative that clinicians are very mindful of the timeframe they are talking about when interviewing clients and need to be conscious that diagnoses are highly time specific and require the identification of the *simultaneous* presence of symptoms. DSM-5 has been criticised as inferior to its predecessors, but this criticism may be largely misplaced because of a difference in assessment methodology.

50   *Part II*

Unreliable assessment prevents the translation of EBTs into routine practice

Evidence-based treatments for psychological disorders are diagnosis specific; thus for example an EBT for borderline personality disorder, dialectical behaviour therapy [Linehan et al. (1994)], is unlikely to be delivered in routine practice because the clinician does not use the appropriate methodology to identify the condition. Indeed it is not possible to specify 'what works' without specifying 'for whom'. Lack of clarity about the recipient of the psychological help means that it is most unlikely that the latter can be effective. The more heterogenous the population addressed, the less credible the intervention.

Alford and Beck (1997) have proposed the cognitive content specificity hypothesis, which states that disorders are distinguished by their cognitive content. In support of this Clark et al. (1989) found that thoughts of loss and failure were specifically associated with depression, whereas cognitions of harm and danger were uniquely predictive of anxiety. The cognitive content specificity hypothesis provides a rationale for the matching of treatment and disorder.

There can be psychological processes that are common to a number of disorders, and this has led to the advocacy of transdiagnostic interventions, e.g. Norton and Barrera (2012). Such interventions are very attractive in that therapists may have to learn only a limited number of skills and it would be possible to include a limited range of diverse presentations, e.g. social anxiety disorder, panic disorder and generalised anxiety disorder, within a treatment group Norton and Barrera (2012). However, the transdiagnostic interventions have not been subjected to independent evaluation or shown any advantage over existing EBTs.

Within a psychological disorder framework, NICE has provided treatment guidelines inter alia on social anxiety disorder (2013) and common mental health disorders (depression, generalised anxiety disorder, panic disorder, obsessive-compulsive disorder and post-traumatic stress disorder [2011]), as well as on psychosis, bipolar disorder, drug misuse, personality disorders, autism, attention deficit hyperactivity disorder (ADHD) and conduct disorders. The language of psychological disorders provides a common language for talking about a person's difficulties. Without agreed definitions as to what constitutes a particular disorder/ difficulty, clinicians are likely to be at cross purposes. From a research point of view it is necessary to carefully specify what problem was addressed and what strategy worked. If positive findings are to be translated into routine practice there has to be clear identification of the target disorder/difficulty and an ensuring of fidelity to the evidence-based treatment for the target.

Whilst this framework mimics the fruitful medical model of treating disorders, it can be objected that it is inappropriate because there are no biological markers for any of the aforementioned disorders/difficulties. Nevertheless it offers a useful heuristic for thinking about and organising treatment. Allen Frances (2013), the leading light in the development of DSM-IV [American Psychiatric Association (1994)], has observed, 'We saw DSM-IV as a guidebook, not a bible – a collection of temporarily useful diagnostic constructs, not a catalog of "real" diseases. . . . People shouldn't worship the DSM categories, but it does make you a better clinician to know them'. Pragmatically, diagnosis offers greater clarity and direction than regarding each person's difficulties as unique, which undoubtedly they are, and distilling an 'appropriate' treatment.

Without recourse to diagnosis, on what basis would a person's treatment be regarded as 'appropriate': the client's or clinician's judgement, or some consensus of clinicians, perhaps a combination of all three? Would such a treatment be evidence based or eminence based? Can the recipient of a treatment be the ultimate arbiter of whether a treatment is appropriate? Does the clinician not have a vested interest in judging the effectiveness of his/her intervention? Abandoning the diagnostic framework raises more difficulties than it solves.

In practice many, (perhaps most, in the author's experience) psychological therapy practitioners operate on the belief that it is sufficient to give the client a questionnaire to complete (self-report), measure and re-administer it at a later date to gauge whether therapy is effective. But clients usually complete these measures in the presence of the practitioners; in some instances the latter reads them out. This is likely to be subjected to demand characteristics, the client wanting to please the therapist and/or convince themselves they have not been wasting their time in therapy or to facilitate an easy exit from therapy. Further, the self-report measures were developed in a particular context, as measures of the severity of a disorder once it was established by independent blind diagnostic interview what that disorder was. Routinely, clinicians do not conduct such an interview, so the meaning of the psychometric tests administered is problematic to say the least. Therapists can be like a sports commentator exclaiming 'What a hit!' at a particular score, but without knowing whether the game being played is cricket, tennis or squash it is pretty meaningless.

Those with recognised psychological disorders are likely to score low on the WEMWBS, but there is no well-being score specific treatment. Whilst tailoring treatment to the individual is necessary in the implementation of every evidence-based treatment protocol, without a diagnostic framework there are no boundaries to the range of treatments. The danger is in succumbing to the Dodo's verdict in *Alice's Adventures in Wonderland* [Lewis Carroll (1865)]: 'Everybody has won, and all must have prizes'.

Beyond psychological disorders

Much of the dismissal of the concept of 'diagnosis' in mental health comes from those in the anti-psychiatry movement, which is heavily populated with psychologists and some leading psychiatrists. Psychology compared to psychiatry is the 'new kid on the block' and a dispassionate judge might wonder about whether not some of the disputes have a territorial quality. It is undoubtedly true that there have been shameful times in the history of psychiatry (see Wertham [1968] for a discussion of appalling behaviour in the Nazi era and Sidley [2015]), but if I were a betting person I would say no group, secular or religious, has been or will be free of such failings. There is a liberal-progressive meta-narrative that society always

52   *Part II*

learns from its mistakes and moves forward, but as McGrath (2015) discusses it is not very convincing. But to highlight simply the misdeeds of a group risks throwing out the baby with the bathwater. Dialogue asks what can we learn from each other, but it is at the expense of a threat to our own worldview, perhaps a necessary cross to bear.

The anti-psychiatry movement is exemplified in the preface to *Tales of the Madhouse* [Sidley (2015)]:

> Psychiatry is a fundamentally flawed discipline routinely delivering a form of institutionalised discrimination that detrimentally impacts on the lives of many people already blighted by distress and misery. The engine room for its deleterious practices is psychiatry's stubborn, fallacious and self serving insistence that the range of human suffering construed as "mental illness" primarily represents the manifestation of some form of biological aberration.

This movement has an almost exclusive focus on those at the psychotic end of the spectrum and their undoubted mismanagement. But I am not at all sure that the same can be said for those with the common mental health disorders (depression, generalised anxiety disorder, panic disorder, obsessive-compulsive disorder and post-traumatic stress disorder). Even at the time of the First World War, soldiers who returned from the front with 'shell shock' could find themselves in hospital with occupational activities and gardening; in this connection the War Poet, Wilfred Owen, whilst in Craiglockhart, (just outside Edinburgh) was encouraged by Dr. Brock to translate the experiences he relived in his dreams into poetry [Scott (2015b)].

It is almost certainly the case that all psychological phenomena have some physical expression (correlate). If I am anxious about giving a talk it will likely be reflected in some butterflies in my stomach, but that is not at all to say that the latter has caused the former, a biological determinism. But that is not to say that a biological understanding of difficulties may not illuminate our understanding and treatment of those difficulties. Some years ago Steve Stradling and I wrote a paper entitled 'Translating the psychobiology of post-traumatic stress disorder into clinically useful analogy' (2001), and more recently Joseph Le Doux, a neuroscientist (2015), has written 'Anxious', the last chapter of which is titled 'Therapy: lessons learned from the laboratory', which is a must-read for clinicians wishing to help clients overcome fears.

It is possible to jettison the idea of mental illness/diagnosis and make a case for simply focussing on mental well-being [see Sidley (2015)], but there is little empirical evidence to suggest that this has yet yielded convincing positive results. Whilst it is true that bodies such as the American National Institute for Mental Health [Winerman (2013)] are no longer funding research based entirely on DSM-defined disorders, and this represents a conceptual shift, the benefits of this have not yet been established. Advocates of the anti-psychiatry movements such as Sidley (2015) place great emphasis on the involvement of clients (service users), use of drop-in centres and a compassionate and informal approach, but seem not to appreciate that this was tried in social work in the 1970s and early 1980s. Working as social workers at that time we could demonstrate no obvious benefit from our family service units/drop-in centres/voluntary agencies, and unsurprisingly social work lost its therapeutic role and became about policing. Sidley (2015) advocates a 'recovery approach' where the emphasis is on 'adherence to a set of values and principles believed to be instrumental in enabling people suffering with mental disorders to live meaningful lives. Active engagement with life, participation in worthwhile activities, the maintenance of hope and the achievement of personal goals are all highlighted to be as important, if not more so, than the elimination of psychiatric symptoms'. This creates a sense of déjà vu in the author; not that I disagree with it in an ethical sense, but historically it is arguable that it has failed to deliver. The issue of what is meant by 'recovery' will not go away, and if it is made fuzzy it will cease to be funded.

The mechanics of recovery from psychological disorder

Recovery from psychological disorders depends partly on the nature of those problems and partly on access to treatment and the quality of that treatment. But treatment itself is dependent on what treatment has been commissioned and the quality-control strategies of a service provider. The context within which a sufferer seeks relief from their difficulties is summarised in Figure 5.3.

Figure 5.3 The mechanics of recovery

54 Part II

The workings of Figure 5.3 can be illustrated by the following example:

At school Janine was regarded as 'slow' and was subjected to bullying. She would absent herself from class because of panic attacks, but she did not tell anyone in school or her supportive family about these attacks. Janine reflected that 'there was no way of telling anyone that you were going mad'. Even at this early age Janine had imbibed the societal prejudice about mental health problems. Unfortunately her teachers saw her simply as disruptive. After leaving school she attended a hairdressing class; when Janine was asked to demonstrate a skill, one of her tutors picked up that she was having panic attacks. She then volunteered that she was also having panic attacks for no reason. The tutor was able to normalise her response, and a less pejorative meaning to her difficulties (bottom cog of Figure 1) was distilled such that she was referred on to a local young person's charity (the middle cog of Figure 5.3). The counsellor at the charity was reasonably competent and taught her controlled breathing to manage her panic attacks. The counselling sessions went on for over a year, with the frequency of the panic attacks gradually subsiding. However because of pressure from the charity (top cog) over waiting lists the sessions were curtailed. Years later she suffered a recurrence of the panic disorder after a minor bump in a car and became depressed because the incident was so minor that it should not have provoked such a reaction. She had not consulted her GP and wondered about the best way forward. She was again a bottom cog concerned about how she would fare interacting with the other cogs.

Mental health apps abound, and it is possible that had these been around at the time Janine first experienced her difficulties, she would not have developed panic disorder. Society also has an input into the 'Mechanics of Recovery' shown in Figure 5.3 in determining the level of funding for mental health services. Recovery is also affected by societal stigma regarding mental illness. Society can help prevent the development of mental health problems in the first place by funding charities such as Silverline, where lonely people have telephone access to a twenty-four-hour helpline and volunteers make regular phone calls to them. Church groups often provide an unrivalled sense of community, with a ready listening ear for personal struggles, whether emotional or practical, e.g. liaison with food banks or credit unions, exerting a preventative mental health function.

Should psychological therapy services be made available to those without a psychological disorder?

Given the limited resources for mental health, is it appropriate to fund counselling for those without a recognised psychological disorder?

Gwen saw her GP over relationship problems; she tended to pursue relationships that she knew could only end in tears and went to extraordinary lengths to maintain them. She was sexually abused on one occasion as a child. Her

GP thought that she might have a personality disorder and Gwen felt that this could well be the case. She was also stressed by her brother's gambling and her inability to help him. Detailed examination using recognised diagnostic criteria for psychological and personality disorders revealed no pathology. She had never previously sought any psychological help.

In DSM-5 such problems can be subsumed under a category of 'relationship problems', but this is not a recognised psychiatric disorder, and the authors of DSM-5 simply suggest that this categorisation may be worthy of further investigation. It could be argued that this represents a creeping medicalisation of everyday difficulties. Yet without a DSM-5 label in the United States it is difficult to justify the provision of and funding for services. But given that funds are limited, should there be a clear demarcation as to the appropriate use of funds? It can be objected that treating Gwen would prevent the development of a DSM-5 disorder, but it would be near impossible to confirm or deny this. In practice, in the UK the lack of a diagnosis is not a barrier to psychological treatment.

Psychoeducation

All the CBT therapies begin with psychoeducation, involving a negotiated description of how the client's difficulties have come about and how they are maintained and a prescription of what can be done. Psychoeducation as part of CBT treatment is located in a framework in which a) the client has had the opportunity to tell the tale of the development of their difficulties; b) a problem list is created which directs attention to enquiry about a range of possible disorders (differential diagnosis); c) the conduct of standardised diagnostic interview; d) assessment of the severity of any identified disorder using a relevant psychometric test, e.g. use of the Beck Depression Inventory to measure the severity of depression. Thus within face-to-face CBT there is a zooming-in on the most appropriate psychoeducational material. Without this lens inappropriate material may be read. Psychoeducation can also take place in other modalities, e.g. through the Internet or Skype.

Screens for psychological disorders can be used to highlight appropriate psychoeducation material. The first step questionnaire [Scott (2011)], reproduced in full in Appendix B, is a screen for the most common disorders. Table 5.2 shows the screening questions for PTSD.

A positive response to three of the symptom questions is an effective screen for PTSD, suggesting that further questioning about each of the PTSD symptoms is required. The final question asks whether the person wants help with the specified difficulties, allowing for a response that indicates ambivalence. If treatment is embarked upon without some resolution of ambivalence, the person is unlikely to fully engage, perhaps defaulting. The first step questionnaire also highlights difficulties that a person might not readily volunteer such as alcohol dependence. Table 5.3 shows the screen for this.

56 *Part II*

Table 5.2 Screen for PTSD

Post-traumatic stress disorder	*Yes*	*No*	*Don't Know*
In your life, have you ever had any experience that was so frightening, horrible or upsetting that, in the past month, you:			
i Have had nightmares about it or thought about it when you did not want to?			
ii Tried hard not to think about it or went out of your way to avoid situations that reminded you of it?			
iii Were constantly on guard, watchful or easily startled?			
iv Felt numb or detached from others, activities or your surroundings?			
Is this something with which you would like help?			

Table 5.3 Screen for substance abuse/dependence

Substance abuse/dependence	*Yes*	*No*	*Don't Know*
i Have you felt guilty about your drinking/drug use?			
ii Have you felt you should cut down on your alcohol/ drug use?			
iii Have people got annoyed with you about your drinking/drug taking?			
iv Do you drink/use drugs before midday?			
Is this something with which you would like help?			

Again the final question of the screen asks whether these difficulties are something that the person would like help with. This question is probably more salient in the area of addiction than elsewhere, and without taking account of ambivalence, treatment efforts are likely to come to naught.

There is some evidence that clients' readiness to adopt change strategies appears to predict the speed with which depressive symptoms resolve in CBT clients with depression and anxiety disorders [Lewis et al. (2012)]. Those who were more contemplative, i.e. seeing advantages and disadvantages in changing their behaviour, were more likely to speedily reduce their depressive symptoms than those who were pre-contemplative, i.e. not recognising their difficulty as a problem that they needed to address. The first step questionnaire and its interview counterpart, The 7 Minute Interview, provide an indication of how contemplative/pre-contemplative the client is, and this can be a useful therapeutic focus.

Any screening instrument necessarily produces false positives, hence the need for further detailed enquiry, but it can at a minimum highlight the educational material that might be most relevant. Scott (2011) has produced survival manuals for depression, each of the anxiety disorders and post-traumatic stress disorder.

Social support   57

For illustrative purposes 'The Depression Survival Manual' is reproduced in Appendix D. The manuals can at least help people anticipate what they can expect in CBT treatment and if their difficulties are mild, and with the support of a significant other may be sufficient to resolve their difficulties. There are however a multitude of other psychoeducational materials available including *Moving on After Trauma* [Scott (2008)] and *Overcoming Depression: A Five Areas Approach* (2014) by Chris Williams, and it remains to be tested which material is better for which disorder.

The screening questions for depression have been found to correctly identify 79% of those who are depressed (i.e. the sensitivity is 0.79) and correctly identify 94% of those who are not depressed (i.e. the specificity is 0.94). Importantly, including the question 'Is this something with which you would like help?' greatly reduced the number of false positives [Arroll et al. (2005)]. This question has therefore been added to the screening for the other disorders. The screening symptom questions for post-traumatic stress disorder [Prins et al. (2004)], obsessive-compulsive disorder [Fineberg et al. (2003)] and substance abuse [Ewing (1984)] have also been subjected to empirical investigation and found to be reliable. Further, the screening questions for generalised anxiety disorder (GAD) symptoms cover the same content area as the two-item GAD scale that has been demonstrated to have high sensitivity and specificity for detecting GAD [Kroenke et al. (2007)]. However, at this time the screening questions for other disorders have only a face validity.

Sometimes a person is not only suffering from one of the disorders covered in the first step questionnaire but may also have a personality disorder; the latter may sabotage standard treatment if not identified and targeted. The Standardised Assessment of Personality Abbreviated Scale (SAPAS), Appendix C, is a screen for personality disorders [Moran et al. (2003)] consisting of just eight items, each item answered with a 'yes' or a 'no'; example items are 'Would you normally describe yourself as a loner?' and 'In general, do you trust other people?' A score of three or more identifies 90% of those with personality disorders. Using a of cut-off of five in a study by Moran et al. (2003) meant that no one who did not have a personality disorder was identified as having one, i.e. there were no false positives. Using a cut-off of five or more, Moran et al. (2003) identified three out of five of those who did have a personality disorder. But the SAPAS is only a screen and it requires detailed further enquiry to establish a personality disorder.

Unfortunately no screen for disorders or personality disorders is in use in routine NHS practice, making it likely that disorders/personality will be missed and treatment at best sub-optimal.

Return to full functioning

Mental health services can be likened to a product on sale in a variety of markets, poundshops, shops and superstores; many services fail trading standards and should be subjected to criticism by the Advertising Standards Authority. The 'product' may be attractively packaged and purchased by an unsuspecting consumer or

58 *Part II*

commisioner of services. This chapter risks being very boring because its task is to increase awareness of how to interrogate claims of mental health effectiveness, rather in the way that a judge might weigh the testimony of expert witnesses in court without himself being an expert in the field in question.

A brief history of evaluating health mental programmes

Up until the 1960s therapies were advocated on the eminence and charisma of the originator of the therapy. This continues to a degree to the present day, but since the 1960s it has been credible to ask the question, 'What works?' albeit this is not a universally accepted question. The author remembers doing a social work course in the early 1970s. Having previously studied physics, I asked whether casework (then a psychodynamically flavoured form of counselling) actually works; this was met with incredulity. Evidence was not the currency of the course. There was a regular, large group meeting of students set up to explore the dynamics of interactions. I arrived late for one such group, and all eyes were on me as I arrived and mumbled, 'Sorry, I missed the bus'. There was a stony silence and I reiterated my apology, but the course leader just glared at me. Therein lies the historical problems with 'therapies'; there is no way of presenting evidence that invalidates them, and attempts to do so are taken as further evidence of the pathology of the dissident. The therapeutic dimension of social work continued through the 1970s but by the 1980s the emphasis had moved to 'task-centred social work'. However, the lack of empirical evidence for its utility and its perceived failure to prevent child abuse led largely to its demise, to be replaced largely by a policing role and my own shift to psychology. In 2005, Marsh and Doel observed, 'Skills at social work are being reduced to an application of administrative proceedings drawn primarily from a substantial agency guidance manual', and their response to this was to re-emphasise the importance of task-centred social work.

Psychiatry has fared rather better than social work. In the 1960s psychiatrist Aaron Beck was concerned that research was impossible because there was little agreement about what was meant by terms such as *depression* and *schizophrenia*. He concluded that the levels of agreement on diagnosis, using the routine psychiatric interview, was between 32% and 54% [Beck et al. (1962)]. This led to the development of the Feighner criteria, which in turn led to research diagnostic criteria in 1972, which acted as a springboard for the operationally defined diagnostic criteria in DSM-III (1980). Kendler et al. (2010) have commented that the team that developed the Feighner criteria made three key contributions to psychiatry: the systematic use of operationalized diagnostic criteria; the reintroduction of an emphasis on illness course and outcome; and an emphasis on the need, whenever possible, to base diagnostic criteria on empirical evidence. Thus the gold standard for evaluating the efficacy of psychotropic medication or psychotherapy was whether the person no longer met diagnostic criteria for the identified condition/s and whether those gains were maintained. The latest refinement of diagnostic criteria, DSM-5 was published in 2013 [APA (2013)] but it is very debatable as to whether this is an improvement on its predecessor DSM-IV-TR [American Psychiatric Association (2000)].

The strengths and limits of self-help

Self-help materials such as mobile-device applications (apps), leaflets, books and computerised CBT can be a very useful way of letting a person know that they are not alone with their difficulties. Further they can create an awareness of coping strategies that are better than currently employed coping strategies. But whilst self-help materials are a useful adjunct to treatment they are usually not sufficient alone. Faced with a pressing need to disseminate psychological therapies the case for self-help materials should not be overstated.

Apps for everything

There are mobile-device applications (apps) for just about every disorder, given the ubiquity of smartphones. This, at least in principle, democratises the availability of psychological help. Entering 'mental health' in the NHS Health Apps website produced twenty-six results, but only two of them referred to any research that demonstrated that they work. An app for depression claimed, 'SilverCloud Health is a clinically proven web and mobile e-therapy programme that uses CBT which you can access 24/7, with weekly feedback and support from your clinician'. This sounds good, but the only evidence offered was a study of an early version of the product by its authors [Sharry et al. (2013)]. In the Sharry et al. (2013) study the average person completing the programme had a ten-point reduction in Beck Depression Inventory Score; however, end-of-treatment data was only available for two thirds of the subjects. Further all participants were university students, and there was no comparison with a waiting list or attention control condition. This hardly merits the epithet 'clinically proven'. The second app to claim that it was clinically proven, 'Sleepio', was for sleep problems, but again the research referred to was by the developers of the app and they did not cite a journal in which the research on this product was published. For an intervention to be evidence based there has to be independent evaluation, i.e. by those independent of the development of the intervention/product using a blind standardised diagnostic interview, i.e. not simply relying on questionnaires completed by the subject (self-report measures). Loucas et al. (2014) made the following comments with regards to eating disorders and apps:

> The complete absence of trials evaluating mobile-device apps demands comment. The fact that there is no evidence to support their use needs to be brought to the attention of clinicians and users as some eating disorder apps promote the idea that they aid recovery. This would not be allowed if they were forms of medication yet, like medication, they have the potential to do harm. For example, people with eating disorders (and those around them) may think that by using an app they are addressing their eating disorder whereas in reality they

60   *Part II*

may be simply delaying their entry into an empirically supported form of treatment. Apps, as with other forms of e-therapy, may have a place in the eating disorder armamentarium, but this needs to be demonstrated empirically.

The above comment is echoed by reviewers of apps for other disorders; for example, Nicholas et al. (2015) comment on apps for bipolar disorder:

> In general, the content of currently available apps for BD is not in line with practice guidelines or established self-management principles. Apps also fail to provide important information to help users assess their quality, with most lacking source citation and a privacy policy. Therefore, both consumers and clinicians should exercise caution with app selection. While mHealth offers great opportunities for the development of quality evidence-based mobile interventions, new frameworks for mobile mental health research are needed to ensure the timely availability of evidence-based apps to the public.

Availability and usage

Given that face-to-face therapy only reaches the tip of the iceberg of sufferers from mental health problems, self-help materials offer the potential of reaching many more. There are self-help materials available for just about every disorder or difficulty. (Norcross et al. [2013] provide a comprehensive guide to books, computerised materials and films.) Early works include 'Control Your Depression' by Lewinsohn et al., first published in 1978, with the most recent update published in 2010. Even more recent self-help books include Steketee and Frost's (2014) volume on hoarding disorder. But despite the scope of self-help materials and their availability for decades, it is rare in the author's experience to come across a client who has used them. However, it could be argued that those who utilised them have found that their problems were resolved and so have no need to present to a therapist, but there is a paucity of evidence that self-help materials alone have this potency.

There are practical difficulties in the use of self-help materials. I'm a user of technology, and it's very definitely a means to an end; the outrage I felt recently when I downloaded Windows 10 to my laptop and within weeks found error messages popping up is second to none. I know there are all sort of fix-it sites on the Internet and computer fix-it books, but I'm not at all sure which are the right ones to address these error messages. A glance at the self-help material reveals the instructions are in English but beyond my computer literacy. I guess the great majority of people have a similar reaction to mental health self-help material. Efforts may be made to increase mental health literacy, but I doubt that public usage of self-help materials is going to change anytime soon. Matters are complicated further because though I can be fairly certain there is an evidence base for the computer fix-it material, 95% of the mental health self-help material has not been subjected to empirical evaluation, and for the 5% that has, the outcomes are very debatable. For the most part self-help materials are products written and

Social support 61

marketed for financial gain, and there is a need to treat them with the same caution as the well-marketed wares of drug companies.

The nature of an individual's difficulties can have a major impact on their usage of self-help. Motivational difficulties are part of a wide range of disorders from depression to substance abuse and psychosis, making it unlikely that an individual will of their own accord pick up self-help materials. Impaired concentration is a diagnostic symptom for depression, generalised anxiety disorder and post-traumatic stress disorder and makes it unlikely that an individual will persist with material even if it is brought to their attention. One way of circumventing these difficulties is by encouraging a would-be reader to recruit a friend or family member to assist, but this requires a degree of motivation not only for the reader but also for the assistant. It may be that some volumes do require the assistance of a therapist, but the latter are likely to be in short supply.

In the self-help book *Moving On After Trauma* [Scott (2008)], the reader is given the following advice to help to help nullify the effects of impaired concentration:

> It is quite possible to read the words on a page but then not be able to recall what you have read. Read in very small doses, just for say ten minutes. To make sure what you have read sticks, summarise important points in a sentence or two (on paper or in your head) before reading further. After ten minutes change gear – have a break, have a cup of tea, go for a walk or have a shower. . . . Discussing what you have read with someone close to you can help clarify what you have read and also help build a bridge of understanding.
>
> (p. 1)

Readability and understandability

Usage of self-help material can be affected not only by difficulties with concentration and motivation but also by the readability of the self-help material itself. Martinez et al. (2008) reviewed the reading ages of six self-help books for depression that are commonly used by therapists and found that the reading ages varied between 12.6 and 15.4, and they suggested that the texts might be problematic for some readers, as 16% of the UK population have a reading age below age 11. But material may be more understandable if it is in story form rather than explanatory text. in *Moving On After Trauma* (2008) the reader is given two options: 'In Chapter 1 you will be introduced to twenty people who have been traumatised by differing events, and who suffer from a variety of disorders. You might find that you identify with some individuals much more than others, and by using the index at the back of this book, you might want to track how they resolve their difficulties. Alternatively you may of course simply read the book from cover to cover'. The narrative way of using a self-help book may be more akin to the sufferer watching a film about themselves employing new coping strategies. It may be that a narrative approach taps more into imagination than the traditional informational way of reading a text.

62   *Part II*

Stand alone self-help and guided self-help

The authors of self-help books that are related to empirically investigated treatments emphasise the value of assisted self-help. In 'Control Your Depression' Lewinsohn et al. (2010) suggest that readers may be able to benefit from the book without assistance, but 'a substantial number of people need some help and encouragement to make use of a self-help book such as this one'. In contrast, David Barlow in the forward to the 'Treatment for Hoarding Disorder Workbook' [Steketee and Frost (2014)] states, 'The programme must be carried out under the guidance of a skilled clinician who has been trained in its use'. Indeed, unless a person's difficulties are mild it may be difficult to make the best use of the material without assistance. But how available is assistance with self-help?

The onset of mental health problems usually leads to a deterioration of close relationships; the person may become more irritable and withdrawn. The sufferer may be less inclined than usual to succour help and less skilful at acquiring it. If it is only the tip of the iceberg of mental health sufferers who can access self-help materials, it may be only the tip of the tip of the iceberg who can secure the type of assistance that they need to profit from the material. Further it is not clear what the 'help and encouragement' referred to by Lewinsohn et al. (2010) should consist of, much less where the reader of the hoarding self-help book [Steketee and Frost (2015)] is supposed to find 'the skilled clinician trained in its use'. Whilst effective guidance is a consummation devoutly to be wished it is rarely available.

A paucity of guidance on helping with self-help

Simply leaving a mental health sufferer with a self-help book might be about as useful as a parent leaving a sex education book with their child, perhaps asking later, 'Did you understand that?' The child replies 'Yes', and that is the end of the story. The child is quite capable of all sorts of misconceptions (terrible pun!) about what has been read. Just as one might empower a parent to be able to appropriately follow up the child's reading, so too it is necessary to enable those close to the mental health sufferer to facilitate understanding of the text.

Below is the guidance that could be used by a person (professional or lay) assisting a trauma victim using the self-help book *Moving On After Trauma* Scott (2008). The format can be easily adapted to other texts, moving from a focus on psychoeducation, decreasing avoidance, managing mood and relationships, which are likely to be germane for most disorders/difficulties:

> *If you are concerned about someone badly affected by a trauma, you could use this guide to help them in* Moving On After Trauma. *Having someone spend ten to fifteen minutes a week going through a self-help book with the person affected can make a world of difference. This can be done just as well by telephone or e-mail. Social support is the biggest predictor of how*

Social support 63

people manage post-traumatic stress symptoms. Try the following weekly brief chats:

Chat 1   *Chapter One—'What's Happening To Me?'*

  1   *How did you get on reading Chapter One? Did it make you feel understood?*
  2   *Did you complete the Trauma Screening Questionnaire (TSQ) on page 10?*
  3   *How many answers of 'yes' did you put? (More than six is probable PTSD.)*
  4   *Did you tell the brief story of what happened by completing the Thumbnail Sketch on page 21?*

Chat 2   *Chapter Two—'Making sense of my reaction'*

  1   *Does it sound right thinking of yourself as having developed an oversensitive alarm that keeps overreacting?*
  2   *Does it sound right thinking of yourself as now living in a bubble?*
  3   *Does it sound right thinking of yourself as a lemonade bottle without the top on, no fizz?*
  4   *Did you find that one or more characters in the book sounded like you?*
  5   *How do you feel about trying to follow in their footsteps to recovery?*

Chat 3   *Chapter Five—'Resetting the Alarm'*

  1   *Did the idea of gradually daring yourself to do things make sense?*
  2   *Did you come up with any little 'dares'?*
  3   *Have you done any dares yet?*
  4   *How will you reset your alarm without beginning to do some dares?*
  5   *Have you read any more about the characters in the book who seemed like you?*

Chat 4   *Chapter Six—'Better Ways of Handling the Memory'*

  1   *What did you think of the idea that blocking the memory doesn't actually work?*
  2   *How did you feel about the idea of creating space for the normal things in life by pigeonholing the memory to be sorted out in a special way at a special time?*
  3   *What way did you think you might try for sorting out the memory in the day so it doesn't disturb your sleep at night?*
  4   *Did you try any special ways of dealing with the memory?*
  5   *You have already made a start confronting the memory of the incident, which is like a bully, by doing the Thumbnail Sketch. There seem to be different ways of getting the bully to back down, such as writing a page a day about the incident and its effects for two to three weeks, after which time you become bored with it instead*

64   *Part II*

of re-experiencing it. Could you have a go at that? If the answer is 'no', what about writing about it just once and reading it over out loud three times a day? If the answer is still 'no', has your way of handling the memory up to now worked? If the answer is 'no', can you be absolutely sure that trying a different way might not work?

Chat 5   Chapter Five—'Resetting the Alarm'; Chapter Six—'Better Ways of Handling the Memory'

 1 Are there still things you avoid that you did before?
 2 Which would be the easiest of the avoided things to have a go at?
 3 What could you say to yourself to make it easier to cope with the dares, e.g. play music or sing? When you tried what you have been avoiding did you spell out the similarities and differences to the incident?
 4 How have you gone on in your special time confronting the bully? Keeping on confronting him/her means he/she backs down. Did it make sense that in writing or talking about it you are coming up with an updated version of it for the mind to work on rather than the old version (which is often fantasy of something worse happening that didn't actually happen)?
 5 Have you read any more about the characters who seemed like you?

Chat 6   Chapters Five, Six and, Seven—'Restoring Relationships'; Chapter Eight—'Managing Mood'

 1 How are the dares going?
 2 Are there further dares you could try?
 3 How is it going at the special time confronting the bully?
 4 Could you invest a little more in relationships?
 5 Could you invest in small doses in doing some things to give you a sense of achievement or pleasure?
 6 How did you go trying to come up with more objective second thoughts when your mood dips?
 7 Did you use the MOOD record on page 95?
 8 After you had come up with the more objective second thoughts, did you get on and do things instead of agonise?

It is also possible to have slightly longer chats, about twenty minutes a week, and cover the material in four sessions of guided self-help.

Does self-help deliver?

Norcross et al. (2013) claim, 'Research reviews have determined that the effectiveness of self-help substantially exceeds that of no treatment and nearly reaches that of professional treatment'. This view reflects the National Institute for Clinical Excellence (NICE) guidelines, which recommended the provision of

Social support 65

cognitive-behavioural therapy (CBT)–based guided self-help (GSH) intervention for anxiety and depressive disorders as part of the stepped care approach [NICE (2007, 2009)].

However a review of thirteen studies for anxiety and depressive disorders by Coull and Morriss (2011) produced less enthusiastic findings; whilst GSH was more effective at post-treatment than a waiting list or no treatment control condition, there was limited effectiveness at follow-up and within routine clinical practice (as opposed to amongst media-recruited individuals). Further, none of the studies examined whether the sufferers were no longer suffering from the initial identified disorder. Rather, outcome was based on self-reported changes on questionnaire measures. In the independent Cochrane review of self-help for anxiety disorders, Mayo-Wilson and Montgomery (2013) concluded that the short- and long-term effectiveness of media-delivered interventions has not been established.

Computerised CBT (CCBT) has the advantage of direct access to treatment, avoiding the embarrassment and possible ambivalence about seeking treatment. For service providers, assisted computerised CBT appears a more attractive treatment option than wholly face-to-face treatment. Gilbody et al. (2015) examined the effectiveness of two computerised interventions for depression, Mood Gym and Beating the Blues, and compared them with treatment as usual by GP, finding no differences. Those who received the computerised interventions received weekly telephone calls to check that they had no technical problems with the programmes and were encouraged to persevere with the programmes and do homework. However, the technical assistant was not a therapist and did not help programme users understand the programme or apply it. Thus, this research was not a test of guided self-help as such, but it is likely indicative of what would happen if apps were subjected to more rigorous examination than has been the case to date. Early research on the effectiveness of Internet-based self-help (sometimes with brief therapist contact) for anxiety, depression, and substance abuse is quite promising [e.g., Andersson and Cuijpers (2009)]. But are the benefits more apparent than real? So et al. (2013) analysed the results of randomised controlled trials of CBT for depression and found that though there was a short-term reduction in depression at post-treatment, the effect at follow up was not significant. Further, there was no significant improvement in functional impairment, e.g. a return to work. There was a high drop-out rate (8–41%), and analysis of data is problematic when more than 20% of subjects drop out. Cochrane (www.mrcbsu.cam.ac.uk/cochrane/handbook) has indicated that in such instances intention to treat analysis (taking the last score as the final score for those who dropped out), which was used by the authors of the trials, is statistically questionable. So et al. (2013) noted that all the studies relied on self-report measures of outcome rather than utilising a gold-standard independent assessor blind to treatment and using a standardised diagnostic interview. Thus it was not known what proportion of those undergoing CCBT no longer met diagnostic criteria for depression at the end of treatment. So et al. (2013) also found that there was significant publication bias, established using a statistical test (funnel plot). CCBT appears a shaky foundation on which to erect an edifice for the treatment of depression.

66   *Part II*

Scope of self-help

It is not just a matter of demonstrating that guided self-help for CBT has internal validity, i.e. it performs better than a control condition, but also of demonstrating that the GSH CBT is useful in the real world, i.e. has external validity. The limited number of GSH CBT randomised controlled trials that have been conducted have had a focus on a specific identified disorder, but in routine practice comorbidity is the norm:

> *Alice had presented to her GP with depression following a road traffic accident and was prescribed antidepressants, which were ineffective. But on more detailed assessment she was found to be suffering from not only depression but also mild post-traumatic stress disorder and binge eating disorder.*

Thus a GSH programme for depression was likely to produce sub-optimal results at best. Though Alice was a reader she would have been unable to pick up a text that comprehensively addressed her difficulties. It can be plausibly argued that self-help materials and GSH CBT are of doubtful external validity.

The dangers of enthusiasm over evidence

Such is the attractiveness of GSH as a solution to the poor availability of psychological therapies that vested interests in developing an app that is researched by the developers may go unnoticed. Unwittingly, to ease the research burden corners may be cut, such as failing to adequately assess comorbidity. Resulting in a misguided rush to market, the app and associated protocol would be widely disseminated, but quality control in routine practice is likely to be much less than in a randomised controlled trial with reliance placed simply on improvements of some psychometric tests (which may have occurred with the passage of time anyway) and are not related to any reliably identified disorder, so that their meaning is highly problematic. Once the genie is out of the bottle it may be impossible to get it back in. It will become a new orthodoxy, with frustrated clinicians at the coalface unable to give voice to their concerns and in some cases stressed by personalising their lack of therapeutic effectiveness.

Part III

The quantity and quality of psychological help available

6 Availability of psychological therapy services

Cognitive behaviour therapy has shown great promise in the treatment of many common psychological disorders and predominates in the list of evidence-based treatments [EBTs Chambless and Ollendick (2001)], but other EBTs include interpersonal therapy and brief psychodynamic therapy for depression, as well as couples therapy. The efficacy of a treatment is measured by the effect size, which is the mean score of clients at the end of treatment subtracted from the mean score of a comparison condition (usually a waiting list control condition), divided by the pooled standard deviation (a measure of the spread of the results). Butler et al. (2006) conducted a meta-analysis of RCTs of CBT and found large effect sizes for depression, generalised anxiety disorder, panic disorder (with or without agoraphobia), social phobia, post-traumatic stress disorder (PTSD) and childhood depressive and anxiety disorders. Marital distress, anger, childhood somatic disorders and chronic pain showed moderate effect sizes. More recently Hofman and Smits (2008) have replicated these findings across the adult anxiety disorders. But translating these results from research contexts to everyday mental health practice has proved difficult.

Treatment is unavailable to the majority of sufferers

There is a treatment gap (TG) between the number of people with mental health disorders and the number of those people who are able to access appropriate services. Mental health has risen up the political agenda in recent years, and there is an emerging consensus that mental health services should be as accessible as physical health services, i.e. that there should be parity of esteem. It has become an article of faith that there is a need to scale up services. But there is a gap between the rhetoric and the reality. On October 21, 2015, BBC 2 televised a programme titled 'Postcode Lottery for Mental Health Talking Therapies' and noted that whilst in some areas 100% of those with anxiety and depression receive a talking therapy within six weeks, in other areas it is 5%. They note that more than one in four of the GP-led Clinical Commissioning Groups (CCGs) are not meeting the target of 75% of patients receiving treatment within six weeks of being referred. One in ten patients experience waiting lists of over a year before receiving any form of treatment, with one in two waiting over three months [MIND (2013)]. One in six of

70 *Part III*

those on waiting lists for mental health services are expected to attempt suicide, four in ten are expected to self-harm and two-thirds are likely to see their condition deteriorate before having the opportunity to see a mental health professional. Because of the limited availability of NHS mental health treatment, three in ten individuals with an untreated mental health issue now opt to pay for private treatment [MIND (2015)].

A Freedom of Information request in July 2014 by Luciana Berger, Shadow Public Health Minister, revealed 67% of Clinical Commissioning Groups (CCGs) spending less than 10% of budget on mental health services, when mental health problems constitute 23% of the burden of illness in the NHS. Professor Simon Wessely, President of the Royal College of Psychiatrists, commented that whilst some variation in funding is to be expected, as some areas will have a higher prevalence of mental health problems than others, there should not be such a difference in funding across CCGs for those with serious mental illness. With regards to mental health, need appears not to dictate the provision of services.

Currently psychological therapies are meeting only 15% of need for adults. The government-appointed Mental Health Taskforce (2016) has recommended increasing access to evidence-based psychological therapies to reach 25% of need so that at least 600,000 more adults with anxiety and depression can access care (and 350,000 complete treatment) each year by 2020–21. But this would still leave three-quarters without treatment for the foreseeable future.

Access to services varies between in-patient, secondary care, specialist unit, IAPT (Improving Access to Psychological Therapies) and primary care, with further differences between adult and children and young persons' services. The availability and scalability of the differing forms of provision are discussed below:

Inpatient

Traditional mental hospitals have a bad press. Dating back to the asylums of old they were often built out of public sight in rural settings. The word *bedlam* gives a clue to their flavour; denoting a state of uproar and confusion, it was a nickname for the Bethlehem Hospital, the predecessor of the current London Institute of Psychiatry. Originally set up by a religious order to serve the poor and homeless at the end of the fourteenth century, the establishment became the first to cater for the mentally ill.

During the First World War the mental hospitals often housed soldiers with 'shell-shock'. Scott (2015b, p. xxvii) gives an indication of the vagaries of the system operating in the lives of the war poets:

> By 1917 Sassoon was highly critical and vocal in his opposition to the War and his friend and fellow poet Robert Graves feared he would be court-martialled and so engineered, without Sassoon's knowledge, via the Under Secretary of State for War, that he be sent to Craiglockhart War Hospital near Edinburgh because of his 'shell shock'. Sassoon was not best pleased with his friend when he discovered the deception after his 'hospitalisation'. Whilst

Availability of psychological therapy   71

there he was under the care of Dr Rivers, who after realising Sassoon was not suffering from shell shock decided to play along with the diagnosis to protect Sassoon. Whilst at Craiglockhart, Sasoon met another war poet, Wilfred Owen who was indeed suffering from shell shock. . . . Owen's doctor, Dr Brock, encouraged Owen to translate his experiences, specifically the experiences he relived in his dreams, into poetry.

By the 1960s and 1970s an anti-psychiatry movement developed in which the mental hospitals were charged not only with not helping those with mental health problems but with making matters worse. In his classic work 'Asylums', published in 1961, Erving Goffman wrote, 'The most important factor in forming a mental-hospital patient is the institution, not the illness, and that the patients' reactions and adjustments are those of inmates in other types of total institutions as well'. In the same year Thomas Szasz wrote 'The Myth of Mental Illness', making the point that there are no biological markers for any of the psychological disorders. This is still the case fifty years later and it does pose a very real challenge to the concept of mental illness, but diagnostic categories do have a utility in that they have facilitated the development of disorder-specific protocols that are evidence based and upon which National Institute for Health and Clinical Excellence [NICE (2011)] guidelines are based.

Between 1998 and 2012 there was a 39% reduction in the number of psychiatric beds, with a 7% reduction between 2010–11 and 2013–14 alone [The Commission on Acute Adult Psychiatric Care (2015)]. A Royal College of Psychiatry report described wards as overcrowded and understaffed, with 15% of wards lacking segregated sleeping accommodation and fewer than 60% having separate lounges for men and women [Royal College of Psychiatrists (2011)]. Patients and carers report that many acute wards are not always safe, therapeutic or conducive to recovery and in some cases could have a negative effect on an inpatient's well-being and mental health [The Commission on Acute Adult Psychiatric Care (2015)], with approximately 5% of admissions having to be made out of area. Such admissions have been associated with increases in patient suicides [National Confidential Inquiry into Suicide and Homicide by People with Mental Illness (2015)]. Such out-of-area moves are not confined to adults; as I write (March 2016), I have just heard of a teenager being moved from the northwest of England to a specialist eating disorder unit in Edinburgh, a logistical nightmare for a single parent visiting with other children in tow.

Crises

The Care Quality Commission (CQC) found that just half of Community Mental Health Teams (CMHTs) are able to offer a twenty-four seven crisis service today [Mental Health Taskforce to the NHS in England February (2016)]. In 2014–15, 1.8 million people in England used mental health services, with 103,840 being admitted to hospital. In a press release from the Royal College of Psychiatrists dated February 9, 2016 titled 'The Way Ahead for Adult Acute Mental Healthcare

72   *Part III*

Provision', it was stated that around 500 mentally ill people have to travel over 50 km to be admitted into hospital every month. These long-distance admissions are mainly due to difficulties in finding acute inpatient beds or suitable alternative services in their home area. This would not be tolerated if a person had a stroke, heart attack or cancer and highlights the Cinderella status of mental health compared to physical care.

Most inpatients have contact with the mental health services in a crisis, but only 14% of patients are happy with the service they receive [Care Quality Commission (2015)]. After an assessment by a psychiatrist a person may be admitted only if there is judged to be a serious suicide risk. Alternatively, if the risk is less severe the person is sent home, with a member of the Community Mental Health Team making weekly visits, most usually for a month or two or, if there is felt to be an ongoing suicidal risk, for as long as such risk obtains. Members of the CMHT rarely provide an evidence-based psychological treatment but play a supportive or monitoring role. In some instances a person presenting in crisis may be judged as low risk, say following what is deemed to be an impulsive overdose after a row with their partner, and there is no follow up by secondary care, but they may be referred to primary care or the Improving Access for Psychological Therapies (IAPT) programme (the latter straddles but is separate from primary and secondary care). Approximately one in twenty-eight of the adult population is in contact with secondary mental health services, which cater largely for those with a psychotic disorder, severe depression and those with a personality disorder. Crisis resolution and home treatment teams have been merged with the generic CMHTs, so that the latter has a wider range of functions. CMHTs are multidisciplinary teams who, in collaboration with service users, draw up a care plan covering the needs and goals of an individual, and coordinate care. Early intervention in psychosis services and assertive outreach teams are specialised community mental health teams focused on providing treatment and support for specific groups, the former for young people between the ages of sixteen and thirty-five who are experiencing their first episode of psychosis, the latter for people with long-term mental health problems with more complex needs and requiring intensive support. However, most assertive outreach teams have been dismantled; there has been much reconfiguration of services to keep costs down but without any obvious clinical benefit. A substantial proportion of people with severe mental health problems have had to wait for more than a year to access treatment, and services are failing to provide sufficient access to the full breadth of evidence-based therapies recommended by NICE [Royal College of Psychiatrists (2014)].

Severe mental illness

Of those adults with more severe mental health problems, 90% are supported by community services [Mental Health Taskforce to the NHS in England February (2016)]. However, within these services there are very long waits for some of the key interventions recommended by NICE, such as psychological therapy, and many people never have access to these interventions. One-quarter of people using

Availability of psychological therapy 73

secondary mental health services do not know who is responsible for coordinating their care, and the same number have not agreed what care they would receive with a clinician. Almost one-fifth of people with care coordinated through the Care Programme Approach (for people with more severe or complex needs) have not had a formal meeting to review their care in the previous twelve months. The Mental Health Taskforce (2016) states that there must also be investment to increase access to psychological therapies for people with psychosis, bipolar disorder and personality disorder.

Secondary care and specialist units

GPs and IAPT can refer complex cases, usually those deemed severely mentally ill or with a personality disorder, to secondary care. Psychiatrists usually act as the gatekeepers for secondary care (they are not employed by IAPT) and are assisted by community mental health workers and psychologists. Secondary care with access to inpatient services is an intended sanctuary for those whom by reason of their mental health problems are a danger to themselves or others. Medication is often a necessary part of stabilising a person when their symptoms are florid, e.g. a person with bipolar disorder who is not sleeping, with flight of grandiose ideas rapidly going from topic to topic. But prescribing should nevertheless, whenever possible, be a dialogue between the psychiatrist and patient, in which a rationale for the medication is given, e.g. 'It is just to help you think straight; without it you can't at the moment'.

Resources for providing evidence-based psychological treatments in secondary care are scarce, with often at most one member of CMHT tasked with providing cognitive behaviour therapy. Of those in contact with secondary care, only half had seen a mental health practitioner in the past month [Dormon (2015)]. Waiting times for psychological treatment in secondary care are particularly problematic. Beck et al. (2015) report a median waiting time from referral to assessment of eighteen weeks, while the median number of weeks between assessment and first session was forty-one weeks. Further sometimes limits of twenty to twenty-five sessions are imposed by managers on the CBT practitioner.

The therapeutic skills of the non-psychiatrists in secondary care are very varied. Whilst NICE recommends CBT as a first line approach to the treatment of psychosis, this very rarely happens in routine practice because of a shortage of qualified staff. With regards to psychosis, Khan and Brabham (2015) report that no service has the capacity to deliver NICE-concordant services to more than 50% of new first episode cases by 2016.

NICE Guidelines (2007) recommend that sufferers from chronic fatigue syndrome (CFS) should be seen in specialist centres, but their poor availability means that they are often referred to generic services such as IAPT. But the authors of the PACE trial, White et al. (2015) have commented that IAPT workers do not have the confidence or competence to deliver the evidence-based CBT protocol for CFS that they developed.

NICE Guidelines (2004) for bulimia recommend a specifically adapted form of CBT, and that the course of treatment should be for sixteen to twenty sessions over

74　*Part III*

four to five months. To the extent that this treatment is available, it is available in regional centres. The hurdles faced by a bulimia sufferer are exemplified in the following anonymised case:

> *Doreen was first identified as suffering from an eating disorder by her GP after she had engaged in self-induced vomiting for a year. She attended her GP with her mother and was vomiting about twice a day. Doreen was referred to a Specialist Service and invited to join a group programme in six to eight months' time – the waiting list for individual therapy was around twelve months. The clinician noted that she was a little hesitant about the prospect of joining the group programme. Two years later it was noted by the same service that she did not attend the group programme or contact them to explain that she would prefer one-to-one therapy. A year later she had sixteen weeks of Cognitive Analytic Therapy. During therapy a traumatic event from childhood was disclosed, the possible psychological sequelae from this were not investigated, and the therapist contented herself with saying that she may benefit from 'a more general intervention'. Doreen stopped binge eating and vomiting for a couple of years, but it was reignited following a minor road traffic accident.*

The above case indicates that not only are there long waits for treatment in specialist units but also that they can be of questionable quality.

Pain-management programmes are provided on a regional basis and tend to be group based, with some requiring almost daily attendance for five days and others weekly attendance for sixteen weeks. Waiting lists are typically six to twelve months and referral from a GP or orthopaedic surgeon is necessary; assessment is by a multidisciplinary team involving psychologists, occupational therapists and pain specialists. Most typically the programmes are based on cognitive behaviour therapy but with a physiotherapy input about the importance of exercise and pacing. The psychological input focuses on teaching participants not to catastrophise about their symptoms.

Every month in England and Wales seven women and two men are killed by their current or former partner. Drugs and/or alcohol are often involved, but the commissioning of alcohol and substance misuse services has been transferred from the NHS to local authorities, leading to the closure of specialist NHS addiction inpatient units. Referral pathways have become more complex, and according to the Mental Health Taskforce (2016), 'Many people with mental health and substance misuse problems no longer receive planned, holistic care'.

Children and adolescents

Half of all mental health problems have been established by the age of fourteen [Mental Health Taskforce to the NHS in England February (2016)]. One in ten children aged five to sixteen has a diagnosable problem such as conduct disorder (6%), anxiety disorder (3%), attention deficit hyperactivity disorder (ADHD) (2%)

Availability of psychological therapy 75

or depression (2%). Children from low-income families are at highest risk, three times that of those from the highest. Those with conduct disorder – persistent, disobedient, disruptive and aggressive behaviour – are twice as likely to leave school without any qualifications, three times more likely to become a teenage parent, four times more likely to become dependent on drugs and twenty times more likely to end up in prison. Yet most children and young people get no support. Even for those that do, the average wait for routine appointments for psychological therapy was thirty-two weeks in 2015–16. A small group need inpatient services but, owing to inequity in provision, they may be sent anywhere in the country, requiring their families to travel long distances.

A fifth of referrals to child and adolescent mental health services are rejected by the services as 'unsuitable', and they are often children who have been abused. It is often suggested that CAMHS rejects cases on the basis that the child/adolescent is not suffering from a diagnosable mental health problem and this can be the reason proferred by CAMHS. But it is not possible to know a child's/adolescent's diagnostic status from a referral letter as the CAMHS assessment framework does not contain a validated, standardised diagnostic interview, and it can therefore not be known with any certainty whether the young person has or does not have a diagnosable mental health problem. The CAMHS website states that people can ask for a second opinion with regard to assessment (and treatment), but there is no right to this, and if it follows the traditional CAMHS format it will be no more reliable. If a second opinion is denied, recourse can be made to a patient advocacy service operated by charities such as MIND, but even if this is successful, it is no guarantor of a reliable assessment. The CAMHS teams are multi-disciplinary with social workers and psychologists performing therapeutic roles with decisions about the appropriateness of treatment beyond eight sessions sometimes resting with the team rather than the individual therapist.

The Mental Health Taskforce (2016) encourages the roll-out of the Children and Young People's Improving Access to Psychological Therapies (CYP IAPT) programme across England by 2018 and development of an access standard for Child and Adolescent Mental Health Services (CAMHS) by the end of 2016–17. Stating that this latter should build on the standard for children and young people with eating disorders announced in July 2015. The Child and Adolescent IAPT service states (March 1, 2016) that it 'began in 2011 with a target to work with CAMHS that cover 60% of the 0–19 population by March 2015, which it has exceeded, achieving 68%. We are now working to achieve 100% coverage by 2018'. The Children's IAPT will encourage self-referral and 'will [use] regular feedback and IAPT's trademark session-by-session outcome monitoring to guide therapy in the room, but using a mixture of goals and symptom measures suitable for all those presenting to community CAMHS, not just anxiety and depression'. Unfortunately, like its adult counterpart, inclusion of a standardised diagnostic interview is not part of the assessment or evaluation making it impossible to gauge the social significance of IAPT's ministrations.

76 *Part III*

Private practice

Psychological therapy is available in the private sector. Given that NHS provision treats at most a fifth of those with mental health problems, there is ample scope for the private sector. Private therapists can be accessed via many routes such as the British Psychological Societies (BPS) directory of Chartered Psychologists, the British Association for Behavioural and Cognitive Psychotherapies (BABCP) website of accredited cognitive behaviour therapists or the British Association of Counselling and Psychotherapy (BACP) list of accredited therapists.

The private sector can make up for the shortcomings of NHS provision:

> *Stefan was given a thirty-minute telephone assessment by his local NHS IAPT service; he was in tears on the phone and pleaded for immediate help. He was put on a waiting list for treatment. Alarmed at the indeterminate wait, he sought and obtained successful private treatment for his panic disorder and depression. Stefan was contacted five months after his initial IAPT contact and offered six thirty-minute telephone sessions. He declined, but was nevertheless sent an appointment which he did not attend and was then sent a discharge letter because of his 'non-attendance', implying to his GP (the source of the initial referral) that he was at fault and not the IAPT service.*

The above case raises the issue of whether current NHS provision is an improvement on what obtained in the past, e.g. fundholding where GP practices could employ their own counsellor or psychologist. Under fundholding the GP practice was a one-stop shop for psychological therapy services with accountability to the GPs, whom the therapist would meet over coffee/lunch. The above case could have been much better served under fundholding.

Distinguishing psychological therapy from guided self-help

The government-funded IAPT (Improving Access to Psychological Therapies Service) is at face value designed to provide psychological therapies, but 61% of their staff are psychological well-being practitioners (PWPS) whose task is to provide guided self-help (GSH) and who are instructed not to drift into therapy [IAPT (2011)]. They see many more people than their high-intensity therapists, who are charged with delivering psychological therapy. Thus by far the bulk of referrals get guided self-help, and only 30% of IAPT clients actually receive psychological therapy (either directly referred to high intensity therapy or stepped up to it) Gyani et al. (2013). When GPs refer patients to an IAPT Service they do not make it clear to patients, perhaps because they are unaware themselves, that the patient will probably get guided self-help and that the provision of psychological therapy is the exception.

About one in four GP consultations are for mental health problems; this is particularly stressful for GPs, with typically seven-minute consultations, and referral to another agency is a welcome relief, hopefully reducing the number of

Availability of psychological therapy   77

attendances to see him/her. But patients can only exercise choice when they are informed what is likely involved in the referral, and the GP may well labour under the illusion that IAPT is, as its name suggests, primarily about the provision of psychological therapy.

But does it matter whether it is GSH or psychological therapy? Briefly, yes, because the strength of evidence in support of each is very different. The methodological quality of studies is assessed, according to the gold standards listed by Foa and Meadows (1997), including a) clearly defined target symptoms (diagnosis and minimum severity required for study entry, inclusion/exclusion criteria discussed); b) reliable and valid measures (rated for each outcome measure used in the study); c) use of evaluators unaware of treatment condition; d) mention of assessor training; e) manualized, specific treatment programs (i.e., a manual was used and followed); f) unbiased assignment to treatment (either random or stratified); and g) treatment adherence (both assessed and reported to be adequate). With regards to the criteria A, clearly defined target symptoms, I have not been able to find an evaluation of GSH for depression or the anxiety disorders in which a standardised reliable diagnostic interview was used at the beginning and end of treatment; by contrast the randomised controlled trials of CBT for depression [Johnsen and Friborg (2015)] and the anxiety disorders [Tolin (2014)] routinely involve such an interview. As such the CBT trials can answer the basic question of the proportion of people that become well, i.e. return to normal functioning, whereas the GSH studies can only proffer the proportion who becomes 'significantly better', whatever that might mean. If I was offered cancer treatment 'X' for which I was informed say 70% become well, i.e. recover, or alternatively I could have the less-demanding treatment 'Y' about which it can only be stated that 70% become 'significantly better', quite unequivocally I would opt for 'X'. But prospective IAPT clients are not informed of the different levels of evidence and in practice for the most part get GSH.

Improvement in GSH studies means improvement compared to a treatment-as-usual comparison condition on a psychometric test. Thus for example in the Williams et al. (2013) study the effect of using the *Overcoming Depression: A Five Areas Approach* book plus three to four short face-to-face support appointments totalling up to two hours of guided support was compared with general practitioner TAU. Inclusion in the study required a Beck Depression Inventory score greater than or equal to fourteen. The GSH was better than TAU, with significantly higher proportions of participants achieving a 50% reduction in BDI-II score in the GSH-CBT arm. At four months, forty-three out of one hundred (42.6%) participants in the GSH-CBT arm achieved this reduction, compared to twenty-five out of one hundred and two (24.5%) at four months (odds ratio 2.28, 1.25 to 4.17, p = 0.008) in TAU. Recovery at twelve months was thirty-one out of sixty-two (50.0%) for GSH-CBT, and twenty out of fifty-five (36.4%) for TAU. But if a friend or relative were thought to be depressed, would you be pleased they were going to get GSH, or more reassured by the opportunity for individual CBT for depression, were the chances of them returning to normal functioning (a socially significant criteria) at least 50%? The likelihood is that many of those undergoing GSH did not meet

78   *Part III*

diagnostic criteria for an anxiety disorder or depression and there would therefore be no credible outcome measure. Inclusion of this 'diagnostic criteria failure' population in a study further reduces the strength of evidence for GSH using the Foa and Meadows (1997) gold standard, (see criteria B above).

Older people

One in five older people living in the community and 40% of older people living in care homes are affected by depression [Mental Health Taskforce to the NHS in England February (2016)]. But depression can be seen as a normal part of ageing and not worthy of treatment both by the sufferer, professionals, friends and family. There are therefore extra barriers for older people to surmount to receive psychological help.

Suicidal behaviour

Suicide is rising, after many years of decline. Suicide rates in England have increased steadily in recent years, peaking at 4,882 deaths in 2014 [Mental Health Taskforce to the NHS in England February (2016)]. The rise is most marked amongst middle-aged men. Suicide is now the leading cause of death for men aged fifteen to forty-nine. Men are three times more likely than women to take their own lives – they accounted for four out of five suicides in 2013. A quarter of people who took their own lives had been in contact with a health professional, usually their GP, in the last week before they died. Most were in contact within a month before their death.

More than a quarter (28%) of suicides were amongst people who had been in contact with mental health services within twelve months before their death, amounting to almost 14,000 people in the ten years from 2003–2013.

Suicidal behaviour tends to be addressed by crisis teams without any direct provision of psychological therapy, but cognitive therapy is effective in preventing suicide attempts for adults who recently attempted suicide. Brown et al. (2005) found that suicide attempters given cognitive therapy were 50% less likely to reattempt than those in the usual care group between baseline and eighteen-month assessment. The central feature of this psychotherapy was the identification of proximal thoughts, images, and core beliefs that were activated prior to the suicide attempt. The author is unaware of any such outpatient treatment in the UK. However, suicides amongst inpatients in mental hospitals have significantly declined over recent years, as a result of better safety precautions, but psychological therapy input is rare.

Disorders/difficulties where motivation is an issue

Motivational deficits are however particularly pronounced in some disorders; for example, in schizophrenia the treatment foci are often on what are termed the positive symptoms: delusions, e.g. believing that one is being followed, and

Availability of psychological therapy   79

hallucinations, e.g. hearing voices. There is less focus on the often more-persistent negative symptoms such as little engagement in productive activity, spending much of the day sitting or lying around, not taking care of basic grooming and hygiene, having little interest in world events or hobbies, and having limited life goals or sense of purpose. These negative symptoms can, long term, sabotage relationships more than the dramatic periods of crisis caused by the positive symptoms. Indeed the affected person may not see them as a problem, albeit that the breakdown of relationships may be a trigger for positive symptoms. The positive symptoms of psychosis are likely to be experienced by an individual as more obnoxious than the negative symptoms and more likely to be the agreed therapeutic target. Insofar as the negative symptoms are addressed, they will be a focus of a support worker visiting twice daily to ensure the individual has a hot meal and some human interaction rather than attended to by a psychological therapist.

Some therapies make more demands on motivation because more than one individual is involved such as in couples therapy or family therapy. To return to the example of Jane whom we first met in Chapter Four, if her partner was willing she may have attended cognitive behavioural couples' therapy. Alternatively, they and Jake could have attended family therapy. The motivational demands of family therapy would be increased further if it were decided to include Jane's mother in this intervention. By contrast in individual therapy there is only a need to focus on the motivation of the client, and this is likely an important factor in the predominance of this treatment modality. But it does rather neglect the fact that a client's problems often have an interpersonal context; for example high levels of expressed emotion (criticism and over-involvement) are a predictor of relapse in depression and schizophrenia [Hooley et al. (1986)], and social support is the largest predictor of recovery from PTSD [Brewin et al. (2000)].

Whose problem is it anyway?

Individuals with severe mental illness/personality disorders can fall between stools. Historically, bodies such as IAPT have seen their prime focus as dealing with anxiety and depression, but hard-pressed secondary care services sometimes refer their own SMI clients to IAPT. The response of some IAPT managers has been to insist that such cases must be taken on, whilst some practitioners indicate that they do not have the training to deliver an evidence-based treatment to this population, and others insist that they have skills to deal with 'complex' cases. A danger for IAPT services is that they could be overwhelmed by such cases, as they require many more than the mean of six sessions [IAPT annual report (2013–2014)] routinely given to their clients and as an agency will be less able to focus on their core task. Unwittingly agencies are likely to enhance the affected individual's sense of alienation.

There has been a long-standing awareness that drug companies will be vociferous in marketing their wares and caution is needed. I've just seen a product advertised on TV for 'dry skin or eczema', a targeting of both the normal and the abnormal. But this extension of the range of applicability of a product is not just

80　*Part III*

a property of Big Pharma; mental health providers that accept self-referral are doing just the same. The IAPT report of 2015 showed that 39% of clients were self-referred in 2014–2015 [HSCIC (2015)]. Wider applicability is associated with a greater likelihood of survival of the product, whether it be a drug or psychological therapy, but the product might not actually be needed. But unlike Big Pharma there is a danger that IAPT will overstretch itself and be seen to fail, particularly as the evidence base for the effective psychological treatment of disorders such as bipolar disorder is much weaker than for disorders like depression and anxiety. A review of randomised controlled trials of psychological interventions for adults with bipolar disorder conducted by Oud et al. (2016) concluded that though there is evidence that psychological interventions are effective for people with bipolar disorder, 'Much of the evidence was of low or very low quality thereby limiting our conclusions'.

'Fuzzies' and agency interaction

Therapists who insist that they can tackle complex cases are open to receive all manner of referrals and are likely to be overwhelmed. Whilst it may be true that a particular therapist can deal with complex cases under ideal conditions of the requisite time and quality supervision, an agency would have to carefully ring fence their work to prevent burnout. With current pressures on waiting lists this is unlikely to happen. For the benefit of all, agency boundaries need to be properly defined, as do terms like *complex* – fuzzy problems cannot be solved.

The problems posed by referrals from secondary care to IAPT may have arisen because of a lack of clarity about diagnosis. IAPT's annual report of 2013–2014 indicates that a provisional diagnosis is made in less than half of cases (46%), in part because clinicians may not feel adequately trained or qualified to provide a diagnosis. Further there is no refinement of the diagnoses, i.e. no definitive diagnosis is proffered. The provisional diagnosis appears very inexact compared to the 'gold standard' diagnostic interview. For example, the IAPT Annual Report of 2013–2014 states that 1% of its clients were suffering from PTSD and 1% from panic disorder, but the comparable figures for patients assessed using the SCID (First et al. 1997) who were attending a psychiatric outpatient department were 14.8% and 17.9% [Zimmerman and Mattia (2000)]. Even allowing that there may be some difference in the IAPT client population and psychiatric outpatients, the prevalence figures are vastly different, suggesting a significant problem with missing cases. In secondary care gold-standard diagnostic interviews are rare and there is likely to be as much inexactitude with regards to diagnoses as in IAPT. Thus when IAPT and secondary care interact they are unlikely to be using a common language, and confusion and difficulties are likely to arise. This raises the question of who is going to make the effort to ensure that the more disturbed clients do not lose out? Both IAPT and secondary care would agree they need much greater resources, which is undoubtedly correct, but it is doubtful that this alone would resolve problems.

7 Quality of psychological therapy services

In December 2015, Healthwatch England reported that 'the quality of mental health services has been raised as a priority by more than half of local Healthwatch, making it the number-one issue for 2016' and observed, 'Yet still too often we hear from those accessing mental health support and their families that they feel the clock is ticking, and that if they are not "better" by the end of their course of counselling they will be left to cope on their own'. A GP can of course re-refer an unsuccessfully counselled patient but in so doing can be censured for clogging up the system.

A failure to engage and maintain clients

In recent years it is common practice in the UK for those referred to a mental health agency to receive a letter asking them to contact the agency to opt in for treatment. This system has been adopted because in the older system about 40% [Trepka (1986)] of referrals dropped out of treatment. Implicit in the opt-in system is a belief that, unless there is some motivation to attend, therapeutic efforts are likely to come to naught. Richards and Borglin (2011) reviewed the treatment of clients with anxiety/depression in routine practice and concluded that there was still a haemorrhaging of clients from routine care, as seen in Table 7.1.

The IAPT Annual Report for 2013–2014 covering referrals in the whole of England indicates a similar picture to Table 7.1, with 37% of those referred not presenting for assessment. An elderly female client of mine with no psychiatric history had been invited by IAPT to ring them for a half-hour telephone assessment; she declined and opined, 'I can't just talk to strangers on the phone. I am not good with words, the thought of talking to someone I can't even see'. It is highly likely that there are many other potential clients who take the view that telephone contact is not the appropriate medium for discussing personal problems. As a consequence a significant minority of clients fall at the first hurdle and are lost to treatment.

Progressing down Table 7.1, 24% attend an assessment session and one or no treatment sessions, leaving just 40% attending at least two treatment sessions – with a recovery rate of 45% for completers, comparable to that found by Richards

Table 7.1 Attrition and recovery in an IAPT programme for anxiety and depression in routine practice from Richards and Borglin (2011)

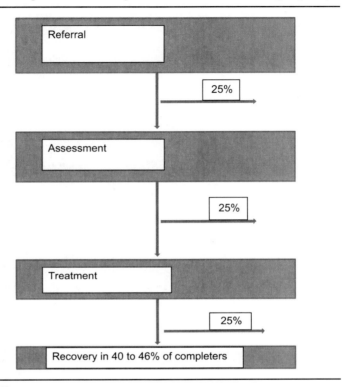

n = 7859

and Borglin (2011). Further the IAPT Annual Report for 2014–2015 indicates that the mean average number of treatment sessions within a finished course of treatment was six sessions. But six sessions of treatment is not an adequate dose of treatment for any evidence-based psychotherapy. It is also a concern that 20% of referrals that ended with a finished course of treatment had the minimum of two. It appears that many potential and actual IAPT clients are often finding the service less than user friendly and are voting with their feet.

Direct access

One way of tackling the haemorrhaging of clients at referral in Table 7.1 would be to allow the public to directly refer themselves to psychological services; indeed, more-recent IAPT Services have done just this. This is an attractive option but it does contain dangers, in that the first contact would be a

Quality of psychological therapy 83

non-medic, and he/she might miss red flags, e.g. a possible thyroid problem [see *Masquerading Symptoms: Uncovering Physical Illnesses That Present as Psychological Problems* (2014) by Barbara Schildkrout New York: John Wiley]. To take an example:

> *Jane's mother Janet was experiencing depression, loss of energy, apathy, fatigue, irritability, emotional lability and difficulty concentrating. Encouraged by her daughter's positive response to CBT, she directly accessed her local psychological therapy service. She scored highly on the PHQ-9 (a measure of the severity of depression) and underwent CBT with the same therapist her daughter had. Unfortunately, therapy was unsuccessful; the therapist considered (formulation) that the root of her problem was that she did not make space for herself but let the demands of her family overwhelm her. Janet, however, asserted that she liked to be useful. She had briefly been on antidepressants some years earlier but gave them up when they were ineffective and did not return to her GP. After Janet had unsuccessful CBT she returned to her GP because of increased tiredness and some confusion. Her GP arranged a blood chemistry screening test, and she was found to have elevated calcium levels and to be suffering from hyperparathyroidism (excessive secretion of the parathyroid hormone). Once her calcium levels were normalised, the symptoms she had had for years fully resolved.*

Whilst most referrals to IAPT are from GPs, there can also be referral from community services and job centres; such referrals suffer from the same deficiency as direct access. In other spheres such as physiotherapy, where direct access has been allowed in some parts of the country, services have folded in some affluent areas because the demands have greatly exceeded the supply. Thus whilst direct access to psychological therapies appears a no-brainer, it remains to be seen whether the gains outweigh the costs.

Credible practitioners

Members of the public can privately refer themselves directly to a mental-health practitioner. Sometimes this occurs because a friend or relative has had a very positive experience with the particular practitioner. However, most people seeking private mental health treatment are unlikely to know whom to contact. Professional bodies such as the British Association of Behavioural and Cognitive Psychotherapies (BABCP) and the British Psychological Society have lists of respectively accredited cognitive behaviour therapists and chartered psychologists whom they deem both reliable and competent to provide therapy. Though they are useful starting points for choosing a therapist, there is a great deal of variability amongst private practitioners; some may provide a service better than the state-funded IAPT but others no better or worse.

84   *Part III*

The voice of practitioners

The British Association for Behavioural and Cognitive Psychotherapies is the UK's lead organisation for cognitive behaviour therapy and has an online forum called the CBT Café. A major thread on this website has been the ubiquity of 'sub-therapeutic doses' of therapy, with sessions sometimes limited to six. Although such a limitation is not IAPT policy, the 3rd annual IAPT Report [HSCIC (2015)] shows the national average number of CBT sessions conducted was 5.8. The BABCP has condemned a 'minimalist' approach to the provision of treatment.

There has been criticism by clinicians working for IAPT (Improving Access to Psychological Therapies, a UK government-sponsored agency devoted to increasing access to psychological therapies), and by other clinicians seeing former IAPT clients, on the CBT Café forum, of the organisation's modus operandi, but there have also been positive comments from IAPT staff that the service has at least increased access to psychological therapy. However, any whistleblower is likely to face a tough time, and expressions of dissatisfaction by staff are likely to be muted. Binnie (2015), a former IAPT worker, expressed the following concerns:

> Junior members of staff (Psychological Wellbeing Practitioners) conduct the initial assessments, often via the telephone and in a very brief and structured manner. . . . The reality is that often inexperienced members of staff without sufficient training or psychological knowledge are left trying to assess complex clients . . . The impulsivity of the assessors is understandable given the context in which they work, where they may have to conduct eight or more of these assessments a day.

He concludes that health ministers and clinical commissioning groups need to hear the voice of clients and treating clinicians and not just that of the providers of services, who, however unintentionally, have to market their services to succeed at the next round of tendering. Every five years providers have to compete in order to win the IAPT tender and deliver the service. Watts (2016) began working for IAPT in 2005 and makes similarly scathing comments to Binnie (2015). In particular he notes that the person providing the treatment is usually different than the person making the assessment and that the former primes the latter on what should be addressed. But a thorough psychological assessment is not carried out, 'nor does the question and answer protocol driven format allow a chance to listen to the patient's complaint'. Watts (2016) states that the majority of sessions are spent on 'eliciting key cognitions', 'eliciting and planning behaviours' and 'guided discovery'. Further homework universally involves 'behavioral change or monitoring existing thoughts to replace them with alternatives'. Watts (2016) has also supervised IAPT workers and states: 'Listening to IAPT tapes sounds like listening to torture – but what I hear is patients giving up what they want to talk about for what the IAPT worker wants to, needs to introduce'.

Quality control

Problems with the metric IAPT use to define recovery are also in evidence when the variability between areas is considered. Layard and Clark (2014) note that in 2012–2013 there was one area with under 30% recovery and another area in which more than 65% recovered. Of 147 areas there were 33 (22.5%) where recovery was under 40%, with 79 areas (53.7%) in which recovery was 40–50%, and in 35 areas (23.8%) recovery was over 50%. Thus, at face value in almost a quarter of IAPT areas, the therapists are doing better than in the controlled trials! Layard and Clark (2014) suggest that the way forward is for areas to ape the practice in the best areas. At one level this is quite reasonable, but when the best are apparently doing better than in the controlled trials, it sounds suspicious. The likelihood is that IAPT is not using a credible outcome measure. This is not to say that there might not be individual therapists who are performing well.

Not only is there a vast disparity in the level of services for physical and mental health, but there is also a disparity in the rigour with which they are evaluated. Mental health treatments in routine practice have been very rarely evaluated with the gold-standard randomised controlled trial involving an assessor that is blind to treatment and using a standardised diagnostic interview. Since the 1960s rigorous efficacy studies of psychological interventions conducted in or by research centres have demonstrated the value of therapies such as cognitive behaviour therapy for common mental health problems, but what is lacking is hard evidence that these interventions have been translated to routine practice without significant loss of potency.

Bogus change

Crisis Intervention Services are common in secondary care. Their remit is to cater for the needs of the suicidal and those with a psychosis. But in attempting to provide talking therapies within six weeks of a referral in primary care, is such a service any more than another crisis intervention service? It is likely that a significant proportion of people either refer themselves or are referred by GPs following some crisis. It is therefore not surprising that overall group means on some psychometric test will reduce as the crisis abates. In such a context changes on some psychometric test are not a reliable indicator of the efficacy of the intervention. To give an anonymised example of this:

> *Gwen was a student nurse. She went to see her GP and said that she had been low for a few months and had been struggling to manage the demands of work and home. The GP administered the PHQ-9 [Kroenke et al. (2001)], a measure of the severity of depression, and she scored 16, which is indicative of depression. Gwen's GP prescribed the antidepressant Citalopram, which she took. On re-examination two months later her PHQ-9 score was 6, which is in the normal region, and this score was maintained at examination a month later.*

86 *Part III*

Whether Gwen above was actually initially clinically depressed is debatable, as no standardised diagnostic interview was conducted, but she attended her GP at a bad patch in her life and with time and medication matters improved. Thus a psychological therapy programme such as IAPT, that evaluates its effectiveness in terms of a metric such as the proportion of clients scoring under 10 on the PHQ-9 at the end of treatment, is on shaky ground. In the evaluation of a large stress group implemented by an IAPT service by Burns et al. (2015), the changes on the PHQ-9 were of a reduction from 16 to 10 during treatment; the best results were for those who attended more than two sessions. Burns et al. (2015) comment that their Stress Control Programme appears 'comparatively clinically equivalent to other IAPT interventions'. But this appears to be no different than the effects of the passage of time: Gilbody et al. (2015) looked at how GP patients with a PHQ-9 score of greater than 10 fare with usual treatment; over a four-month period, their mean PHQ-9 score reduced from 16 to 9 (the usual treatment included, antidepressants 85% and IAPT 13%; 6% had been in contact with secondary care).

A study by Guo et al. (2015) shows the benefits that can accrue simply from the appropriate prescribing of antidepressants. This study found that for depressed clients, 28.8% remitted (Hamilton Depression score of 7 or less) with medication dose chosen by the clinician (routine care) and 73.8% remitted with measurement-based care (guideline and rating scale-based decisions), i.e. with a bona fide treatment. Measured against these yardsticks the claims for the added benefits of psychological therapies look somewhat dubious. Further, the Guo et al. (2015) study is more reliable in that an independent diagnostic interview has been conducted in the former. Thus the claim of the Improving Access to Psychological Therapies to a 45% recovery rate [Richards and Borglin (2011)] would be hard to defend in a court examining reliable methodology, and it would be even more difficult to defend the proposition that as presently delivered the psychological therapies constitute an added value.

Levels of evidence

Efficacy studies (can it work in principle?) are conducted predominantly with the gold standard of blind, randomised, controlled trials using a standardised diagnostic interview; effectiveness studies (which ask, 'Can it work in practice?') are usually not. Thus the level of evidence for routinely available mental health treatments is not compelling.

Grades of recommendation relate to the strength of the evidence on which the recommendation is based. Thus the Scottish equivalent of NICE, SIGN (2013) in giving a 'C' recommendation for CBT for chronic pain, were simply saying CBT 'should be considered' for this difficulty; this reflected their inability to draw on any randomised controlled trials, but they had sufficient well-controlled case studies, which were sufficiently free from bias, and there was a moderate probability that the CBT made a difference to pain management. SIGN uses four grades of recommendation; A–D, where A is the most recommended and D the least. There

Quality of psychological therapy 87

are eight levels of evidence used by SIGN with randomised controlled trials, with a very low risk of bias at the top to expert opinion at the bottom – a spectrum from evidence-based treatments to eminence-based. But there are mental well-being interventions that are beyond this spectrum which I will term 'ultratherapies'; included in this category are app-based, self-delivered treatments. Leigh and Flatt (2015) reviewed fourteen apps, only two of which had used an NHS-accredited performance metric, in these two instances a self-report questionnaire. Four of the apps offered evidence to support effectiveness.

In the legal system the burden of proof in the criminal system is 'beyond reasonable doubt', but in the civil system (e.g. personal injury) it is 'on the balance of probabilities'; routine mental health services operate in a way analogous to the civil system. Just as in the civil system, there are endless debates between expert witnesses arising from differences in methodology. There is similarly considerable room for disagreement about the effectiveness of routine mental health services because of methodological concerns and biases.

Specialist NHS facilities often fail to address comorbity

Specialist facilities are set up with a particular difficulty in mind, such as pain or eating disorders, and unsurprisingly do not address co-existing problems, despite impeding their core function by not doing so. There is rarely facility for treating any comorbid condition such as post-traumatic stress disorder, and this can cause problems as the following anonymised example indicates:

> Sharon suffered a lower back injury when she was thrown backwards by an electric shock in work. She had gone into a storeroom, leaving the door open, to look at the electrics and see why the power had failed in part of the store and inadvertently touched a wire that had become loosened from its connection. After the accident she was off work for twelve months, partly because of her fear of returning to work and partly because of her back injury. Sharon suffered from flashbacks and nightmares of lying on her back on the floor 'in full view, surrounded by customers, not comprehending what had happened'. On her first day of the group pain management programme, she became distressed when others asked her how her pain had come about, felt 'surrounded' as she had done in the incident and left the building.

In the above example Sharon's post-traumatic stress disorder was not catered for in the treatment of her pain.

Ambivalence to randomised controlled trials

Practitioners' attitudes to randomised controlled trials tend to range between ambivalence and hostility, with comparatively few using them as a signpost for daily practice. (In the next chapter it is proposed that without RCTs as a satnav,

88 *Part III*

claims of evidence-based practice are questionable). Though the psychological therapies have a good evidence base in research settings [see the NICE guidelines], reproducing these results in routine practice is likely to be problematic, not least because of attitudes to outcome studies. Binnie (2015) observed, 'I have heard on numerous occasions "NICE guidelines are just a guide"'.

More generally there is a gap between published research and replication. Laboratory findings in the psychological sciences are often not replicated. The Open Science Collaboration, [Aarts et al. (2015)] conducted replications of 100 studies published in three psychology journals and found that the mean effect size of the replication effects was 0.197, which was only half the magnitude of the original effects' 0.403. These authors state, 'Potentially problematic practices include selective reporting, selective analysis and insufficient specification of the conditions necessary or sufficient to obtain the results'. Whilst the studies under consideration were not psychological therapy interventions, they do highlight the fact that when there are methodological problems with either the original study or with a replication, findings will be different, leading to confusion and dismay.

Mis-attribution of treatment failure to the treatment rather than to primarily unreliable diagnosis

It is likely that insufficient attention to diagnoses in routine practice will mean that poorer results are obtained than in a randomised controlled trial. In this connection Johnsen and Friborg (2015) conducted a meta-analysis of seventy cognitive behaviour therapy (CBT) studies for depression and concluded that CBT did not seem to be helping reduce depression symptoms as much now as it did when it was first pioneered in the 1970s. But inspection of Table 1 of this study showed that from 1977 up to and including the millennium, 85% of studies were randomised controlled trials (RCTs), but from 2001 to 2014 the comparable figure was 65%. One of the hallmarks of an RCT is blind assessment, using a standardised interview. Thus there was no certainty that treated populations post-millennium were comparable to those before. Post-millennium there were ten times as many field studies (FS) as prior to the millennium. However, FS studies are much more a mirror image of evaluations and treatments that take place in routine practice, e.g. Westbrook's (2005) IAPT where there is sole reliance on a psychometric test as a metric. In the Johnsen and Friborg (2015) study, outcome from non-diagnostically guided treatments was poorer. The results of Johnsen and Friborg's (2015) meta-analysis could be most parsimoniously interpreted as indicating that CBT does not work well when the population being addressed is poorly defined. An ill-defined population is precisely the situation that obtains in routine practice when psychological therapies are delivered. In Aart et al.'s (2015) terms there is a failure to provide sufficient information to determine treatment, i.e. a reliable diagnostic assessment is not made. Thus there can be no expectancy that CBT in routine practice will produce results comparable to those found in randomised controlled trials.

Publication bias and eminence-based treatment

Treatments are likely to be published if they yield positive results; there is a penchant for novelty and originality, and journal editors do not favour negative results. Further it is more difficult to get funding to replicate findings, and even if funding is secured, negative findings might well not see the light of day. A publication bias can therefore exist, sometimes exacerbated by peer reviewers who do not declare a conflict of interest when considering the worthiness of a paper with negative findings for publication. Thus for a treatment to be truly evidence based it needs to be independently replicated, with the same degree of rigour as in the original trial and with transparency about conflicts of interest; regrettably these caveats are often not in place. As a consequence there is an espousal of so-called 'best practice', determining the form and funding of service provision, relying more on the status and influence of the purveyors of the particular form of service provision than on evidence.

The case for careful monitoring rather than precipitous intervention

Though the talking therapies service was intended for those with anxiety and depression, the term is used very loosely. A GP can readily make a case that any heartsick patient falls in this category if they are not obviously psychotic, and there is a possibility that if referred elsewhere they may attend to see them less. Anybody who feels stressed can readily subsume their difficulties under an anxiety-and-depression umbrella and seek to take shelter in the talking therapies.

This raises the question of whether instant availability of talking therapies is in fact a good use of resources; would a 'wait and see' policy be better? Would a more rigorous initial assessment be appropriate? Does the very act of improving access also carry within it the seeds of its own destruction? Frances (2013) recommends a process of stepped diagnosis involving 1) Gathering baseline data; 2) Normalizing problems – take them seriously, but reformulate positively as expectable responses to the inevitable stresses in life; 3) Watchful waiting – continued assessment with no pretense of a definitive diagnosis or active treatment; 4) Using minimal interventions, education, books, computer-aided self-help therapy; 5) Utilising brief counseling; 6) Offering definitive diagnosis and treatment. Such a process is already enshrined in the NICE guidelines for dealing with trauma responses; Frances (2013) appears to be recommending a more general extension of this approach. His book is titled *Saving Normal,* and his thesis is that we should not prematurely medicalise normal stress responses. As I write, I have just reviewed the records of two patients who were prescribed antidepressants by their GP. In one case the patient's ex was seeking custody of their children and in the other case a parent was distraught at learning that one of her children had been diagnosed as autistic. In neither case was a wait-and-see policy applied. Drugs were the immediate response, robbing both patients of the opportunity to test whether their own resources, supplemented perhaps by drawing on the support of friends and family,

90   *Part III*

would be equal to the challenges. A watchful waiting policy would apply equally to proferring a psychological therapy, concentrating limited resources where they are needed. The dominant model should be one of temporary destabilisation by life events and a naturally occurring restitution.

In some instances, such as an acute psychotic episode, where the person is incoherent, experiencing delusions and/or hallucinations or is actively suicidal, watchful waiting would be inappropriate. But such cases are very much the exception rather than the rule, albeit that medication might be appropriate in such instances. However, the antipsychotics are not restoring normal functioning; they are offering an altered state of consciousness, which admittedly in some instances the affected individual may regard as preferable to the self-harm that may accrue from not having them prescribed.

Charities and the NHS

As a consequence of the shortcomings of NHS provision, people often seek the support of charities such as MIND or the Richmond Fellowship. Sometimes CCGs link up with a particular charity to provide a service, but the charity is then dependent on that source of funding and can have difficulties resisting demands to take on ever-more-complex cases using a minimalist intervention, e.g. such as guided self-help. Nuttall (2016) was involved in a London charity that linked up with IAPT to provide a service, but as he indicates this can be problematic for the charity: 'There was also the survival fear that if the "partners" (the charity) did not conform to the IAPT system either in its operations or its model of therapy, NHS funding would be withdrawn, the system imposed and NHS referrals that would otherwise sustain the partner be diverted. It is unlikely within this scenario that local charitable agencies could survive, putting in jeopardy both client choice and training facilities for would-be counsellors and therapists'. It thus makes it difficult for charities such as MIND to openly challenge IAPT. Nuttall (2016) notes his charity is meeting the target of seeing 15% of the population affected by mental health problems and as such is being held up as an exemplary model, but he questions the IAPT criteria for success: ' "Attending to" is defined as patients meeting the criteria of two clinical contacts – one of which is always telephone triage and the second might be only a letter of appointment. Neither of these in psychotherapy practice would be considered clinical contact of any benefit'. Nuttall (2016) adds that although managers from his charity are 'invited' to IAPT board meetings, they have little say in the implementation of the strategic directives handed down.

Stepped care and mental health

Currently, when people are given low-intensity interventions few are stepped up to high intensity [7.7% Richards and Borglin (2011)] and only 6% [Richards and Borglin (2011)] are sent to high intensity without going through low intensity. It could be argued that this is because the 'minimalist' intervention is so effective, but this has not been demonstrated by an independent assessment using a standardised

Quality of psychological therapy   91

diagnostic interview. There is at least a suspicion that many of the serious cases are actually 'lost'; these cases may return to the GP, who then re-refers, and the GP may be scolded for clogging the system! De facto there is a minimalist psychological service, with mental health refugees seeking asylum where they can. The ratio of the numbers attending low-intensity to high-intensity interventions varies enormously throughout the country from 22:1 to 0.5:1 [Richards et al. (2012)], but the ratio of those with supposedly serious problems to mild problems should not show such a wide variation; it ought to be more or less constant.

A numbers game?

It is now a matter of political correctness to involve clients/service users in the provision of services, and although this is a move in the right direction, paid staff nevertheless have greater power to engage Clinical Commissioning Groups, health ministers and the media and to hold sway. The survival of service providers depends on their marketing and ability to process the largest number of clients per staff member. But independent quality control is absent; there is no 'Trading Standards Authority' applying the rigorous outcome measures utilised in randomised controlled trials that were the basis for establishing evidence-based psychotherapies, as recommended by NICE.

How service users are actually faring in IAPT

As luck would have it, I have had independent access to IAPT clients and the opportunity to use a standardised diagnostic interview to chart how they have fared. I have been an expert witness to the court for over twenty years. Between 2010 and 2015, I conducted 866 medico-legal examinations; I have had no axe to grind in gauging the impact of services on individuals. I have not been employed by any of their service providers. As an expert witness my primary duty is to advise the court on a person's functioning and treatment needs. In this capacity I have necessarily had to use the most reliable assessment methodology available [see Scott (2002, 1998)]. In reviewing the mental health histories as an expert witness I have been wholly independent of any service provider and have had the space to make the most reliable assessment using a) an open ended interview, b) standardised semi-structured diagnostic interview SCID, c) a screen for malingering and d) review of medical and counselling records.

Nevertheless, there are problems with generalising from my findings. All have been seeking compensation for some trauma, from slips to coach crashes involving fatalities and with trauma responses ranging from no discernible psychological effect or exacerbation of a pre-existing condition, to adjustment disorder, specific phobia, depression, panic disorder, post-traumatic stress disorder and most commonly, combinations of disorders. Whilst the range of disorders identified does cover the whole spectrum of disorders, there is an over-representation of those with PTSD, so the case mix is slightly different than that of routine mental health services. Nevertheless it is possible to gauge how those with different disorders have

92 *Part III*

fared in the mental health system. Most people do seek compensation for injury when they are not at fault; as such they are a fair representation of the general population.

In some cases their contact with IAPT had been before the index event that led them to seek compensation and in others afterwards. Ideally I would have seen an entirely random sample of IAPT clients, but this is not the case and there has therefore has to be some caution in interpreting my findings. But my findings are more reliable than any other yet available, in that current assessments of routine practice are a) not independent of the service provider – APT has always marked its own homework, b) do not review medical and counselling records, c) often do not involve an open-ended interview so that the client has the time to fully tell their story and d) do not include a standardised diagnostic interview to make a reliable diagnosis.

Study sample

Over the past five years I have assessed 866 compensation cases, of whom 88 (10.2%) were children. In 34 (3.9%) cases the person had at some point made a suicide attempt. Of adults, 65 (8.3%) were involved at some time with an IAPT service either before or after the event that led to my medico-legal assessment and 176 (22.6%) were involved in non-IAPT counselling. Thus approximately 1 in 3 (30.5%) adults had been referred for counselling. The GP records documented that 25 (3.2%) adults had declined counselling.

The reach of IAPT

How people fare in the IAPT service is of particular importance because it is heralded as the way forward, and agencies are encouraged to follow an IAPT template. In the area in which I work, the northwest of England, 8.3% of my sample were dealt with by IAPT. Lord Layard, a prime mover with regard to IAPT, in a Kings Fund document [Layard (2015)] dated January 23, 2015] stated that the immediate goal of IAPT was to see 15% of those with mental health problems with a 25% target by 2020. Lord Layard expressed fulsome praise for IAPT: 'The journal *Nature* has called IAPT world beating and I think it probably is the best effort to deliver evidence-based psychological therapy that there is anywhere in the world at the moment. And we have got ten countries now considering introducing their own version of the IAPT arrangements'. But even if IAPT were as potent as Lord Layard claims and achieves its access targets, it would still mean that three out of four people with a mental health problem would, in his view, have at best a sub-optimal service for the foreseeable future.

Embarking on the IAPT care pathway

IAPT operates an opt-in system requiring a person to ring in and arrange an assessment, and some may find this too difficult, Ms. A. was referred by a local psychiatric service to IAPT; she had a history of depression and was asked by the service to opt in but did not do so. That this referral was made indicates a paucity of

Quality of psychological therapy 93

psychotherapeutic services in secondary care. It also casts doubt whether an opt-in service is appropriate for depressed clients for whom oftentimes a major problem is motivation.

The IAPT experience begins with a thirty-minute telephone assessment by the most junior members of IAPT staff, usually psychological well-being practitioners (PWPs). The 2014–2015 IAPT Annual report shows that 27% of people do not proceed beyond this initial assessment. In my review of sixty-five consecutive IAPT cases the comment of Ms. B. may help to flesh out why there is such a loss of clientele at this early stage: she felt the telephone assessment was rushed, the lady was abrupt and the only available treatment appointment was in an evening rush hour; she feared heavy traffic and had to cater for her young children, so she did not turn up for treatment. This raises the question of whether a thirty-minute telephone conversation is an appropriate way to welcome anyone into a therapeutic service. It is likely to be difficult for most to tell the story of their difficulties within thirty minutes, explain the practical difficulties they face and at the same time feel understood and safe with the person at the other end of the phone. These difficulties are compounded if part of the client's difficulties is that they mistrust others.

Offering a low-intensity intervention is the default option in IAPT unless it is abundantly evident that a high-intensity intervention is required, but this can be very off-putting. Mr. C had a telephone assessment with IAPT two months after a serious road traffic accident; the PWP offered group therapy which he declined, and so he was offered appointment for computerised CBT Beating the Blues. He declined this also, saying that he felt he couldn't fit it in with his busy work schedule, and didn't respond to further scheduled appointments. The IAPT documentation recorded him as suffering from depression, which I confirmed in my diagnostic interview, but he was also suffering from post-traumatic stress disorder. This failure to identify PTSD meant that he was referred to inappropriate low-intensity intervention.

A referring GP wrote to an IAPT Service thus:

> I was extremely worried seen last week by colleague of yours issued with a number of leaflets on managing anxiety and depression not had the motivation to read the leaflet concerned that this approach should be used to people who are already depressed and lack motivation next appointment was arranged by telephone in 3 weeks further intervention would have been more appropriate she appears to have lost confidence in the system.

Sometimes people are inappropriately discharged from the service on the basis of an inadequate assessment, as exemplified by the case of Mr. D., for whom the following letter was sent by IAPT: 'Telephone assessment PHQ-9 5/27 GAD-7 6/21 he does not feel therapy required currently and happy to be discharged from the Service'. Whilst the scores on the PHQ-9 and GAD-7 are indicative of no problems with anxiety or depression (indeed he had mentioned that he no longer felt low), my diagnostic interview revealed that he nevertheless had a phobia about driving and travelling as a passenger in a car, and wanted this addressed; this was not identified by IAPT, and he was inappropriately discharged after assessment.

94　*Part III*

There are, it seems, fundamental problems with the embarkation process in IAPT. The training of PWPs is much less intense than that of their high-intensity counterparts; the latter undergo a year-long training involving two days a week in college and three days a week in an IAPT placement. Further, the high-intensity therapists are more likely to be more highly qualified. For example, approximately 50% of those undergoing the Institute of Psychiatry's (IoP's) year-long training were already clinical or counselling psychologists [In *Press Behavioural and Cognitive Psychotherapy* 'What IAPT CBT High Intensity Trainees Do after Training'], albeit those completing the IoP course were also more likely to be more highly qualified than most high-intensity therapists nationally.

Telephone guided self-help

Telephone guided self-help sessions usually last less than thirty minutes and are a cost-saving option compared to the traditional face-to-face fifty-minute individual session. In IAPT they are sometimes delivered following one face-to-face session, but use of the telephone can make interpersonal matters difficult to sort. The case of Ms. E. shows this; she felt the therapist did not understand and dropped out. There was no IAPT diagnosis, and my diagnostic interview revealed that she was suffering from depression. Table 7.2 shows an anonymised abstract from the IAPT documentation:

Table 7.2 Anonymised example from IAPT documentation

Date		PHQ-9	GAD-7	Social Phobia	Agoraphobia	Specific Phobia
Telephone assessment	Very difficult time a month ago when fell down escalator embarrassed shocked anxiety in past school phobia home schooled for a year aged 9/10 bullied at school	11	9	3	2	3
Session 1	Guided self help 45 min. difficult time 3 months ago when fell down escalator feeling outside due to religion brought up in anxiety on/off many years worse last 3 months	11	9	3	2	3
Session 2	Guided self help 30 min. strong fear of being judged by others	–	–	–	–	–
Session 3	Guided self help 25 min. agreed stepped up for further treatment of social anxiety	13	12	5	1	3
Session 4	Assessment and treatment stepped up	–	–	–	–	–
Session 5	CBT 60 min. stated social anxiety main problem due to fall anxieties have returned assessment will continue	15	13	4	0	0

Table 7.2 shows that her depression score (PHQ-9) did not reduce with treatment and her social phobia score rose. But neither the social phobia, agoraphobia or specific phobia scales are standardised validated measures. The records and Ms. E.'s comments show a failure to identify the correct target; it seems likely that this was at least in part due to the mode of treatment delivery and poor assessment.

Treating normality

But it is not the case that telephone-assisted guided self-help never works. Ms. F. had congenital scarring on her face. Whilst she did not meet diagnostic criteria for any psychological disorder, she was self-conscious and her PHQ-9 and GAD-7 score reduced from 18 and 16 respectively to 0 for both following IAPT treatment. Within IAPT's criteria for full recovery (initial scores both above 10, and a reliable change [an improvement of at least 6 on the PHQ-9 and 4 on the GAD-7] such that the final scores are below 10 and 8 on both). But it appears that IAPT have in fact treated normality; she had no disorder initially. She had concerns, which are part of normal life. It is doubtful that intervention in this case was an appropriate use of resources.

Restricted field of vision in IAPT

IAPT was set up to treat primarily mild to moderate depression and anxiety, but there is nothing in the assessment framework that makes it possible to identify uncommon disorders such as avoidant personality disorder, body dysmorphic disorder and excoriation (skin picking) disorder. Such uncommon disorders may or may not be associated with depression or anxiety disorder, but if such clients are treated simply as cases of anxiety or depression they are likely to feel shortchanged. At diagnostic interview I found that Ms. G. was suffering solely from excoriation (skin picking) disorder. She was referred by her GP and had an eight-week wait for an IAPT face-to-face assessment session. Ms. G. was then passed to high intensity and had five sessions in total with three different therapists. No mention had been made by any of the professionals about excoriation disorder, and when I saw she was much relieved to learn that there was such a disorder and a protocol for dealing with it. The therapists had simply asked her to monitor the intensity of her craving to pick. Ms. G. was also asked to complete thought records, as well as the depression and anxiety measures PHQ-9 GAD-7 each week and in the presence of the therapist. These two measures are mandatory in IAPT even when, as in Ms. G.'s case, they had no relevance to what she was suffering from. The therapists seemed unaware that completion of psychometric tests by a client in the presence of the former may in any case give a misleading result, as the client can score to please the therapist.

Limited sessions

It appears that sometimes the number of sessions in IAPT is determined by managerial edict rather than client need. Mr. H. experienced workplace bullying and at my diagnostic interview I found that he was suffering from depression. Mr. H was

96   *Part III*

given six counselling sessions and pleaded for more sessions; he was given an extra session. Though he had found the sessions helpful there was no change in his diagnostic status. He was still depressed. There was no evidence that an evidence-based treatment for depression had been embarked on. Ms. I. said that she had seven sessions with IAPT because that was all she was allowed to have and not because she was better. My diagnostic interview suggested that she was suffering from PTSD, and this was unchanged by the IAPT intervention. However, she was also suffering from depression and this resolved with IAPT (her PHQ-9 score reduced from 21 to 9 and GAD-7 from 18 to 10). Both Mr. H. and Ms. I. received sub-therapeutic doses of treatment.

Dropping out of IAPT

The IAPT Annual Report 2014–2015 states that 41.8% of those entering treatment complete it (they define completing as attending at least two treatment sessions); thus at face value almost 60% of people do not complete treatment. But IAPT applies the term *recovery* to just those who complete treatment and consider that half of these recover, i.e. of ten referrals who *begin* an IAPT programme, just two would recover. The IAPT results sound much better if reference is made simply to 'completers'. When an intention to treat analysis is performed the results are poor; approximately four out of five do not benefit from IAPT.

IAPT does not use the term *dropout*, and in normal parlance it refers to a person dropping out before the evidence-based treatment is complete. Thus, considering only the 'completers' group in IAPT, given that those completing treatment attended an average of six sessions and no evidence-based psychotherapy involves so few sessions, probably at least half of these so called 'completers' would actually be considered dropouts. Mr. J. said that he had seven or eight therapy sessions; he was tempted to make a complaint about the therapy but could not face a confrontation and dropped out of treatment. He said that he never felt comfortable enough with the therapist to volunteer the fact that he had nearly made a suicide attempt. Mr. J. said that he felt uncomfortable with the therapist and could not understand her explanation of his difficulties. He said that the therapist talked to him about his belief system and asked him did he 'believe in Santa Claus'. He felt demeaned but not confident enough to complain. Mr. J. said that the therapist focused on his relationship with his father, who he said had been somewhat heavy handed on occasions when he needed to be, and there was an implication that his father was somehow responsible for the way he was currently. He said that this made him very angry because he is very fond of his father, but he did not feel able to voice this to the therapist. Mr. J. said that the therapist also focused on his unusual first name, and though he did experience some bullying in relation to this, in his view it was not significant; however, the therapist seemed to make much of this. My diagnostic interview revealed that he was suffering from post-traumatic stress disorder, alcohol abuse and depression, but there was no evidence that these had been addressed with an evidence-based psychotherapy.

Quality of psychological therapy   97

Ms. K. described her treatment by a psychological well-being practitioner as 'hopeless' and said she had been asked to put smiley faces on activities she had completed. She dropped out after three sessions, but her PHQ-9 score reduced from 23 to 14 and GAD-7 from 21 to 10. Despite this my diagnostic interview suggested no change in her diagnostic status, in that she was still suffering from depression. Mr. L. attended two appointments. According to the IAPT documentation he had 'mild PTSD' and was introduced to EMDR psychoeducation. He declined the offer of further appointments, and in fact he only had a travel phobia according to SCID interview.

Arbitrary criteria for discharge

Discharge from IAPT is not based on diagnostic status but often on an arbitrary focus on some particular symptom that has in fact improved. Mr. M. was appropriately treated with trauma-focussed CBT for his post-traumatic stress disorder, and though he improved with this treatment my diagnostic interview revealed that he was still suffering from PTSD. He was discharged on the basis that his flashbacks were no longer as disturbing. Mr. M.'s depression had not been identified or treated by IAPT and was still present at the end of his treatment with them.

Client satisfaction

There can be a desynchrony between clients' expression of satisfaction with treatment and a failure to respond to treatment. Mr. N.'s score on the PHQ-9 improved from 17 to 13 with treatment; his GAD-7 score remained constant at 15. Of therapy he said, 'I find it helps me a lot; I am having a very difficult time and I always feel better after seeing my therapist'. Diagnostic interview revealed that his PTSD and depression had not improved with treatment. Further, there appeared to have been no setting and reviewing of homework, no teaching of skills to confront what is feared nor strategies taught for dealing with flashbacks and nightmares, i.e. an evidence-based treatment protocol had not been followed.

Quantitative evaluation of IAPT

The outcome of IAPT treatment as assessed by independent diagnostic interview is detailed in Table 7.3.

The levels of recovery depicted in Table 7.3 fall far short of the UK Government's aspiration [Layard and Clark (2014, p. 199)]: 'From clinical trials a reasonable expectation is that 50% of those diagnosable should recover and that was the target which Alan Johnson set for IAPT' (Mr. Johnson was the Labour Health Minister in 2007). Whether or not the person had at the time gone through litigation made no difference to treatment outcome. The levels of recovery showed little variation from disorder to disorder, as seen in Table 7.4.

The levels of recovery shown in Tables 7.3 and 7.4 are no greater than would be expected with the passage of time or from a placebo effect.

98   *Part III*

Table 7.3 IAPT outcome (n=65)

- Consecutive subjects who had used the UK, Improving Access to Psychological Therapies Service (IAPT), either before or after personal claim, revealed: 15.6% overall recovery rate
- No difference in recovery rate of those who had been treated before their personal injury (n=14) to those treated after (n=51)
- A mean of 1.6 disorders.

Table 7.4 Little variation in recovery rate by disorder

- Approximately half (thirty-three) were found to be suffering from post-traumatic stress disorder (PTSD), of whom five (15.1%) no longer met DSM diagnostic criteria for PTSD by the end of IAPT treatment
- Almost half (thirty-two) suffered from depression, with seven (21.9%) no longer meeting DSM criteria by the end of IAPT treatment.
- Twenty-six people suffered from disorders other than PTSD and depression [panic disorder six; specific phobia twelve; GAD one; OCD two; social phobia; body dysmorphic disorder one; excoriation disorder one; chronic adjustment disorder twelve; and alcohol abuse one], with 2 (7.7%) no longer meeting criteria by the end of treatment.

(n = 65)

IAPT's dubious yardstick

IAPT measures outcome using the PHQ-9 and GAD-7 as their primary measures, but such psychometric tests were developed in a context in which a) people were given a standardised diagnostic interviews for depression and anxiety and b) they were administered to a population (psychiatric outpatients) [Kroenke et al. (2001)] in which the prevalence of depression and anxiety was likely higher than in IAPT. PHQ-9 and GAD-7 scores without the anchor of a diagnostic interview are of doubtful validity. For example, what does a PHQ-9 score of 12 mean if the person is suffering from a simple phobia about driving or travelling as a passenger in a car or from skin picking (excoriation) disorder? IAPT's client population contains 40% self-referrals; as such it is likely to have a much lower prevalence of sufferers from disorders pertinent to their key measures PHQ-9 and GAD-7, than in psychiatric outpatients where the instruments were validated. This means that the use of cut-offs derived in one context (psychiatric outpatients) are likely to be inapplicable in the IAPT context. Employment of these cut-offs will result in many false positives, i.e. clients unnecessarily treated for depression or generalised anxiety disorder. (Historically IAPT have used a score of 10 or above on the PHQ-9 to

Quality of psychological therapy   99

define a case of depression and 8 or above on the GAD-7 to define a case of anxiety).

The mis-identification of disorders in IAPT is likely to be ubiquitous. IAPT effectively operates a stand-alone test screen for depression and anxiety, but the National Institute for Health and Clinical Excellence recommended against routine depression screening [NICE (2010)]. In 2013, the Canadian Task Force on Preventative Health Care also recommended against screening adults for depression [Joffres et al. (2013)]. IAPT's usage of psychometric tests is misplaced.

IAPT in its data handbook (2012) lists psychometric tests that may be used for other conditions such as social phobia, PTSD and obsessive-compulsive disorder (OCD), but as their usage is not determined by a reliable standardised diagnostic interview, their appropriateness is questionable despite the specification of cut-offs to establish caseness. But the author's review of sixty-five cases found that none of these additional psychometric tests were used in any case. A review of the practice of high intensity therapists [Behavioural and Cognitive Psychotherapy (In Press)] revealed that in less than a quarter of cases (23%) were disorder-specific outcome measures discussed in supervision. Psychometric tests as used in IAPT are a navigational tool that oftentimes leads nowhere.

Overdiagnosis and overtreatment

The main effect of using the PHQ-9 and GAD-7 cutoffs for 'caseness', in lieu of a reliable diagnostic interview, is that many people with normal transient life difficulties become subject to psychological therapies. As a consequence psychological therapy services become overburdened and less able to focus on those who really do need an evidence-based treatment for psychological disorder. There has been a pathologising of normality. This parallels what has happened with the prescription of antidepressants for depression. Mojtabai (2013) found that only 38.4% of those prescribed antidepressants met the DSM diagnostic criteria for major depression. As Frances (2013) has argued, there is a need to 'save normal', to restrict psychological therapies to those disorders for which they are known to work. The case of Albert illustrates this:

Albert fell from a ladder at work, landing on his heels; his injuries were such that he could no longer work as an electrician. He had worked in this capacity for forty years. His mood was low, and his GP prescribed antidepressants (Mirtazepine), which he took briefly but gave up because of perceived side effects (aching joints). (He had also been prescribed antidepressants, Citalopram, eight years earlier when his father died, and took them for three of the six months they were prescribed). SCID diagnostic interview [First et al. (2015)] revealed that he had not met diagnostic criteria for depression since the fall, but initially suffered from chronic adjustment disorder with depressed mood. This had transmuted into DSM-5 defined intermittent explosive disorder (IED) for the past five months and excoriation

100 Part III

(skin-picking) disorder for the past nine months. His PHQ-9 score was 16, his GAD-7 score 17, and on the PTSD checklist he scored 52 (above the usually employed cut-off for PTSD). If the psychometric test scores had been used in isolation (in IAPT fashion) he could easily have been a candidate for psychotherapy for depression or PTSD, neither of which he had. Further, treatment would have been immediate giving no opportunity for natural adaptation. An adjustment disorder diagnosis suggests a period of watchful waiting and taking psychotherapeutic action only when diagnosable conditions come into view, in Albert's case the IED and excoriation disorder.

It can be argued that intervention as soon as there are difficulties prevents disorders from developing, but there is no evidence of this. To the contrary, Bisson et al. (1997) found early emotional debriefing of burn victims increased the likelihood of developing PTSD.

IAPT: no cognitive assessment

In the author's review of sixty-five IAPT cases, no therapist performed a cognitive assessment, i.e. used a standardised measure of cognitions for a particular disorder, e.g. Obsessive Beliefs Questionnaire or Post-traumatic Cognitions Inventory. This casts doubts as to whether salient cognitions (a key target in CBT) were identified in treatment. The IAPT Handbook (2011) offers no measures for cognitive assessment, conveying an implicit message that this is unimportant.

Fitting therapy to the client rather than the client to therapy

Evidence-based treatment protocols have been established in randomised controlled trials, in which there are a proscribed number of treatment sessions conducted over a specific period. Whilst it can be reasonably argued that significantly less than this number of treatment sessions would constitute a sub-therapeutic dose, it is tempting to use this number of sessions as an upper limit on what number of sessions should be provided when as is invariably the case, there is a scarcity of therapeutic resources, with consequent managerial pressure. Further during the course of treatment there can be serious adverse events, as the following case illustrates:

Barbara was referred for treatment following two suicide attempts. She had had ECT many years ago and was troubled by memories of this. Barbara was also being tested for possible multiple sclerosis, which was confirmed after the second session of CBT for depression. After the third CBT session she had a heart attack, and her daughter had told her that she was leaving her partner to return home. The therapist decided that Barbara's distress at recent events was 'normal' and that simple contact through a period of watchful waiting was appropriate, with therapy recommencing when Barbara felt ready. But the therapist was told by the independent CBT Clinic for which she was working (the clinic was funded by insurers) that further treatment sessions could not be guaranteed and there was a need to 'complete' the case.

In the randomised controlled trials of CBT, a significant minority of clients do not recover (return to normal functioning) or respond by the end of the established treatment protocol but may yet respond with an extended period of treatment. To provide this extra treatment imposes an extra financial burden on the providers of psychological services but with limited prospects of success. A dose-effect relationship [Howard et al. (1986)] appears to operate in psychotherapy with most of the gains of therapy occurring in the first eight sessions, with 50% of clients improved by this stage and gradually diminishing returns in outcome thereafter, with 75% improved by twenty-six sessions. Hollon et al. (2014) examined whether CBT combined with antidepressants conferred any added benefit to the second group of clients alone, when treatment was continued for up to forty-two months until recovery was achieved. This follows the more normal routine practice of treating a person until they recover (and not to a predetermined point as in RCTs). Interestingly there was only added benefit for those with a severe but non-chronic depression. Further, those clients with a co-existing personality disorder took longer to recover. Thus in this instance, fitting the client to therapy would involve a) consideration of the severity of depression and b) determining whether they in addition had a personality disorder. In the Hollon et al. (2014) study, therapists could if necessary also draw on the protocols for clients with personality disorders contained within Beck's work for personality disorders [Beck et al. (2003)] as well as follow the standard Beck depression protocol [Beck et al. (1979)]. Combined CBT and antidepressants resulted in 72.6% recovery eventually compared to 62.5% recovery with antidepressants alone. The approach of Hollon et al. (2014) is one of personalised medicine, continuing treatment until full normalisation. In practice this is a difficult goal for cash-strapped service providers, particularly as therapists also met weekly for ninety minutes to review cases.

Within IAPT clients are often given the cheap off-the-peg solutions in the first instance without any clarity of the problem that they are attempting to solve. Few (approximately 10%) progress to a more bespoke service staffed by more experienced staff and fewer still will undergo treatment to recovery as exemplified in the Hollon et al. (2014) study.

Whether or not therapy is fitted to the client or the client to therapy depends on the diagnostic acumen (and thereby training) of the clinician. This in turn depends on what training is funded and the agenda of service providers and Clinical Commissioning Groups (CCGs). Fitting clients to therapeutic services rather than vice versa is likely to be a factor in the unprecedented levels of staff stress amongst psychological therapists in the UK [see Chapter Ten].

Part IV

Realising the potential of psychological therapies

8 Creating a mental health system fit for purpose

The current mental health system is not fit for purpose; the public do not get what it says on the tin. Only 30% get psychological therapy in the government-funded Improving Access to Psychological Therapies Service [Gyani et al. (2013)]. IAPT has always marked its own homework. There has been a failure of governance within the mental health system.

Stepping away from inappropriate treatment

The PHQ-9 has been pressed into service as a metric to evaluate routine mental health services. Wittkampf et al. (2009) compared the performance of the PHQ-9 with a gold-standard diagnostic interview – the SCID [Spitzer et al. (1992)] – and found using the PHQ-9 cut-off of 10 and above to denote a 'case' resulted in a third of people being diagnosed erroneously as depressed. Thus a third would be given inappropriate treatment. Wittkampf et al. (2009) concluded that the PHQ-9 is not specific enough to be used as a diagnostic instrument and advise that it should always be followed by a formal diagnostic procedure [a point reiterated by Reynolds (2010)]. However there is no reliable diagnostic interview conducted in IAPT. IATP personnel have used the PHQ-9 as a measure of how much they make a difference, but Wittkampf et al. (2009) found that it had only a moderate correlation with the interview-based gold standard of change – the Hamilton Depression Rating Scale – and concluded that the PHQ-9 does not seem appropriate as a severity index or a measure of change.

Stepping away from bogus reassurance about the effectiveness of intervention

When there are comparatively short waiting lists, as in IAPT, people are coming at their worst. For some there will be improvement as the crisis passes. Such changes are not evidence of the success of IAPT. The Wittkampf et al. (2009) study was based on patients seeing their GP, but 40% of IAPT patients are self-referrals. Thus it might be anticipated that the overall prevalence of depression in the IAPT population will be lower; this in turn means the positive predictive value of the PHQ-9 will be even less, i.e. there will be many more than the 33% false positives,

106   *Part IV*

resulting in an even greater wasting of treatment resources. A psychometric test only has validity when it is tapping a relevant construct. Thus at least in principle the PHQ-9 could be used as a metric for reliably diagnosed depressed patient, but such a metric is meaningless if the patient has no disorder or some other disorder. IAPT's use of the PHQ-9 and its companion the GAD-7 (a measure of generalised anxiety) is irrelevant for patients with other primary diagnoses, despite IAPT's pressing them into service. Within its own terms of reference IAPT has not demonstrated that it makes a real difference to people's lives, but it is extremely well marketed and backed by many eminent people. Of course, the same has happened in the past with some of the psychotropic drugs of pharmaceutical companies.

Demanding socially significant change

There is a distinction between a clinically significant improvement in symptoms (in depression studies, which use a diagnostic interview, a 50% reduction in depression symptoms on the interview-based Hamilton Depression Rating Scale, [HDRS]) and remission (achieving a score less than 7 on the HDRS, Thase et al. [2001]). But these authors note that those who have simply 'improved' as opposed to 'remitted' are much more liable to relapse. IAPT have made a similar distinction between improvement and remission but use the self-report measure PHQ-9 as the measure, and apply this as a measure without reliably knowing what the disorder is. The PHQ-9 is not a valid outcome measure in these circumstances.

Further, the Thase et al. (2001) results do suggest that the socially significant goal for treatment should be full remission; they found that at best this was achieved by various antidepressants less than half the time, and further, 25% remitted with placebo. IAPT has not demonstrated that its mode of service provision is any better than placebo [see Table 7.3].

Lessons from history

'Those who cannot remember the past are condemned to repeat it', wrote George Santanya (1905–1906) in his five-volume work *The Life of Reason*. Whilst Aaron Beck can be rightly credited as a prime mover in the development of what has come to be known as evidence-based psychological therapies, the context in which his cognitive behaviour therapy was developed appears to have been forgotten, leading to a widespread failure to deliver EBTs in routine practice.

In their earliest published work, Beck et al. (1962) were concerned that meaningful research on psychotherapy was made impossible by a failure to agree what target the therapy was meant to be addressing. Different clinicians would have different understandings of terms such as *depression* and *schizophrenia*, some emphasising one particular symptom over another. Thus the standard psychiatric interview was very unreliable with levels of agreement between 32% and 54%. Reliability can be assessed in a number of ways. In the distillation of the DSM-5 reliability was assessed by furnishing clinicians with a computer checklist of symptoms; one clinician would assess a patient and another clinician would assess

Creating a mental health system 107

the same patient a week or two later, and the levels of agreement between the clinicians was calculated, for various disorders. The level of agreement is expressed by the kappa statistic. The more uncommon a disorder is in a particular population, agreement is less likely; the kappa statistic adjusts for this. In the DSM-5 field trials the kappa statistics indicated over 85% agreement for disorders such as PTSD assuming 10% prevalence in the population. Thus having a standardised reliable diagnostic interview makes research possible. (Actually there are arguments about the best way to calculate reliability: in the DSM-IV field trials the two clinicians were given the same information, i.e. the second clinician viewed the videotape of the first clinician's interview and made his assessment on this data. The kappa values with this mode of calculating reliability tend to be higher than in the test-retest modality. Thus, whilst kappa for depression appeared respectable in the DSM-IV field trial it was not in the DSM-5 trial, which resulted in a kappa of 0.28.) Beck et al. (1962) made the point that it was important to control for two types of variance in an interview: information variance, i.e. the range of information considered pertinent; and criterion variance, i.e. the threshold above which a symptom can be considered to be present at a clinically significant level. Their concerns led to the development of Research Diagnostic Criteria [Spitzer and Robins (1987)] which were in turn a stepping stone to the DSM criteria, without which there would have been scarcely any foundation for the construction of EBTs. (There is an alternate set of criteria ICD 10 used by the World Health Organisation [2010], but these have generally not been used by psychiatric researchers because of their vagueness.) Beck's initial study of CBT for depression showed over 50% of people fully recovered, i.e. returned to normal functioning by the end of therapy.

Keeping in mind the yardstick for evidence-based treatment

Given that EBTs are diagnostic specific and predicated on an accurate diagnosis, it is likely that attempts to replicate the findings from randomised controlled trials with non-academic therapists in routine practice will founder in the absence of a reliable diagnostic framework. Chambless and Hollon (1998) [see Appendix E] have detailed the requirements for a psychological therapy to be termed an evidence-supported treatment as inter alia including 'b) a population, treated for specified problems, for whom inclusion criteria have been delineated in a reliable, valid manner; c) reliable and valid outcome assessment measures, at minimum tapping the problems targeted for change'. Routine NHS psychological therapy as conducted by IAPT does not reflect those aspects of EBTs i.e. b) and c) above, that are needed to translate the benefits of research into practice. Tolin et al. (2015) have suggested, however, that Chambless and Hollon's (1998) criteria need updating to include also i) evidence of effectiveness in at least one study in a non-research setting, using non-academic therapists; ii) evidence of impact on functional impairment, e.g. a return to work and not just symptom improvement. Thus the recommendations of Tolin et al. (2015) represent a heightening of the bar for what should be considered an evidence-supported treatment, but their emphasis

108　*Part IV*

on impacting functional impairment is a welcome attempt to bring in a real-world (social) significance.

The price paid for expediency

Since the millennium, research studies on CBT for depression (and indeed other disorders), have been characterised by a desire to reduce the research burden by employing psychometric tests rather than conducting the more-costly blind diagnostic interviews. Thus in the Johnsen and Friborg (2015) meta-analysis of CBT studies for depression, there are ten times as many field studies (FS) after the millennium as before. The more recent studies produced a less-positive outcome, suggesting that CBT is sub-optimal in a poorly defined population. The way in which clients are triaged in routine practice is a closer parallel to the FS studies than the diagnostic-based studies in the randomised controlled trials, and consumers are therefore likely to be short-changed.

Treatment without a reliable foundation

Recent UK, CBT texts such as Grant et al. (2008) suggest that though standard diagnostic interviews may be of assistance to the novice or a therapist assessing an unfamiliar problem, they see them as being much less relevant to the experienced CBT practitioner. Grant et al. favour a 'Functional Analysis Assessment' [pp. 14–16], the 'Mental Health Status' section of which refers simply to 'appearance, speech, mood, appetite, sleep, libido, anhedonia, irritability, self-worth and self-image, hopelessness, risk/self-harm/suicide, psychosis, concentration, orientation and memory'. These are much the same domains as those covered in the standard routine psychiatric interview that Beck et al. (1962) considered necessary but found to be insufficient to establish a reliable diagnosis. Grant et al. (2008) observe, 'In the absence of knowledge about the reliability and validity of case formulation, its use constitutes an act of faith on the part of both therapist and client – in our view a worthwhile one'. But if oftentimes CBT therapy is conducted without recourse to a diagnostic interview, then there can be no case formulation, which is a specific example of the cognitive model of a disorder, i.e. when there is no case, what remains is a formulation, and we are back full circle to precisely the sort of idiosyncratic formulations that graced psychoanalysis in the 1950s and 1960s and which Beck distanced himself from. Formulation has been found to have low reliability [see Kuyken et al. (2005) and Kuyken (2006)].

Writing in the United States in the same year as the Grant et al. (2008) UK work, Persons (2008) asserts that 'diagnosis can aid in formulation, treatment planning and intervention decision making' [p5] and recommends the use of the relevant parts of a standard diagnostic interview after generating a problem list from the client's narrative. Persons adds, 'Diagnostic error can contribute to treatment failure. For example, if the treatment plan is founded on the notion that the patient has unipolar depression and GAD when she actually has bipolar disorder and a substance abuse disorder, the treatment plan is likely to be misguided and the outcome poor' [p225]. Nevertheless, in routine practice it is extremely rare to find a practitioner incorporating a standardised diagnostic interview in their assessment and evaluation.

The poor press of standardised diagnostic interviews

The common riposte to advocacy of standardised diagnostic interviews is that they are mechanical and involve an unnecessary labelling of clients. This view is unfortunately promulgated on many professional training courses. But the evidence is that clients find them valuable. Further, without using diagnosis there can be no hard evidence that a treatment works. Without diagnosis, reliance is placed on surrogate outcome measures such as psychometric tests. This is at best like evaluating a medication for its cholesterol-reducing properties rather than whether it reduces number of deaths; the former is a much easier hurdle to surmount when marketing a product, drug or CBT in routine practice. I have never met anyone who is opposed to the inclusion of a standardised diagnostic interview in assessment and evaluation and who has actually tested the SCID or ADIS out and certainly not in more than a handful of cases. To pronounce on their merits without conducting the experiment is to say the least unscientific. It seems that diagnostic interviews are actually by-passed for ideological reasons with an anti-psychiatry/anti-medical model flavour.

Ideology also plays a part in the treatment of clients in routine practice who are held to be more complex than the patients featuring in controlled trials, and consequently the single disorder protocols of the trials are seen as inappropriate. But advocates of this position have not, at least in my experience, put this to test. They have not tried to interweave protocols for each of the disorders from which a person suffers, and certainly have not done this for more than a handful of cases. The result is a license to rely entirely on clinical judgement, and once again we are back full circle to the pre-CBT days. Just as it is not legally acceptable these days for a clinician to claim he simply exercised his clinical judgement when things go wrong, so too psychological therapists cannot be allowed to hide behind clinical judgement; there has to be transparency and accountability.

The social significance of psychological therapy

Labour Health Minister Alan Johnson announced:

> On 10 October 2007, World Mental Health Day . . . we will build a groundbreaking psychological therapy service in England. . . . the service will be capable of treating 900,000 additional patients suffering from depression and anxiety over the next three years. . . . around half are likely to be completely cured.

The promise for society is a very clear and laudable one: half of those with anxiety and depression 'completely cured' is an unequivocal standard. This should be

110 *Part IV*

contrasted with IAPT's translation of this standard. The IAPT Annual Report of 2014–2015 claims a 'reliable recovery of' on average 42.8% (with variation among sites between 69.4% and 18.8%). But this is not recovery based on a standardised diagnostic interview administered at the beginning and end of treatment. Such an interview reliably asks the person how impaired they are in their functioning. Had such an interview been conducted, one could meaningfully specify the proportion that had recovered from whatever disorder had been initially identified. It would thus have been possible to gauge the social significance of the psychological therapy programme, but not so with the IAPT programme. Instead, IAPT has relied on a dubious measure of clinical significance which serves to obscure its real performance.

IAPT has operationalised its notion of 'recovery' to mean a particular size of change on a psychometric test and the end of treatment score falling below a particular cut off, i.e. they rely on a measure of clinical significance. Measures of clinical significance were developed in a context in which it was known from diagnostic interview what disorder the person was suffering from, and a psychometric test used was specific to the disorder in question; thus in the depression studies reviewed by Beck et al. (1979), the Beck Depression Inventory was used. Further, in these studies a diagnostic interview was used at the beginning and end of interview and it was therefore possible to state that over 50% were cured, i.e. no longer met diagnostic criteria for the disorder. Such findings can be meaningfully complemented with clinical significance results to give a more fine-grained analysis as in Scott and Stradling (1991). However, clinical significance results without a reliable diagnostic context are close to meaningless; what does 'reliable recovery' on the PHQ-9, a measure of the severity of depression, mean if the person did not have depression but suffered from say a specific phobia, excoriation disorder or an adjustment disorder?. It is not the mathematical formula to operationalise 'clinically' significant that is in question but the validity of the concept. Psychometric tests assess symptoms; they do not assess functional impairment. It is the impairment in social and occupational roles that is distilled in a diagnostic interview and in which particular symptoms have to clear a threshold of impairment to be regarded as present. Thus the findings of a diagnostic interview have a real-world meaning. This is not to say that it is not useful, as Scott and Stradling (1990) did to make distinctions between clinically reliable recovery, clinically significant improvement and clinically significant deterioration and ascertain what aspects of therapy might be associated with each. But from the client's perspective the question is 'Am I back to normal functioning?' The diagnostic interview gives the client the opportunity to fully tell their story and elaborate on their functioning. The SCID [First et al. (2015)] begins with an open-ended interview, then proceeds to examine each symptom of a diagnostic set, and there is a determination of whether a particular symptom is present at a clinically significant level.

Diagnostic interviews are time consuming but without them reliance is placed on an 'alleged clinical significance'; applied to a population this results in very anomalous findings. For example, IAPT success rates vary across location between 69.4% and 18.8%, according to the IAPT report of 2014–2015. If there was such

Creating a mental health system   111

a variation in morbidity from say cancer treatment, very serious questions would be asked about the skills of oncologists, or more likely it would be asserted that there is something radically wrong in how the deaths attributed to cancer are calculated. Politicians, Clinical Commissioning Groups and professional bodies need to ensure psychological therapies are clearing the bar of social significance and that professionals do not, for whatever reason, obscure matters. To date there has been inadequate governance of mental health.

Since the inception twenty years ago of criteria for determining what should constitute an evidence-supported treatment [see Chambless and Ollendick (1998), Appendix E], there have been moves by Tolin et al. (2015) to refine the criteria to make them more socially relevant. Tolin et al. (2015) suggest that only treatments that have a demonstrated impact on functional impairment, e.g. return to work, should be deemed an EST. Further an EST must have been demonstrated to have been effective in at least one non-research context using non-academic therapists. The Tolin et al. (2015) recommendations heighten the bar as to what would constitute an EST. For likely most people with a psychological disorder, losing their diagnostic status would be socially significant. However, for some difficulties such as suicidality, the 'success' of an intervention might be reasonably measured by the extent to which it reduces suicide attempts rather than say overcoming an underlying depression. For some disorders such as schizophrenia in which the impact of psychological therapies is small (reducing further when sources of bias, particularly masking, are controlled for) [Jauhar et al. (2014)], rather than having a goal of recovery from schizophrenia, an improvement in say social functioning may be a credible goal.

'All therapies are equal but my therapy is more equal than others'

The Dodo in *Alice in Wonderland* [Lewis Carrol (1865)] was asked to judge the winner of a race around a lake and declared, 'Everybody has won, and all must have prizes'; this is a position espoused by many practising therapists when challenged as to whether they utilise evidence-based treatment protocols. It tends to run in parallel with a belief that their particular practice is worthy of imitation, with an implicit assumption that it is superior. Such therapists often have strong misgivings about the applicability of randomised controlled trials to routine practice [contradicted by the Stirman et al. (2005) study], and rather than implement these protocols they prefer what is termed 'evidence-based practice' as opposed to 'evidence-based treatment'. In private practice there is, in principle, more scope for evidence-based practice, but even within the UK Government service IAPT, there are no measures of treatment fidelity either for CBT or other evidence-based treatments such as interpersonal psychotherapy, brief psychodynamic therapy or couples therapy and no measure of fidelity either when counselling takes place under this umbrella. Thus therapists at the coalface have flexibility without fidelity and are unlikely to be reigned in by the traditional model of supervision, which stresses the primacy of continuing professional and personal development.

Re-visiting evidence-based practice

Evidence-based practice is defined as consisting of three components of information: best available research evidence, clinical expertise and patient characteristics [The APA Presidential Task Force on Evidence-Based Practice, EBP (2006)]. But this allows any clinician who likes to claim that their treatment reflects their judgement based on experience. Another clinician (e.g. a supervisor) might claim different experiences and make a different judgement, but there is no means of arbitrating between them. Further, they might both claim that they are taking into account the research evidence and patient characteristics, but this will not resolve matters. The dispute will most likely be resolved by who has the most power, e.g. a supervisor or an organisation. An appeal to clinical expertise/experience runs the risk of using an information-processing bias such as the availability heuristic [see Kahneman (2011)], where a particular case is recalled for its vividness and exceptional quality rather than whether it is prototypical of the response to a particular treatment. What is lacking in the common model of EBP is any notion of primacy or hierarchy.

The prime mover for EBP has to be research evidence; this is then filtered by the therapist's clinical expertise and then the patient characteristics. Unless pride of place is given to research evidence, the danger is that almost anything can be justified. To give an example of how this hierarchical model of EBP operates, there is good evidence that exposure therapy for PTSD is effective [see Roth and Fonagy (2005)], but Scott and Stradling (1997) observed that it did not go down too well in routine practice, and they found that homework compliance with an exposure tape was only just over 50% in a sample of predominantly working-class patients. Thus the research evidence is the product of scientist-practitioners testing out protocols in randomised controlled trials, whereas the determinants of EBP are engineers testing out the utility of research at the coalface. Evidence-based practice is a mode of behaviour that incorporates the knowledge and practice elements in Figure 8.1.

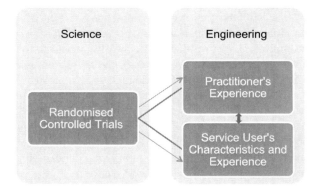

Figure 8.1 A model of evidence-based practice

Creating a mental health system 113

Figure 8.1 shows the supremacy of science in determining evidence-based practice, reflected in the gold-standard randomised controlled trials as the fuel for the application of the findings (engineering). (This is not to say that evidence from single case designs cannot be important, but they cannot be sufficiently relied upon in the absence of RCTs.) The therapist's experience of implementing the science in routine practice is important data, albeit that care has to be taken that it is not skewed by information-processing biases, for example being unduly influenced by a distinctive but exceptional case. The service user's characteristics, including diagnosis, should as far as possible be matched to an RCT. This match need not always be perfect. For example a client with PTSD who is on the autism spectrum would undergo treatment based on the NICE-approved, trauma-focussed CBT, but would likely need adaptations to the protocol in practice. It is the service user's experience of the service which is the ultimate arbiter of the utility of dissemination efforts. Without independent inquiry into a service user's experience of psychological therapy, the social significance of the latter is in doubt. It is commonplace these days to have service users represented in mental health bodies, but this is mere tokenism without systematic careful listening to each client engaging in a service and those declining to do so. There should be a bi-directional relationship between therapists and service users so that services can be appropriately re-configured, e.g. noting that some would-be service users see a telephone assessment as inhospitable and a therapist would recommend a different organisational modus operandi. Evidence-based practice, however, takes place in a particular climate, and if it is such that the therapist is micro-managed, or ill equipped because of skills or time resources, then evidence-based practice is rendered impossible.

Figure 8.1 represents a particular case of the more general dynamic interplay of science and engineering. Consider the development of the personal computers: it was scientists who post-World War II developed semi-conductors (transistors) which led to printed circuit boards, but it was engineers who assembled these boards to develop personal computers in the early 1980s. Such computers were then refined in response to the feedback from consumers, making wider dissemination possible.

From Figure 8.1 claims of evidence-based practice can be dismissed, if there are no randomised controlled trials to support the intervention. Thus, a practitioner using Solution-focussed Therapy (SFT) might claim that his/her practice produces very good results and feedback is good, but given the paucity of RCTs for this treatment modality it would be a doubtful claim. The Database of Abstracts of Reviews of Effects (DARE) [from the Centre for Reviews and Dissemination at the University of York] in 2014 concluded that the claimed effects of Solution-focused Therapy by Gingerich and Peterson (2013) were 'based on very variable evidence and appear to overstate the potential benefits; they should not be considered to be reliable'. SFT studies have historically been the main empirical justification for Task-centred Social Work [Marsh and Doel (2005)]. It can be asserted that if reliable trials of SFT were conducted they would show great benefit. But should practice be funded on such maybes?

114   *Part IV*

Failure to detect the superiority of CBT over other psychotherapies for depression and anxiety disorders can, according to Tolin (2014), be attributed to including studies of poor methodological quality, according to the gold-standard criteria of Foa and Meadows (1997). Tolin's (2014) review suggests that the power of CBT is most in evidence when studies use evaluators unaware of treatment condition, assign patients randomly to treatment and use outcome measures that are reliable and valid for the intended purpose. For example, the three studies suggesting an advantage of EMDR over CBT did not use evaluators unaware of treatment condition, and two of the three studies suggesting an advantage of EMDR appear not to have used random assignment. But the Dodo verdict is not only inapplicable to depression and anxiety disorders; it is also inapplicable to bulimia. In the Poulsen et al. (2014) study patients with bulimia were randomly assigned either two years of weekly psychoanalytic therapy or twenty sessions of CBT spread over five months. After five months, 42% of the CBT group had stopped binge eating and purging; for those receiving psychoanalysis the figure was 6%. Further, after two years, the proportion of the psychoanalysis group who were free from bulimia had risen to 15% whilst the comparable proportion by for the CBT group was 44%. These findings are particularly salient as the leading researchers in the study did not have an allegiance to CBT.

Therapists' belief in the Dodo verdict can sabotage clients receiving an evidence-based treatment. But supervisors and organisations can also operate as if the Dodo verdict is true, reinforcing a therapist's belief and making for an uphill struggle to ensure clients get appropriate treatment. The American Psychological Associations Division of Clinical Psychology website (www.div12.org) contains updates on psychological therapies in terms of the strength of evidence supporting them; *strong* denotes therapy in which well-designed studies conducted by independent investigators converge to support a treatment's efficacy. Research support is labelled 'modest' if there is just one well-designed study or two or more adequately designed studies to support a treatment's efficacy. In addition, this site labels research support 'controversial' if studies of a given treatment give conflicting results. This website can help offset psychological therapists' penchant for attending workshops or reading how-to books rather than perusing the research literature. The popularity of both workshops and how-to books depends much more heavily on marketing and charisma than evidence. But in the UK psychological therapy courses pay little attention to providing students with a framework for distinguishing the wheat from the chaff of therapies. Few for example teach the Chambless and Hollon (1998) criteria (see Appendix E).

Groups

For depression and the anxiety disorders group CBT and individual CBT appear equally effective [Scott (2011)], but the interventions examined have largely been diagnosis specific. The cost savings for a diagnosis-specific group are as much as 50% [Scott and Stradling (1990)] and when properly implemented widens the benefits of CBT. It is not however a panacea, and there can be problems with

Creating a mental health system 115

assignment to and retention in group CBT. Scott and Stradling (1990) addressed these difficulties by offering up to three individual sessions to run alongside the group programmes. In later work Scott (2011) has suggested that though groups should be diagnosis specific, the presence of additional disorders can be addressed by using e-mail/telephone calls, using freely available self-help materials for the comorbid disorders available from the Routledge website.

But CBT groups conducted following an evidence-based treatment protocol are rare in routine practice. Groups are an attractive option to managers because of the increased throughput of clients; it is tempting to run a group for depression/anxiety disorders, but such transdiagnostic groups are not evidence based. Although there have been studies of transdiagnostic groups they have been of a very limited range of disorders; for example Norton and Barrera's (2012) 'transdiagnostic' intervention was confined to clients with panic disorder, social anxiety disorder and generalised anxiety disorder. The more heterogenous a group the more difficulty therapists have in giving each member sufficient attention. A further concern is the external validity of the transdiagnostic groups in the Norton and Barrera (2012) study; 74% of those in the study had completed some or all of a degree/professional course that is not at all the sort of population encountered in routine practice. In the running of groups care has to be taken that clients with a significant personality disorder are not entered into a group. Those with personality disorders have major problems managing relationships, and these interpersonal difficulties could sabotage a group. Thus assessment for a group requires a reliable assessment that includes a screen and assessment for personality disorder. It may be that a group can accommodate those with an anxious personality disorder (avoidant, dependent, obsessive compulsive), but not those with a dramatic personality disorder (borderline, antisocial, histrionic, narcissistic) or odd personality disorder (schizoid, paranoid, schizotypal).

Judgements about the effectiveness of a group intervention have to be as informed by the Model for Evidence-based Practice in Figure 8.1 as similar judgements in relation to individual therapy. In this connection Brahler et al. (2013) performed the first randomized controlled evaluation of Compassion Focussed Therapy (CFT). Adults with a schizophrenia-spectrum disorder were randomized to group CFT (sixteen, two-hour sessions) or to treatment as usual. The authors concluded that CFT appeared 'safe, acceptable and promising' but added 'psychiatric diagnosis was based on case note review not on diagnostic interview'. Thus in terms of Figure 8.1 there is not a reliable controlled trial to draw upon in the practice of CFT and it is not therefore a catalyst for evidence-based practice, however enthusiastic a practitioner might be about it.

Large group

The Stress Control programme of White et al. (1995) is more of a public health intervention than a psychotherapeutic group. It is run as a night school class, and though there are questions and answers between attendees and presenters, personal problems are not discussed. In a recent implementation of the programme Burns

116 *Part IV*

et al. (2015) had a mean group size of seventy-four and a range from twenty-three to 106, with six weekly, two-hour sessions. The programme consisted of week 1, introduction to psychoeducation and the cognitive behavioural model; week 2, management of physiology; week 3, management of mental events; week 4, management of behaviour; week 5, management of panic attacks and sleep; and week 6, self-care. At the end of each session, material for the next session was distributed containing homework exercises. At the final session, relapse prevention materials were distributed. Three quarters of the 1,062 clinical cases [PHQ-9 greater than or equal to 10 and/or GAD-7 greater than or equal to 8] attended three or more sessions. Of those attending pure stress control alone 37% 'moved to recovery', defined as an improvement of 6 points on the PHQ-9 and 4 points on the GAD-7. With mean PHQ-9 scores for the clinical case sample reducing from 15.50 to 11.58. Burns et al. (2015) claim that 'SC appears comparatively clinically equivalent to other IAPT interventions'. However Gilbody et al. (2015) looked at how GP patients with a PHQ-9 score of greater than 10 fare with usual treatment, over a four-month period; their mean PHQ-9 score reduced from 16 to 9. It is thus not at all evident that the Stress Control programme is of social significance. The methodological quality of the stress control studies are poor when assessed by the Foa and Meadows (1997) criteria, in that there are no clearly defined target symptoms, no diagnostic interview was conducted to establish which if any disorder the person was suffering from and the proportion 'cured' by the end of the intervention. Further there is no independent evidence that six or fewer sessions constitute an adequate dose of psychotherapeutic intervention.

It can be objected that the psychological well-being practitioners providing the intervention are not therapists but coaches, but there is still no evidence that the coaching has made a socially significant difference. Such large-group interventions are an attractive option to managers, greatly increasing access, and may be disseminated because of the enthusiasm of the IAPT authors, but they serve only to divert resources from the provision of evidence-based psychotherapy.

9 Maintaining the social significance of psychological therapy

If psychological therapy does not make a real-world difference (social significance) then it counts for naught; there is a danger of agencies using the term *clinical significance* to muddy the waters. It is rather like the manufacturer of a particular consumable claiming it lowers cholesterol, on its face not an unworthy goal, but it is not at all clear whether this change is related in any meaningful way to the likelihood of one's dying of heart disease. The manufacturers use a surrogate measure rather than a hard measure, blurring the distinction between the two. The acid test for any service provider is the proportion of people fully recovered from a psychological disorder as assessed by an independent assessor using a standardised diagnostic interview.

The dangers of substitute tests for social significance

When psychometric tests alone are used as a measure of clinical significance, it is the service provider's operational definition of the term that becomes the foundation for its marketing strategy. It rarely occurs to politicians, commissioners, service providers, professional bodies and therapists to look beyond the term *clinical significance*. But to properly exercise good governance it is imperative that they do. The position is somewhat akin to what used to obtain in court, where an expert witness could hide behind his or her clinical judgement; nowadays there is much more enquiry on what that judgement is based on; it has to be evidence based, not eminence based. The provision of psychological services has arguably not yet caught up with these developments.

In a curious way, employing CBT therapists as G4S intends [job advert February 2016] – to 'provide return-to-work advice and guidance regarding health issues. . . . Targeted on the level, number and effectiveness of interventions in re-engaging customers and customer progression into work' – is focussed on a more visible outcome of a CBT therapist's ministration: 'return to work' rather than 'clinically significant change', but it is not a valid measure of the effectiveness of a psychological therapist's intervention. Not only does the outcome of psychological therapy have to be socially significant, it also has to be valid. Consider the following case:

> *Andrew was very stressed by the behaviour of his boss. Other colleagues at his level had been the targets of his maltreatment and they suspected he had a drug*

118   *Part IV*

> *problem, but nobody wanted to grass him up. He had had a messy divorce and*
> *he had a lifelong habit of blaming himself whenever anything went wrong.*
> *Andrew saw a more senior manager and Personnel; he was advised to take*
> *leave and was referred for counselling. On examination with a standardised*
> *diagnostic interview he met criteria for depression. Whilst off work he attended*
> *for CBT, kept social contact with friends at work and discovered that nothing*
> *was changing at work. Returning him to the toxic environment at work would*
> *in the therapist's view have produced a depressive relapse.*

The above example illustrates the importance of CBT therapists not getting distracted from their primary task of restoring a person's normal functioning as *they,* not their employer or provider of psychological therapy, deem it. This is not to say that psychological therapy may not play a part in reducing absenteeism. On April 5, 2016, under a Freedom of Information request, the BBC revealed that that the number of policemen on long-term sick leave (more than twenty-eight days) for mental health problems had increased by a third in the previous five years. This has taken place in a context where strapped-for-cash forces have greatly reduced the number of force welfare officers, and external referral to psychologists is either rare or non-existent. It is possible to tackle such absenteeism using psychological therapists, but great care has to be taken that the therapist is independent of the person's employer and that their primary goal is to return the person to their normal level of functioning. Thus, whilst a reduction of absenteeism is a likely by-product of referral to a psychological therapist, using an evidence-based treatment, it cannot be a prime intent.

The person absent from work on mental health grounds has to be given the space to narrate the whole story of their difficulties, so that they can feel listened to and understood (not just a thirty-minute telephone interview in which the clinician completes a checklist), followed by a diagnostic interview. This results in a diagnosis/ diagnoses that reflect the level of functional impairment. Further there is the distillation of a goal of return to normal functioning, the achievement of which is determined by a repeat of the diagnostic assessment.

Moving to best practice assessment

A study by Ehlers et al. (2013) offers a template that might be a stepping-stone to a more reliable evaluation of service provision. In this study Ehlers et al. (2013) evaluated the effectiveness of an NHS trauma clinic. At initial assessments, clinicians conducted the Structured Clinical Interview for DSM-IV (SCID) to assess Axis I First et al. (1997) and II diagnoses [First et al. (1995)]. The clinic's focus was on treating clients with diagnosed PTSD. The primary outcome measure was the change in PTSD symptoms on the Posttraumatic Diagnostic Scale [PDS, Foa et al. (1997)]. Thus a valid outcome measure was used in that it was relevant to the identified patient population. The PDS was administered at the first and last treatment session and at follow up; of those completing treatment, 84.5% showed reliable improvement and 65.1% clinically significant change, with an overall dropout rate of just 13.9%. Such results give some confidence that the service was making a socially significant difference. However, this confidence would have been increased had the SCID diagnostic interview been conducted post-treatment, in which case it would have been possible to indicate the proportion of people who recovered, i.e. had lost their diagnostic status. Doubtless the re-administration of the SCID was not done to ease the research burden, and Ehlers et al. (2013) believed they had struck a reasonable balance between cost and research rigour. There is inevitably a trade-off between the two.

Flexibility in the mode of treatment delivery

Psychological treatment should begin with an initial reliable, comprehensive, face-to-face assessment and should conclude with the same. These two assessments are like bookends; without them the intervening treatment materials are likely to fall off the shelf. The findings of the initial assessment influence the content of the supported 'books/materials'. The comprehensive post-treatment assessment sign-posts what if any further interventions are necessary.

The mode of delivery of materials between the bookends is not restricted to the traditional individual, weekly, face-to-face therapy session. The author has found that where clients are suffering from a single disorder such as a phobia, panic disorder or obsessive-compulsive disorder, it is possible to negotiate check-ins obviating the need to attend a therapist's office (save largely for the initial and end of treatment assessments). The mode of the check-ins is the product of a negotiation between the client and therapist. For example, one client with OCD, living in a remote area but running his own business, opted for a pre-arranged weekly telephone call followed by an e-mail summarising the session and confirming the homework. In another instance a client with a phobia about driving and travelling as a passenger agreed to daily check-ins in the week she was to hire a car and practise overcoming her fears with 'dares'; this concentrated approach to tackling her phobia was dictated by the devastating effect not driving was having on her business. She and the therapist agreed to a daily exchange of texts (except on Sundays). Clients with panic disorder can benefit from a two-day group intervention. But a check-in approach is unlikely to be viable if the person seems likely to have a personality disorder (see Appendix C and Chapter 5) and/or significant comorbidity. Whilst self-help materials can be included between the bookends and referred to, this approach is not primarily guided self-help but still less costly than traditional treatment. There is no reason why clients should not ask about the viability of a check-in in their case, even if it takes the therapist out of their comfort zone. This approach widens patients' choice and increases affordability.

'I'm too busy to make a reliable assessment'

It can be objected by service providers and therapists alike that the number of referrals is too great to make possible the fine-grained distinctions between disorders that I have advocated in these pages. But the evidence-based psychotherapy

120   *Part IV*

advocated by NICE is diagnosis specific, and it follows that not to make a reliable diagnosis means that treatment is not evidence based. It can be further objected that the cases encountered in routine practice are so complex that treatment has to be based on the clinician's formulation (judgement). But this position means in effect that there are no boundaries on what the clinician might do in good faith. It becomes an exercise in unbridled clinical judgement. Further, it has not been demonstrated that most cases are complex. Stirman et al. (2005) mapped charts of individuals seeking treatment under managed care to the criteria of nearly one hundred RCTs and identified that 80% of these individuals would be eligible for at least one RCT, and the majority did not have more complex diagnostic profiles than participants included in RCTs.

Demanding credible mental health assessments

Imagine you are taken into hospital on a Saturday night with excruciating pain. A&E is very busy with those worse for alcohol, and you overhear the nurses discussing your case; they say that the doctors are too busy to distinguish appendicitis from a possible kidney problem. You are given antibiotics and sent on your way. On leaving, the nurses reassure you that you could be stepped up to doctors if the antibiotics don't work. You would rightly write a letter of complaint, insisting that a) you should have been reliably assessed at the outset and b) taken by lift to the correct floor for your difficulties, e.g. surgery for your rupturing appendix or dialysis for your kidney problem, and not experimented with in a stepped care programme. But current NHS mental health assessment is akin to this scenario.

The above analogy illustrates the lack of parity in organisation between physical and mental health services. Such organisational issues need tackling by politicians, Clinical Commissioning Groups, professional bodies and service providers. If those in power do not take on board these structural changes, the individual therapist might be at a loss as to how to provide an adequate service within the constraints of the organisation. Because a psychological therapist is with a client at the coalface there is some wriggle room, and they might perhaps complete the seven-minute interview screen [Appendix B], but if for example they work in IAPT, post the session they would still need to spend fifteen minutes after each session doing the administrative work of entering psychometric test results into a computer, etc. The latitude an individual therapist would have will depend also in part on his/her manager and supervisor. But quality control also needs to be assured at the micro-level of individual therapist's actions.

It is not just recent mental health initiatives that are failing

Whilst much of this volume has been devoted to a critical re-appraisal of the UK government mental health initiative IAPT, the great majority of people with mental health problems are untouched by it and are also poorly served, as the following anonymised example illustrates:

Aidan was present at the 1989 Hillsborough football disaster. He saw bodies carried across the pitch on improvised stretchers, a child passed over the top of the crowd only to be pushed back in by a policeman. Almost thirty years later he found his original statement to the police had been doctored to present the latter in a more favourable light. He had been a self-employed window cleaner at the time of Hillsborough but couldn't maintain his business, initially partly because of his physical injuries. Aidan experienced considerable financial difficulties, life became very stressed at home and he felt he had let his children down. He was placed under the care of a consultant psychiatrist following two suicide attempts and saw a clinical psychologist. The latter recommended he attended a support group, which he attended for twenty years. He enjoyed attending the support group; he felt understood there, but his functioning continued to be significantly impaired within his family, socially and economically. Thirty-one years later a clinician had access to all his records, revealing that no diagnosis had been made and no evidence-based psychotherapy had been conducted. On examination, using the SCID diagnostic interview he was found to be suffering from PTSD and depression (he had been on antidepressants since shortly after Hillsborough). At interview he said that he could recall no one ever making a diagnosis and had never heard of cognitive behaviour therapy. Aidan stated that his life was in ruins.

This is a scandalous indictment of our mental health system, or lack of it.

Ensuring psychological therapy meets 'trading standards'

Alleged CBT abounds, but much of it would fail the Trades Descriptions Act. Clients may well believe that they have already had CBT for their disorder/ difficulty and as a consequence be very reluctant to countenance the possibility of further CBT. In addition, feelings of failure may be compounded by the knowledge that they have not responded to an evidence-based treatment.

This raises the question as to how one can distinguish authentic from fake CBT. The wrapping of the fake usually depicts variously thought records, edicts to think straight or activity records, sometimes a collage of all three. The same present is handed out largely irrespective of the disorder/disorders the recipient is suffering from. It is a generic CBT that is being peddled, without any evidence base but oftentimes given in good faith with the donor's belief that it is specially tailored to the needs of the individual recipient. Further they 'know' their approach works because of the psychometric test results that they administered. The likelihood is that the donors are unwittingly using information processing biases that fuel a mis-selling scandal. For example, recalling in detail the delight of a client who did really well in therapy with only a vague recollection of those who have not done well or defaulted – this is termed the availability heuristic. Such rules of thumb can be pressed into service at times of uncertainty; whilst this can serve to motivate the therapist, it can be a disservice to the most commonly encountered clients. A therapist can also unwittingly operate a confirmatory bias by asking clients to

122 *Part IV*

complete a psychometric test in front of them. Neglecting the client's desire to please the therapist (or exit from therapy as soon as possible), the therapist then takes the test result as confirming his judgement that the client is improving, without collecting any evidence from a different source, e.g. diagnostic interview, that might disconfirm his/her hypothesis. A full set of such biases, 'Cognitive Dispositions to Respond', is detailed in Scott (2014) and it is suggested that they should be a focus in therapist supervision.

Fidelity and flexibility

There are two elements to fidelity: adherence and competence. *Adherence* refers to tackling the appropriate treatment targets for the identified disorder with the relevant treatment strategies. *Competence* refers to how skilfully the clinician completes this task. To illustrate the features of fidelity, the fidelity scale for depression is reproduced below from Scott (2014)

Inspection of Table 9.1 shows that it is not possible to rate competence, outside of the context of adherence. Thus, attempts to assess therapist competence by listening to an audio recording of a therapist's treatment session without knowing which disorder/disorders have been reliably identified is meaningless. Young and Beck (1980) developed the Cognitive Therapy Rating Scale (CTRS), which has been found to relate to outcome in cognitive therapy for depression [Shaw et al. (1999)], but the effect is modest, accounting for just 19% of the variance in outcome on a clinician-administered measure and with no relation with self-report outcome measures. Further, the aspect of competence that was most associated with outcome was structure (this referred to setting an agenda, assigning relevant homework and pacing the session appropriately). By contrast general therapeutic skills or specific CBT skills did not predict outcome. The CTRS has been pressed into service in routine practice for disorders other than depression and in contexts in which there has been no reliable diagnoses. This is of doubtful validity, yet it is the common metric used to evaluate a therapist's performance, encouraged by CBT training courses with little regard to the validity issue.

A study by McManus et al. (2012) looked at the levels of agreement between therapists and supervisors using the CTRS; whilst there were moderate correlations between the two, the ratings of the less-competent therapists were significantly more in agreement with those of their supervisors than the ratings of the more competent therapists! These authors posit several possible explanations for these strange results. But the received wisdom is that supervisors' ratings of clinical performance are thought to have the greatest validity because they bear the closest relationship with client outcomes [Chevron and Rounsaville (1983) and Kuyken and Tsivrikos (2009)]. Further the inter-rater reliability of the CTRS has been found to be poor, with one study showing intra-class correlation of less than 0.1, unless the assessors are trained together [Jacobson and Gortner (2000)]. It is unlikely that in routine practice raters will have been trained together, so that in the use of the CTRS disagreements are likely. This raises the question of whether the penchant for using the CTRS has been a matter of the tail wagging the dog.

Maintaining social significance 123

Table 9.1 Treatment fidelity scale for depression

Treatment Adherence and Competence: Depression

Adherence: How thoroughly were specific treatment targets and techniques addressed in the session?							Competence: How skilfully was the target addressed using the particular techniques? Rate 1–7, Where 1 is no competence and 7 is total competence
1 *2* Not done	*3* Some discussion	*4*	*5* Considerable Discussion	*6*	*7* Extensively Discussed		
Treatment target	*Technique*				*Score*		
1 Depression about depression	Focus on responsibility for working on solutions and not on responsibility for problem.						
2 Inactivity	Developing a broad investment portfolio, wide-ranging modest investments.						
3 Negative views of self, personal, world and future	Challenging the validity, utility and authority by which these views are held. Use of MOOD chart.						
4 Information-processing biases	Highlighting personal biases and stepping around them using MOOD chart.						
5 Overvalued roles	Valuing multiple roles, renegotiation of roles in social context.						
	Mean score						

Perhaps the CTRS should not be regarded as a gold standard in the present state of knowledge; rather, it is a silver standard and we are without a gold standard.

In specialist units there can be excellent adherence to a protocol, but without a comparable monitoring of competence, as the following example illustrates. A therapist in a trauma unit followed a trauma focussed CBT protocol for a client, Constance, with PTSD, but the therapist showed little evidence of competence, persisting with the protocol for thirty-two sessions, despite the client's non-response and ongoing distress. The therapist then switched to EMDR, which was continued for twelve sessions despite no evidence of benefit and Constance's ongoing distress. The client's associated panic disorder was not addressed systematically using any protocol. The unit had not performed a comprehensive assessment nor utilised a measure of fidelity.

Countering infidelity

Clinical Commissioning Groups need to ask agencies how they will ensure fidelity to EBTs. The agencies will likely reply via supervision, but CCGs need to drill further, asking how supervisors ensure fidelity. Traditionally the primarily role of

124 Part IV

the supervisor has been to provide support for the clinician and ensure their professional development. Thus though supervision has long been mandatory it has not been a guarantor of quality control. Scott (2014) has suggested that the primary role of a supervisor is to act as a conduit for evidence-based treatment and argues that the necessary flexibility of a clinician must take place within a context of fidelity. If agencies are not using fidelity measures, it is doubtful whether much of the output would pass trading standards. The examples of supervision described in Scott (2014) show that it can be conducted in such a way that the clinician is not micro-managed and stressed out.

A three-dimensional view of competence

Historically the notion of 'competence' has been uni-dimensional, focussing on a general measure of therapeutic skill (generic competence in Figure 9.1), such as the CTRS. Scott (2014) has argued that this is inadequate and has recommended the three-dimensional model below:

The competence engine is housed in an adherence body and both are needed for the CBT 'car' to take clients in the direction of a return to their full, normal functioning. The diagnosis-specific competences rest on an accurate assessment of the presence of a disorder/s, and attempts to implement the evidence-based protocol/s for the particular disorder/s. For depression and the anxiety disorders, a set of disorder-specific treatment targets and techniques are reproduced in the appendix of Scott (2014); Table 9.1 of this chapter gives an exemplar. Stage-specific competences are competences that therapists need to display at key points in the

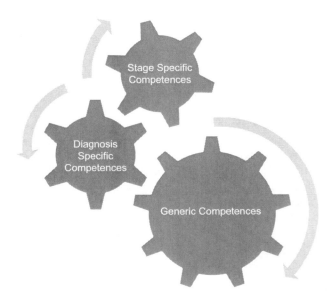

Figure 9.1 The competence engine

Maintaining social significance   125

client's trajectory through therapy. These include those required for the initial evaluation, presentation of a credible rationale for treatment, engagement (including addressing motivational issues), re-evaluation at various points in therapy and relapse prevention towards the end of treatment. Failure in any one area of competence means the engine grinds to a halt. The supervisor's task can be conceptualised largely in terms of helping the clinician motor; this is not to say that there are no other important aspects of supervision such as providing support, ensuring self-reflection and facilitating professional development.

Documentary evidence

It is routine for medics to have to account for their practice in their notes; if they have done something and it is not recorded and anything goes wrong, they are unlikely to avoid professional or legal sanction. But it is usually extremely difficult to judge from psychological therapists' notes exactly what has been done in therapy. The notes are rather like an open-ended interview in which germane matters may be touched upon, but it is not possible to gauge adherence to any evidence-based treatment protocol. Further it is also usually impossible to assess the skill (competence) with which a particular treatment target is addressed. Given the much-vaunted status of homework in CBT it is strange indeed to rarely find any clear written statement of the client's homework; at most there may be an inscription of 'Homework, thought records, activity scheduling' but with no personalisation of such tasks and nothing that could form the basis for detailed review at the next session. Psychological records routinely have a disturbing vagueness.

It can be argued that a therapist demonstrates his or her accountability by periodically recording a session and having it assessed by their supervisor, with usually the cognitive therapy rating scale [Shaw et al. (1999)]. But there are a number of problems with this: a) the chosen session may be atypical, chosen to present the therapist in the best light; b) the therapists' behaviour in most of the sessions is still unknown; c) treatment protocols are diagnosis specific, and it is possible to score well on the CTRS despite using an inappropriate protocol and d) the CTRS has some validity with regards to depression, but its validity for other disorders is unknown.

Connection difficulties

It is not just the in-session written records that are a problem; the communications of psychological therapists often lead other professionals, medics and lawyers baffled. GPs will often skip to the final paragraph of the letter, seeking out what if anything they are being asked to do. Medics and lawyers will for good or ill operate on a medical model: 'This person was suffering from x; are they still suffering x, yes or no'. Psychological therapists are often uncomfortable with this, and their utterances lead other professionals muttering under their breaths. Professional training, at least for psychologists, does stress the importance of being able to communicate with other professionals but is light on what constitutes evidence of this.

126 *Part IV*

In fairness in recent years psychological therapists have become better at alerting other professionals to the possibility of suicide risk. Further in-session notes will refer in detail to discussions around this topic.

Psychological therapists are rarely these days working in a context in which they have face-to-face contact with the referring GP. In the days of GP fundholding (which expired in 2000) psychologists would be attached to a particular practice, meeting with the GPs both formally and informally, and this itself conferred greater accountability. The GP would often have a greater knowledge of the client's social context and could be a relatively permanent reference point, or at least his/her practice would be. Arguably something is lost by positioning IAPT services somewhere between primary care and secondary care. Multi-disciplinary teamwork has suffered. As far as a psychological therapist is concerned, a GP is an independent arbiter of whether the patient's difficulties have been meaningfully addressed, and this can be important feedback for the therapist. Completion of a self-report measure by the client in the presence of the therapist is subject to demand characteristics and whether that instrument is an appropriate metric. With current service provision, accountability, such as it is, resides primarily in the writings of the psychological therapist, which oftentimes do not stand up in the court of critical professional evaluation.

Research domain criteria – a step forward or backward somersault?

It is a concern that for all the research, biological markers for psychological disorders as defined in the DSM have yet to be found and that these disorders rest largely on a consensus. Whilst the DSM criteria may have attained reliability, from a biological perspective they are of questionable validity. This has led the United States National Institute for Mental Health [www.nimh.nih.gov] to move away from an exclusive focus on the aetiology of DSM disorders but to also fund research on phenomenon that cross diagnostic behaviours, such as repeated checking (prominent in OCD and to a lesser degree in GAD and PTSD). The NIMH asserts that neuroscientists are much more confident about finding the neurobiological basis of such a discrete phenomenon than for the more multi-faceted disorders. To this end they have developed Research Domain Criteria (RDoC), which highlight the expressions of mental health that they deem worthy of focus. The RDoC are not intended as an alternative diagnostic system; it is acknowledged that for current clinical services the DSM is the best way forward, but it does provide a new direction for research and may lead to psychological treatments that are more targeted at the actual joints of mental health problems. But it is all a definite 'maybe', and there appears no alternative to DSM-based treatment anytime soon.

10 Wounded healers

On February 3, 2016, The British Psychological Society reported on a 2015 survey of over 1,300 psychological therapists working in the NHS. The survey found that 46% reported depression with half (49.5%) feeling they are a failure. One-quarter considered that they now have a long-term chronic condition, and 70% said that they find their jobs stressful. Reported stress at work was up 12% in 2014: 'The overall picture is one of burnout, low morale and worrying levels of stress and depression . . . the majority of respondents made negative comments about their work environment, 10% of comments were more positive', citing the following exemplars:

'Being target driven is the bane of our lives'.

'IAPT is a politically driven monster which does not cater for staff feedback/input in any way. All we are told is TARGETS!!! And work harder'.

'It is invigorating to work in a team where thoughtfulness, understanding, support and compassion are central to what we do, not seen as optional extra or a luxury'.

'I am so disappointed I have just resigned'.

'I carry my resignation in my diary now as I feel that I'm on the verge of giving up the battle'.

Common themes identified by the survey were a managerial fixation on targets, complained about by 41%, and workplace environments creating stress and burnout, complained about by 38%. Extra administrative demands, an increase in having to work unpaid hours and staff being prevented from providing adequate therapy due to resource cuts were other frequent themes.

The survey shows that psychological therapists have lower levels of job career satisfaction than other NHS staff. It is difficult to believe that this will not impact the service to clients. IAPT however claim a recovery rate of 38–39%, almost comparable to that in controlled trials; see Layard and Clark (2014, p. 199): 'From clinical trials a reasonable expectation is that 50% of those diagnosable should recover, and that was the target which Alan Johnson set for IAPT. Recovery rates have been somewhat below this level. But they are rising and are quite impressive'. This seems implausible given the low morale, and the true figure is more likely to

128 *Part IV*

be the 15% established by the author in an independent assessment using a standardised diagnostic interview. To put this into some sort of context, the placebo response rate for full remission in cases of depression is 25% [Thase et al. (2001)].

Charities, social services and the NHS are an obvious pathway to resolving mental health issues. But the climate is often such that mental health practitioners have difficulty delivering an effective service because of impossible organisational demands, e.g. to provide just six therapy sessions, and a toxic environment. The NHS absenteeism rate is 50% greater than in the private sector, placing greater demands on those still at work. In part, working conditions in the NHS are more difficult in that twenty-four-hour care is provided, but there is often a culture of 'no egg on our face', which has meant that concerned individuals within the NHS have been marginalised and sometimes lose their jobs. The classic example of this is consultant paediatrician Dr. David Drew from Walsall who despite litigation lost his job [(2014)]. His initial complaint was that the heating was inadequate on a ward for poorly newborn children. It transpired that the powers that be were saving on heating costs as they were within a year or so moving to a new building. The forward to Dr. Drew's book is written by the journalist, doctor and broadcaster, Dr. Phillip Hammond, who wrote:

> Whistleblowers should be the heroes of our time, praised and rewarded for speaking up and putting patients before corporate, political and personal interests. Yet too often they are vilified for doing the right thing. They become professionally isolated, rumours are circulated about their mental health and counter accusations are made (and often invented) against them. Unsurprisingly, whistleblowing is very bad for your health. Stress-related illnesses, relationship breakdown and financial hardship are common. Even if you win it can feel like a defeat. More often it is the whistleblower who has to leave their job and finds it near impossible to get another in the NHS. Usually they are poorly represented by their unions and professional bodies, savaged by NHS lawyers paid out of the public purse and end up heavily in debt.

In the author's experience social service departments, publicly funded non-governmental agencies and charities fare no better than NHS staff:

> *Malcolm was a support worker escorting two men with learning difficulties across a road, when a car drove into them. He was severely injured and one of the men died. Afterwards Malcolm was given no support from the charity that employed him; in particular there was no attempt to give him a physically less-demanding role or offer him any treatment for his depression. He felt that the agency was simply concerned to present itself in a good light so that it could continue to attract monies from the public purse. Malcolm eventually had counselling from a publicly funded non-governmental agency and found it helpful, but the therapist was only allowed to provide six treatment sessions. He was so distressed at the last treatment session the agency allowed him one extra treatment session. Detailed assessment revealed that Malcolm was*

suffering from depression and post-traumatic stress disorder. He also had flashbacks about his maltreatment by his employer, reliving interviews with the personnel manager and avoiding the location of the charity.

The very bodies tasked with assisting those with mental health problems can cause them. There is a regrettable tendency for agencies to blame the traumatised employee when things go wrong:

Mary was a social worker who made a surprise home visit to a couple who were known drug abusers with a young child, and she was badly assaulted. Far from being supported by her employer she was disciplined for making an unaccompanied visit, which did technically break the rules but given the shortage of staff had become a common practice. She felt she couldn't face returning to her work and gave up her career.

Gleaning the true quality of mental health service provision is made very difficult to determine by walls of silence and the marketing skills of organisations.

When demands exceed resources

Mental health practitioners will become stressed if the tasks demanded of them exceed their resources of training and facilities. Those seeking help may not fit the remit of service providers and the latter may not recognise this or if they do soldier on with the referral because of pressure from line managers and the organisation.

Demands might include the perceived expectations of others, perceived workload and perceived standards. Threats may be external, e.g. a perceived hostile environment, or internal, e.g. danger signals from the body. Resources include the person's self-esteem, perceived social support and coping skills. Too few demands/threats, and the seesaw in Figure 10.1 moves clockwise and the person is under-stressed; too many demands and the seesaw moves anti-clockwise and the person is over-stressed. If the person continues to be over-stressed the likelihood of developing depression or an anxiety disorder increases. Ideally there should be a balance between perceived demands/threats and resources. The position of the fulcrum is determined by the individual's characteristic ways of thinking. Such is the position of some individuals' fulcrum (very far to the right in Figure 10.1) that it takes very little demand/threat for them to tip into the stressed region. The operation of Figure 10.1 is illustrated by the case below:

Martha was working as a mental health practitioner when a client, Genevive, was re-referred by her GP to the agency. Whilst Martha had performed the initial assessment on Genevive, previously she had not been responsible for her treatment for the identified depression. At re-assessment Martha again identified depression and she was also tasked with treating her. After a few sessions it became apparent that though Genevive was doing everything Martha asked her to do, it gradually dawned on her that not only was Genevive

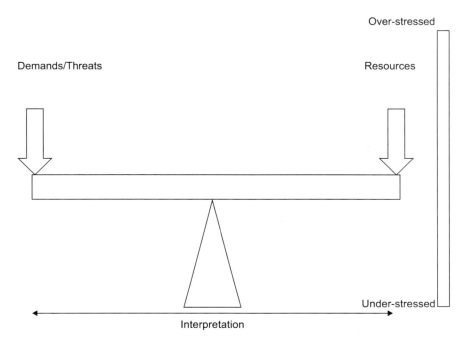

Figure 10.1 Stress – when demands exceed resources

depressed but she also had an avoidant personality disorder. Martha had had no training to address personality disorders, and her line manager reminded her that they were not within the remit of the organisation. Nevertheless Martha felt obliged to continue to try to assist Genevive. At home Martha was having problems with her partner with regards to his infidelity and drinking. Thus there were increased demands at home and at work. At the same time Martha felt inadequate; she had in effect moved the fulcrum of Figure 10.1 to the right and the seesaw tipped up to the stressed region. Her line manager was well meaning and suggested she take time off, which she did, but at home during the day she was 'alone, with the four walls', with no demands on her, and the seesaw tipped downwards to the under-stressed region.

A better awareness by managers, supervisors and organisations of how stress operates could help prevent absenteeism and impaired work performance by mental health practitioners. But organisations tend to have a primary interest in their survival and oftentimes market their wares very well. Protests from individuals within the workforce are likely in the first instance to be seen as evidence of personal pathology, and a black mark is awarded that stymies progression. Psychological therapists have no collective voice with their employer. Therapists may belong to professional bodies such as the British Association for Cognitive and

Wounded healers 131

Behavioural Psychotherapies and the British Psychological Society, but the former is simply a special interest group and the latter a professional association. Further both have lent their credentials to IAPT, involved in the development and monitoring of the psychological well-being practitioner role. IAPT luminaries regularly present at their conferences, with the voice of dissenters unheard to date. I have direct experience of an IAPT worker having to move site because he protested to his Manager that an eight-session group programme consisting of four sessions on anxiety and four on depression was not evidence based; he was supported in this by his supervisor, and indeed I re-iterated this to his manager, who replied that I didn't know it wouldn't work! The issue of appropriate advocacy for psychological therapists needs to be urgently addressed; it may be that they need a union to represent their needs

Impossible goals

Half of psychological therapists feel a failure [British Psychological Society February (2016)]; it seems likely that they are the ones who have personalised their inability to reach the unreliable goals of their employer. There may be better and worse ways of managing a toxic environment, for example insisting on breaks, insisting on keeping evening and Saturday work to a minimum and not personalising treatment failures. If a therapist feels that their employer is not listening to their concerns they may well exhibit 'presenteeism', turning up for work, going through the motions and keeping their heads down. It is highly likely that as a consequence of presenteeism clients will lose out. Long-term therapists are unlikely to endure the toxic environment and will leave or at least go on long-term sick leave. Openness and agreeableness are two facets of personality likely to be at the fore amongst therapists. However, openness (what you see is what you get) is likely to be an own goal in a toxic environment; the more detailed and reasonable the explanations given, the more ammunition that is given to others to seize on a minor aspect of what is being said and derail the whole discussion. Further the desire to please others may result in impossible demands on the therapist. For many therapists having to work essentially as an undercover policeman to survive will be a great personal strain (it is noteworthy that comparatively few policeman have a personality suited to working undercover).

The rate of burnout amongst mental health workers ranges from 21–67% [Morse et al. (2012)]. Further burnout is associated with negative attitudes towards the organisation, low levels of performance, higher rates of absenteeism and increased likelihood of leaving. Burnout is defined as 'overwhelming exhaustion, feelings of cynicism and detachment from the job and a sense of ineffectiveness and lack of accomplishment' [Maslach (2003), p. 190]. Maricutoiu et al. (2016) reviewed the effectiveness of interventions on employees burnout, and found that a) when only controlled studies were considered, i.e. where there was a comparison waiting list condition, the effects were much less than thought hitherto; b) the interventions (cognitive-behavioural interventions and interventions based on relaxation techniques) were effective only in reducing emotional exhaustion and had no effect on

132 *Part IV*

personal accomplishment. These authors suggest that lack of personal accomplishment and de-personalisation are difficult to target with CBT. It may be that a sense of personal accomplishment can only be generated by giving the psychological therapist the skills and time to make a real-world difference to a client's life. Whether a psychological therapist is provided with these means is in the proximal gift of the employing organisation, and the distal gift of Clinical Commissioning Groups and politicians. It is however also the responsibility of the Health and Safety Executive to ensure the provision of a safe workplace; it would be sad indeed if the only redress for psychological therapists was through the courts.

Postscript

When I began writing this book it was originally titled 'Pathways to Mental Health', but then I made four discoveries:

1 Within current mental health service provision, I could find few paths that would result in a socially significant difference in sufferers' lives, differences that they would see as meaningful.
2 If a friend or family member was in psychological difficulties I could not recommend that they avail themselves of NHS provision.
3 As an expert witness to the court in personal injury litigation I could not recommend NHS provision.
4 Those charged with delivering psychological therapy were themselves very stressed.

These discoveries were disorientating for me in writing the book: What sort of guide could I be? But they also flagged matters of serious concern that were as much in the domain of politicians and Clinical Commissioning Groups as practitioners and clients. I decided that the only way forward was to construct steps 'towards a mental health system that works', hence the present volume.

I am conscious that the work challenges many cherished ideas, including stepped care, low intensity interventions and IAPT. But I have no doubt that these developments were a brave attempt to address the vexed problem of how we can make psychological therapies available to more than the tip of the iceberg of sufferers. Unfortunately, only the tip of the iceberg of IAPT clients is found on independent assessment to have recovered, and there is therefore a pressing need for a rethink. Just as it is not credible to take a drug company's word for the potency of its product, so too providers of psychological services must be subject to rigorous independent assessment.

The first part of the book asserts that mental health services do not exist in a vacuum and that the societal climate undoubtedly influences mental health. There is then the intriguing possibility that community-based interventions, e.g. funding various support groups, might be a better use of resources than employing therapists. Such community interventions can clearly reach many more people than therapists could have contact with. But the evidence base for this community

134 *Postscript*

approach is weak and in many ways it seems it is a re-enactment of what many social workers did in the 1970s and 1980s and to which I reacted in 1989 with my first book: *A Cognitive Behavioural Approach to Clients' Problems* (London: Routledge). Nevertheless I have retained a belief that this social dimension to mental health is very important; for example the biggest single predictor of recovery from PTSD is perceived social support. Whilst it is not clear what the relative balance of investment in community psychology and therapeutic intervention should be, I do not doubt that they are both important. Sometimes one can't prove something is important, e.g. food banks, but faith in such enterprises is, I believe, legitimate. Research depends on researchers being honest; there is pressure on researchers to publish positive results, and oftentimes there has been difficulty in replicating positive findings. It seems that the scientific paradigm alone is not sufficient to guarantee 'real findings' and recourse must also be made to a complementary ethical framework.

The question of evidence is critical to evaluating the relative merits of low- and high-intensity interventions. High-intensity interventions often rest on a research base of randomised controlled trials, involving an independent assessor using a standardised diagnostic interview; low-intensity interventions are rarely based on research with such methodological rigour. In the rush to disseminate interventions it is important to be cautious and very conscious of the different levels of evidence. However there does seem to be at least moderately reliable evidence that group and individual therapy are equally effective for depression and the anxiety disorders, yet group CBT is rare in the UK and much less so judicious combinations of group and individual therapy.

Practitioners have to be aware that the population used in a research study can be very different to the client before them; the difference might be demographic, e.g. in education or in a subtly different diagnosis. Competence in diagnosis is as important as the ability to deliver skilful therapy, and the two have to match. The prime purpose of supervision is to ensure fidelity to an evidence-based treatment protocol and to ensure the blending of protocols when, as is usually the case, there are co-morbid disorders.

The stress levels of psychological practitioners make it unlikely that they are currently able to routinely deliver effective treatment. Far from being scientist-practitioners, they are more like engineers at the coalface trying to deliver something useful but oftentimes frustrated by their employer. Unfortunately their voice is really heard in the public arena.

Appendix A
Warwick-Edinburgh Mental Well-being Scale

Below are some statements about feelings and thoughts.

Please circle the number that best describes your experience of each over the last 2 weeks STATEMENTS	None of the time	Rarely	Some of the time	Often	All of the time
I've been feeling optimistic about the future	1	2	3	4	5
I've been feeling useful	1	2	3	4	5
I've been feeling relaxed	1	2	3	4	5
I've been feeling interested in other people	1	2	3	4	5
I've had energy to spare	1	2	3	4	5
I've been dealing with problems well	1	2	3	4	5
I've been thinking clearly	1	2	3	4	5
I've been feeling good about myself	1	2	3	4	5
I've been feeling close to other people	1	2	3	4	5
I've been feeling confident	1	2	3	4	5
I've been able to make up my own mind about things	1	2	3	4	5
I've been feeling loved	1	2	3	4	5
I've been interested in new things	1	2	3	4	5
I've been feeling cheerful	1	2	3	4	5

WEMWBS

WEMWBS is very simple to score. The total score is obtained by summing the score for each of the fourteen items. The latter ranges from 1–5 and the total score from 14–70.

Appendix B
First step questionnaire/interview

Name: Date:

D.O.B.:

The first step questionnaire

This questionnaire is a first step in identifying what you might be suffering from and pointing you in the right direction. In answering each question just make your best guess; don't think about your response too much, there are no right or wrong answers.

1.	Yes	No	Don't know
During the past month have you often been bothered by feeling depressed or hopeless?			
During the past month have you often been bothered by little interest or pleasure in doing things?			
Is this something with which you would like help?			

2.	Yes	No	Don't know
Do you have unexpected panic attacks, a sudden rush of intense fear or anxiety?			
Do you avoid situations in which the panic attacks might occur?			
Is this something with which you would like help?			

3. In your life, have you ever had any experience that was so frightening, horrible or upsetting that, in the past month, you	Yes	No	Don't know

   i. Have had nightmares about it or thought about it when you did not want to?

   ii. Tried hard not to think about it or went out of your way to avoid situations that reminded you of it?

   iii. Were constantly on guard, watchful or easily startled?

   iv. Felt numb or detached from others, activities or your surroundings?

Is this something with which you would like help?

4.		Yes	No	Don't know

Are you a worrier?

Do you worry about everything?

Has the worrying been excessive (more days than not) or uncontrollable in the last six months?

Is this something with which you would like help?

5.		Yes	No	Don't know

When you are or might be in the spotlight say in a group of people or eating/writing in front of others do you immediately get anxious or nervous?

Do you avoid social situations out of a fear of embarrassing or humiliating yourself?

Is this something with which you would like help?

6. Obsessive-Compulsive Disorder		Yes	No	Don't know

Do you wash or clean a lot?

Do you check things a lot?

Is there any thought that keeps bothering you that you would like to get rid of but can't?

Do your daily activities take a long time to finish?

Are you concerned about orderliness or symmetry?

Is this something with which you would like help?

7.		Yes	No	Don't know

Do you go on binges where you eat very large amounts of food in a short period?

Do you do anything special, such as vomit or go on a strict diet to prevent gaining weight from the binge?

Is this something with which you would like help?

8.		Yes	No	Don't know

Have you felt you should cut down on your alcohol/drug use?

Have people got annoyed with you about your drinking/drug taking?

Have you felt guilty about your drinking/drug use?

Do you drink/use drugs before midday?

Is this something with which you would like help?

9.		Yes	No	Don't know

Do you ever hear things other people don't hear or see things they don't see?

Do you ever feel like someone is spying on you or plotting to hurt you?

Do you have any ideas that you don't like to talk about because you are afraid other people will think you are crazy?

Is this something with which you would like help?

10.	Yes	No	Don't know

Have there been times, lasting at least a few days, when you were unusually high, talking a lot, sleeping little?

Did others notice that there was something different about you?
If you answered 'yes', what did they say?

Is this something with which you would like help?

Appendix C

Standardised assessment of personality – abbreviated scale

Only circle Y (yes) or N (no), in the case of question 3 if the client thinks that the description applies *most of the time* and *in most situations*.

1 In general, do you have difficulty making and keeping friends?........... Y/N
   (YES = 1, NO = 0)

2 Would you normally describe yourself as a loner? .... Y/N
   (YES = 1, NO = 0)

3 In general, do you trust other people? .... Y/N
   (YES = 1, NO = 0)

4 Do you normally lose your temper easily? .... Y/N
   (YES = 1, NO = 0)

5 Are you normally an impulsive sort of person?.................................... Y/N
   (YES = 1, NO = 0)

6 Are you normally a worrier? .... Y/N
   (YES = 1, NO = 0)

7 In general, do you depend on others a lot? .... Y/N
   (YES = 1, NO = 0)

8 In general, are you a perfectionist?.. Y/N
   (YES = 1, NO = 0)

Appendix D
Depression survival manual

1   How depression develops and keeps going

Depression usually involves loss of a valued role, for example in a relationship or job. But by itself that is not sufficient; the person also has to become inactive giving up on what they used to do and making sure they take a picture of most things from the worst angle (negative spin).

> What have you stopped doing that you used to enjoy?
> What is it that puts you off doing some of what you used to enjoy?
> Is there something in particular making you go on strike for better pay and conditions?

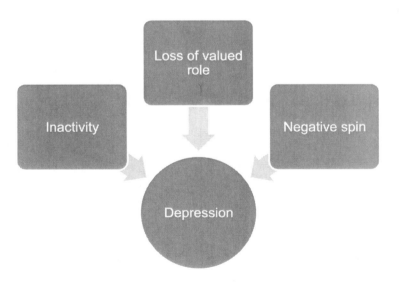

Figure 1 Lighting the fire of depression and keeping it going

Depression is kept going by a negative view of self, personal world, the future and depression about depression.

How do you feel about yourself?
How do you feel about others?
How do you feel about the future?
How do others feel about you?
Does the way you feel about yourself square with how others see you?
Are you sure that you are wholly responsible for your depression?
Are you responsible for working on a solution to your depression?
What sort of things could you timetable yourself to do?
Would you be more able to do them, if you did them in small doses, e.g. phone call to friend rather than spend an evening with them?

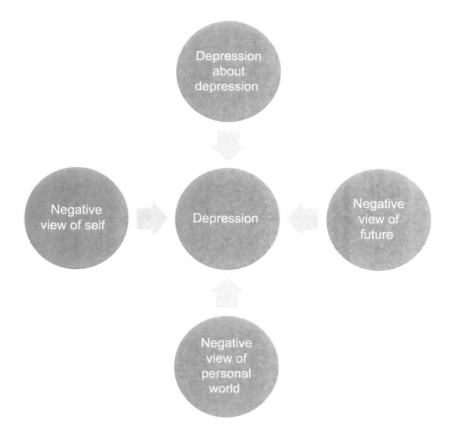

Figure 2 Fuel for the fire

2 No investments, no return

In depression it is as if the person stops investing in what might give them a sense of achievement or pleasure. The dice feel loaded against you, like a boxer knocked to the canvas thinking, 'What is the point in getting up? I will only get knocked down!' If not investing is combined with putting a negative spin on your previous investments, e.g. 'That just showed how stupid I am!' then the result may well be depression; as seen in Figure 3, the negative spin often involves seeing hassles as catastrophes.

But if you don't invest there can be no return; it is rather like having some money, putting it under your carpet and then complaining because it has lost value with inflation. You might well think these days that the banks are not to be trusted. But you would probably advise a friend with some money to make lots of small, low-risk investments in very different places or maybe just deposit accounts in different banks. Many people with depression have had all their investments in just place, a relationship or a job. They may have been encouraged to keep investing in the one place because the returns were good. But it is just a question of time before any one investment runs out of steam; for example the person might lose a job or their partner might die. You can choose not to invest, but it is a choice.

> What investments are you making at the moment?
> Is there a balance between things that might give you a sense of achievement and those that might give you a sense of pleasure?

Figure 3 Putting your money under the carpet and seeing hassles as catastrophes

Figure 4 Investing in achievement and pleasure

Appendix D   143

Sometimes the investments that you think will be good don't come off and sometimes ones that you don't expect to deliver do; could you see yourself making a wider range of investments?

Is there a pattern to your mood? Is it worse at certain times in the week?

Is there anything you could plan to do at the particular times you tend to feel low that might lift your mood a little?

If your major investment didn't work, what do you take that to mean about you?

Use the ruler below to indicate how distressed you have been each day, morning, afternoon and evening and what, if anything, you were doing at the time:

Activity and mood

	Monday	*Tuesday*	*Wednesday*	*Thursday*	*Friday*	*Saturday*	*Sunday*
Morning 0–10 Activity							
Afternoon 0–10 Activity							
Evening 0–10 Activity							

Looking at your activities and mood above, is there a pattern, e.g. worse in the morning, or when you are not doing things?

Could you come up with a better way of arranging your activities, e.g. get up with the alarm and go for the morning paper before you have a cup of tea rather than lie in bed?

Keep a record of any positive experiences in great detail, e.g. not just that 'it was great to bump into an old school friend' but 'it was great for John to remind me that when we were making a noise and the librarian said "this table out", we picked it up and began walking with it'.

3   On second thoughts

The first thoughts of those who are depressed are usually more negative than they need to be. Cognitive behaviour therapy is not only about becoming gradually more active but also about standing back and pausing at your first automatic thought and checking out to see if there is a better second thought.

When you got up this morning what were your first thoughts about coming to the group?

Were these first thoughts more negative than they needed to be?

144   *Appendix D*

Did you or could you come up with better second thoughts?
Do you often think, 'I think too much'?
Is it thinking that you do, or is it agonising?

Once you have reasonable second thoughts don't pick at them; decide what to do and do it. Become an actor, not a ruminator. The more objective second thoughts might feel uncomfortable and take a lot of acting upon before they become second nature; don't get distracted by agonising, and refuse to play the ruminator.

To help you manage your moods pass them through the MOOD chart below: 'M' stands for monitor your mood; 'O' stands for observe your thinking, what it

Table 1 MOOD chart

Monitor Mood	Observe Thinking	Objective Thinking	Decide What to Do and Do It
1 Mood dipped standing drinking coffee looking out of the window.	Life is passing me by like the cars.	It is passing everyone by, it depends on what I do with it.	I could do some painting and decorating or maybe visit my sister. I'll do the painting/decorating today and visit my sister tomorrow.
2 Mood dipped when I received a letter that I am not getting any unemployment benefit.	It's going to be awful.	It is going to be difficult; I will not be able to pay child maintenance, but I do have a really good relationship with my daughter. My ex will not be happy though. I will not be able to afford car insurance but mum will not mind loaning it to me.	I will appeal against the decision with the help of my solicitor and ring mum and ex.

Appendix D 145

sounds as if you have said to yourself; 'O' is for objective thinking, more realistic second thoughts, and 'D' is for deciding what to do and do it.

In the first example of the use of the MOOD chart, the person is daydreaming, gazing out of the window when they notice that their mood has dipped. Daydreams can be like a poisonous gas without a smell in that because nothing has actually happened, such as an argument, it can be difficult to pinpoint exactly what the person has said to themself to feel the way they do.

To identify the toxic negative thought the individual has to do a slow-motion action replay of the situation they were in when the upset occurred to get something of a clue to their reflex/automatic thought Their observed thinking (column 2) may be nothing more than an informed guess as to what it sounds as if they have said to themselves to feel the way they do. It should be noted that in the first example, in column 3, the objective thinking, the person acknowledges that there is, as is often the case, a grain of truth in the observed thinking, i.e. it has some validity. But in column 3 the person is challenging the utility of thinking 'life is passing me by'. Finally in column 4 the person comes up with some investments: painting/decorating and visiting his sister.

In the second example the person encounters a hassle, the stopping of his benefit, but typically in depression any hassle is immediately viewed as a catastrophe: 'It is going to be awful'. A catastrophe can be shrunk back to a hassle by the client asking themselves, 'What specifically is so bad about what has just happened?' and the person identified two issues: an inability to pay maintenance or car insurance. Because these concerns were made very specific they were then open to re-appraisal and the person was able to reflect that at least his relationship with his daughter would not be harmed and there was possible financial help from his mother.

You can cross-examine your automatic negative thought in three different ways. You can ask:

How true is this?
How useful is this way of thinking?
Who says I should look at this in this way?

4   Just make a start

If you are depressed, waiting until you feel like doing something is like waiting for a big lottery win. Depression is like dragging a ball and chain; to do anything is a major achievement.

You have to give yourself permission to break any task, e.g. cleaning the house into small chunks, hoover the living room, then have a break with a cup of tea and then do the next small task – empty and fill the dishwasher.

When you are doing the tasks, either those intended to give you a sense of achievement, e.g. cleaning the house, or pleasure, e.g. going for a walk, you will likely feel you are going through the motions. If you continue to invest the taste of life will likely come back, but you can't say exactly when. It's a bit like

146 *Appendix D*

Figure 5 Depression and the ball and chain

beginning to exercise in the gym; all you get to begin with is aches and pains with little to show, and it takes some weeks to notice a difference.

> What thoughts have put you off doing things?
> Have you been expecting yourself just to do things as you did before you became depressed and then because this all seems too much not doing anything?
> If you put the thoughts that have sabotaged your activity through the filter of the MOOD chart, what more objective second thoughts (column 3) could you come up with?

5   Expectation vs. experience and recalling the positive

In advance of an activity the depressed person usually predicts that they are not going to enjoy the activity, but they usually feel a bit better from doing the activity than if they don't.

Figure 6 Expectation vs. experience

On a scale 0–10 where 10 is the best you have ever felt and 0 is the worst, how did you feel getting ready to come to the group today?
On a scale 0–10, how do you feel right now?

If you felt say 3/10 before coming out today and 6/10 now, you could use the numbers 3 and 6 as a reminder that there is a gap between expectation and experience and that you can trick yourself into inactivity by relying on your expectation rather than your experience.

But there is another problem in depression: what to do with how you remember your experience. Tonight if your partner or a friend asked you how you got on in the group today, what would you likely say?

Probably most would say one word: 'Okay'. A bit like asking your children what they did in school today, the reply is invariably 'Nothing'; you know they must have done something! 'Nothing' is shorthand for 'I can't be bothered plugging in my brain, switching on and coming up with an answer', but if then a friend rings your child goes into graphic detail about something good that happened. If you are suffering from depression, you tend to recall the good things in a vague way, e.g. 'Okay, my team drew'; you do not go into detail, e.g. 'It was superb when Liverpool equalised in the last minute of extra time'. So tonight if you talk of the group session don't just say 'okay' or even some expletive. Try and recall in detail some good moment, e.g. a chat with a group member over coffee as the group was assembling. Then follow this up with keeping a detailed record of the positives in your week.

6 Negative spin or how to make yourself depressed without really trying

Imagine that you wanted to make someone depressed by what you say, so that for example if a child tells you enthusiastically that they got a B in their maths exam, what would you say? Remember you are trying to make them depressed.

One possibility is 'You should have got an A'; you hone in on the negative and discount the positive getting a 'B', and this is called using a mental filter.

148 *Appendix D*

Other possibilities are 'You didn't try hard enough'; this is called jumping to conclusions, as without being inside the child's head you can't know how hard they tried. To make the child depressed you just focus your camera in such a way that the lens, setting and filter give a negative spin. You might feel like smashing the camera of an adult who makes a child depressed in this way. But if you are depressed you are probably using a camera with these odd settings to make yourself depressed. The first step in taking an objective picture is to become aware of the ten settings of the camera that cause problems, then to step around them.

There are no water-tight distinctions between the information-processing biases, and many people who are depressed customarily use a number of them.

Do any of these ring bells for you?

Which ones do you think you need to make a note of, to make yourself aware of what you might be doing when you are getting upset?

You might want to get hold of David Burn's book Feeling Good: The New Mood Therapy *from the library or buy it from amazon.co.uk for about £6 to read more about these ten biases in Chapter Three. It has also got lots of other useful information on depression.*

Table 2 Information processing biases

1 Dichotomous (black and white) thinking, e.g. 'I'm either a total success or a failure'.
2 Mental filter, focussing on the negative to the exclusion of the positive, e.g. 'How can you say it was a lovely meal; how long did we have to wait for the desert to be served?'
3 Personalisation, assuming just because something has gone wrong it must be your fault, e.g. 'John did not let on to me coming into work this morning; it must have been something I said'.
4 Emotional reasoning, assuming guilt simply because of the presence of guilt feelings, e.g. 'I can't provide for the kids the way I did. I've let them down; what sort of parent am I?'
5 Jumping to conclusions, e.g. assuming that being asked to have a word with your line manager means that you are in trouble.
6 Overgeneralisation, making negative predictions on the basis of one bad experience, e.g. 'I've had it with men after Charlie; you cannot trust any of them'.
7 Magnification and minimisation, magnifying faults or difficulties minimising strengths or positives, e.g. 'I am terrible at report writing and I am lucky to have got good appraisals for the last couple of years'.
8 Disqualifying the positives, e.g. brushing aside compliments and dwelling on criticism.
9 *Should* statements, overuse of moral imperatives, e.g. 'I must do . . . I should . . . I have to . . .'
10 Labelling and mislabeling, e.g. 'If I make a mistake I am a failure as a person'.

7 An attitude problem?

A person's attitude to life can be fine for many circumstances but runs into problems if certain types of events (Key Events) occur; there are some examples in Table 3: Attitudes and Problems

> Do you see yourself as being as being addicted to approval (sociotrope)?
> Do you see yourself as addicted to success (autonomous)?

Most things that people are addicted to are fine in themselves but are a problem when they dominate their life. If you are a true sociotrope or autonomous you might want to consider weaning yourself off; there will be withdrawal symptoms and you may always find them tempting. There might be the odd slip, but you can prevent it becoming a full-blown relapse by using the MOOD chart and spotting whether the upset is really to do with an attitude from the past. Today's upsets and past attitudes overlap to some extent,

Table 3 Attitudes and problems

Attitudes	*Problems (Key Events)*
'I must be liked all the time and in all circumstances' (a sociotrope – addicted to approval)	A relationship breaks up
'If I am not the top I am a flop' (the highly autonomous person may be addicted to achievement)	Fails to get promotion or an exam or is made redundant
'Everything has to be done just so' (the perfectionist)	No longer given the time to get everything perfectly right
'To be happy you have got to have . . .' (excessively rigid)	When you cannot achieve what you judged necessary for happiness

Figure 7 Today's upsets, past attitudes and key events

150   Appendix D

Figure 8 Strategies unequal to the task of lifting low self-esteem

What has upset you today might be a key event in that it opens the door to a particular attitude (e.g. a key event for a sociotrope might be not being praised by her boss for a piece of work today) and upset. Using the MOOD chart the sociotrope might come up with a more useful attitude (objective thinking), e.g. 'approval is nice but no one can rely on it; it is not like oxygen', and then stop depressive rumination using the 'D' of the MOOD chart and get on and do something, invest.

Your attitudes might be about perfectionism or extreme rigidity about how things should be. There is nothing wrong with these attitudes in the right place, but if certain key events occur they can be your undoing.

Use the MOOD chart for monitoring your mood, but try and be alert for any key event that has called onstream an 'attitude problem' and come up with/ use your antidote to this 'gremlin'; in the objective thinking column, don't stew on your upset once you have sorted it get on to the 'D' of MOOD and '*D*o'.

If you are weighed down by a low opinion of yourself, as seen in Figure 7, you might play the sociotrope, autonomous or perfectionist to lift it for you, but long term it's too heavy. Alternatively you might numb the pain of low self-esteem by being very rigid, e.g. if I can continue this job or this relationship then just maybe I can think of myself as okay, but the anaesthetic (an overvalued role) eventually wears off, exposing the nerve.

By realising where your low self-esteem comes from, you can begin to tackle it.

8   My attitude to self, others and the future

Your attitude to yourself, others and the future can play a major role in maintaining depression. The depressed person usually has a negative view of themselves; for some low self-esteem is very long standing but became much worse after the loss of a valued role, e.g. children leaving the nest or losing your job. For others the negative view of self is of more recent origin.

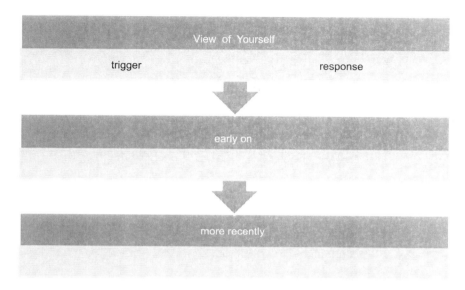

Figure 9 What makes me think about myself the way I do?

    How has the view of yourself changed?
    If your low self-esteem goes way back, what do you wish had been said to you that might have made a difference?
    Do you think you would have been as bothered by recent upsets if your self-esteem was already in tact?
    Do you equate your worth as a person with an achievement or perhaps with the approval of someone important to you?
    Is it possible to be worthwhile without this achievement or approval?
    Do you think a jury would return a 'not guilty', 'guilty' or the Scottish 'not proven' verdict on you?
    What is the story you carry round with you of how other people are?
    Do you need to update the story, say in the light of your experiences in the group?
    Do you use dichotomous thinking about yourself and others, e.g. they are either 'saints or sinners'?
    Do you dwell on the mistakes of yourself or others, leaving the positives out of the reckoning and employing a mental filter?

With a negative view of yourself, you may be reluctant to let others get to know you. You might also think others are going to be critical of you and that you'd better stay in your shell. The negative views of yourself and others conspire to produce a negative view of the future.

152 *Appendix D*

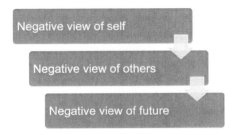

Figure 10. Negative view of the future

The negative view of the future leads to inactivity, a failure to invest and thereby depression.

> Can you be certain that the future is going to be negative?
> Have there been good times in the past?
> Can you be certain good times cannot come again?
> Can you commit to constructing a future, despite life being a bit of a bomb-site at the moment?

9 Be critical of your reflex first thoughts not how you feel

In depression the person tends to criticise themselves for what they have been feeling and yet have an uncritical acceptance of their automatic negative thoughts. To overcome depression the person has to climb a number of stepping stones, accepting without criticism what they are feeling, identifying negative automatic thoughts, distilling objective thoughts, then investing in life, as seen in Figure 11.

> Do you often think 'I shouldn't be feeling . . .'?
> How useful has it been to blame yourself for what you have been feeling?
> Who, other than yourself, says you should be blaming yourself for what you feel?

Sometimes people are so afraid of what they feel that they try to distract themselves by feverish activity that ends in exhaustion, at which point the feelings return. This emotional avoidance is self-defeating and needs to be replaced by an acceptance of experienced emotion. However within cognitive behaviour therapy the emotion experienced does not necessarily have the last word. To climb out of depression a first step is to acknowledge what you feel without apology, avoiding depression about depression. Depression is challenge enough without double depression.

Appendix D   153

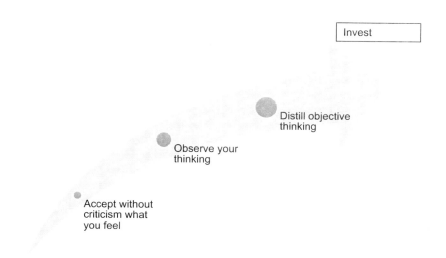

Figure 11 Stepping stones out of depression

10   Preventing relapse

The more episodes of depression you have had the more likely you are to have another one. However with the skills learnt in this programme, you may well be able to stop a slip becoming a full-blown relapse. When you are feeling better, you may want to forget about the skills you learnt in the group because they remind you of the bad times in your life. But depression tends to create a fault line; you could again crack along the fault line if you came across a similar set of circumstances. But if you have your own survival manual and take active steps to use your skills at the first signs of depression, you can nip it in the bud. So that you are prepared, it is useful to have fire drills even when there is no fire – reading your survival manual at good times.

Some common early warning signs are in Figure 12.

Are there any other signals you get when you are beginning to slide?

The temptation is to deny that you are beginning to slip (this is called cognitive avoidance) because the memory of last time is so painful. But if you acknowledge you are beginning to slip and use the tools from the programme, you can stop the depression gathering momentum. Depression is like a rock running downhill. Stopping it near the top as it begins its descent is relatively easy.

> What situations do you think might be most dangerous for you?
> What would your game plan be in the event of such triggers?
> What changes to your week would you need to make?

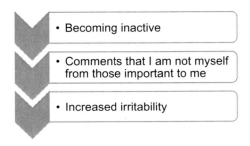

Figure 12 Early warning signs

What activities/contacts would you need to make?
What thoughts would be the best antidotes to the negative automatic thoughts that would come onstream?
How would you remind yourself to be patient with yourself while you give the tools a chance to make a difference?
How would you avoid blaming yourself that you are experiencing signs of depression?
Which resources would you call upon: this survival manual, a supportive friend, a self-help book, your therapist?
What thoughts might get in the way of accessing the help you need?
How would you answer the thoughts that might sabotage you seeking help?

Appendix E

Summary of criteria for empirically supported psychological therapies – Chambless and Hollon (1998)

1. Comparison with a no-treatment control group, alternative treatment group, or placebo a) in a randomized control trial, controlled single-case experiment, or equivalent time-samples design; and b) in which the EST is statistically significantly superior to no treatment, placebo, or alternative treatments or in which the EST is equivalent to a treatment already established in efficacy, and power is sufficient to detect moderate differences.

2. These studies must have been conducted with a) a treatment manual or its logical equivalent; b) a population, treated for specified problems, for whom inclusion criteria have been delineated in a reliable, valid manner; c) reliable and valid outcome assessment measures, at minimum tapping the problems targeted for change; and d) appropriate data analysis.

3. For a designation of efficacious, the superiority of the EST must have been shown in at least two independent research settings (sample size of three or more at each site in the case of single-case experiments). If there is conflicting evidence, the preponderance of the well-controlled data must support the EST's efficacy.

4. For a designation of possibly efficacious, one study (sample size of three or more in the case of single case experiments) suffices in the absence of conflicting evidence.

5. For a designation of efficacious and specific, the EST must have been shown to be statistically, significantly superior to pill or psychological placebo or to an alternative bona fide treatment in at least two independent research settings. If there is conflicting evidence, the preponderance of the well-controlled data must support the EST's efficacy and specificity.

References

Aarts, A.A., Anderson, J.E. and Anderson, C.J. (2015) Estimating the reproducibility of psychological science. *Open Science Collaboration Science*, 349, n.p. DOI: 10.1126/science.aac4716

Alford, B.A. and Beck, A.T. (1997) *The Integrative Power of Cognitive Therapy*. New York: Guilford Press.

Altamura, A.C., Dell' Osso, B. and Fumagalli, S. (2006) Is duration of untreated illness a poor outcome factor in Generalized Anxiety Disorder? *International Journal of Neuropsychopharmachology*, 9, 119.

Altamura, A.C., Santini, A. and Salvadori, D. (2005) Duration of untreated illness in panic disorder: A poor outcome risk factor? *Neuropsychiatric Disorder Treatment*, 1(4), 345–347.

American Psychiatric Association (1980) *Diagnostic and Statistical Manual of Mental Disorders*. Fifth Edition DSM-III. Washington, DC: American Psychiatric Press.

American Psychiatric Association (2000) *Diagnostic and Statistical Manual of Mental Disorders*. Fifth Edition DSM-IV-TR. Washington, DC: American Psychiatric Press.

American Psychiatric Association (2013) *Diagnostic and Statistical Manual of Mental Disorders*. Fifth Edition DSM-5. Washington, DC: American Psychiatric Press.

Andersson, G. and Cuijpers, P. (2009) Internet-based and other computerized psychological treatments for adult depression: A meta-analysis. *Cognitive and Behavior Therapy*, 38, 196–205.

Anti-Bullying Alliance (2015) Serious mental health consequences for children and young adults as a result of bullying in schools, Press release November 21st 2015.

APA Presidential Task Force on Evidence-Based Practice (2006) Evidence-based practice in psychology. *American Psychologist*, 61, 271–285.

Arroll, B., Goodyear-Smith, F., Kerse, N., Fishman, T. and Gunn, J. (2005) Effect of the addition of a 'help' question to two screening questions on specificity for diagnosis of depression in general practice: Diagnostic validity study. *British Medical Journal*, 331, 884–886.

Basco, M.R., Bostic, J.Q., Davies, D., Rush, A.J., Witte, B., Hendrickse, W. and Barnett, V. (2000) Methods to improve diagnostic accuracy in a community mental health setting. *American Journal of Psychiatry*, 157, 1599–1605.

Beach, S.R.H. and O'Leary, K.D. (1986) The treatment of depression in the context of marital discord. *Behavior Therapy*, 17, 43–49.

Beck, A., Burdett, M. and Lewis, H. (2015) The association between waiting for psychological therapy and therapy outcomes as measured by the CORE-OM. *British Journal of Clinical Psychology*, 54, 233–248.

References 157

Beck, A.T., Freeman, A. and Davis, D.D. (2003) *Cognitive Therapy of Personality Disorders*. Second Edition. New York, NY: Guilford Press.

Beck, A.T., Rush, A.J., Shaw, B.F. and Emery, G. (1979) *Cognitive Therapy of Depression*. New York, NY: Guilford Press.

Beck, A.T., Ward, C.H. and Mendelson, M. (1962) Reliability of psychiatrics diagnoses: A study of consistency of clinical judgements and ratings. *American Journal of Psychiatry*, 119, 351–357.

Bentall, R.P. (2009) *Doctoring Mental Health: Why Psychiatric Treatment Fails*. London: Allen Lane.

Binnie, J. (2015) Do you want therapy with that? A critical account of working within IAPT. *Mental Health Review Journal*, 20, 79–83.

Bisson, J.I., Jenkins, P.L., Alexander, J. and Bannister, C. (1997) Randomised controlled trial of psychological debriefing for victims of acute burn trauma. *British Journal of Psychiatry*, 171, 78–81.

Bolier, L., Haverman, M. and Westerhof, G.J. (2013) Positive psychology interventions: A meta-analysis of randomized controlled studies. *BMC Public Health*, 13, 119.

Boonstra, N., Klaassen, R. and Sytema, S. (2012) Duration of untreated psychosis and negative symptoms: A systematic review and meta-analysis of individual patient data. *Schizophrenia Research*, 142, 12–19.

Brahler, C., Gumley, A. and Harper, J. (2013) Exploring change processes in compassion focussed therapy in psychosis: Results of a feasibility randomized controlled trial. *British Journal of Clinical Psychology*, 52, 199–214.

Brewin, C.R., Andrews, B. and Valentine, J.D. (2000) Meta-analysis of risk factors for post-traumatic stress disorder in trauma exposed adults. *Journal of Consulting and Clinical Psychology*, 68, 748–766.

British Psychological Society (2016) Psychological therapies staff in the NHS report alarming levels of depression and stress – their own. Press release February 3rd 2016.

Brown, G.K., Have, T.T. and Henriques, G.R. (2005) Cognitive therapy for the prevention of suicide attempts. *Journal of The American Medical Association*, 294, 563–570.

Brown, N.J.L., Sokal, A.D. and Friedman, H.L. (2013) The complex dynamics of wishful thinking: The critical positivity ratio. *American Psychologist*, 68, 801-813.

Bruchmuller, K., Margraf, J., Suppiger, A. and Schneider, S. (2011) Popular or unpopular? Therapist's use of structured interviews and their estimation of patient acceptance. *Behavior Therapy*, 42, 634–643.

Burns, P., Kellett, S. and Donohoe, G. (2015) "Stress Control" as a large group psychoeducational intervention at Step 2 of IAPT services: Acceptability of the approach and moderators of effectiveness. *Behavioural and Cognitive Psychotherapy*, 44, 431–443. http://dx.doi.org/10.1017/S1352465815000491

Butler, A.C., Chapman, J.E., Forman, E.M. and Beck, A.T. (2006) The empirical status of cognitive-behavioral therapy: A review of meta-analyses. *Clinical Psychology Review*, 26, 17–31.

Campbell, R., Ahrens, C.E. and Sefl, T. (2001) Social reactions to rape victims: Healing and hurtful effects on psychological and physical health outcomes. *Violence and Victims*, 16, 287–302.

Care Quality Commission (2015) Right here, right now – help, care and support during a mental health crisis. London: Care Quality Commission. Available at: www.cqc.org.uk/content/new-report-looking-peoples-experience-care-during-mental-health-crisis (accessed on 2 November 2015).

158 *References*

Carey, M.P., Carey, K.B. and Meisler, A.W. (1991) Psychiatric symptoms in mentally ill chemical abusers. *Journal of Nervous and Mental Disease*, 179(3), 136–138.

Chambless, D.L. and Hollon, S.D. (1998) Defining empirically supported therapies. *Journal of Consulting and Clinical Psychology*, 66, 7–18.

Chambless, D.L. and Ollendick, T.H. (2001) Empirically supported psychological interventions: Controversies and evidence. *Annual Review of Psychology*, 52, 685–716.

Chevron, E. and Rounsaville, B.J. (1983) Evaluating the clinical skills of psychotherapists: A comparison of techniques. *Archives of General Psychiatry*, 40, 1129–1132.

Chmielewski, M., Clark, L.A., Bagby, R.M. and Watson, D. (2015) Method matters: Understanding reliability in DSM-IV and DSM-5. *Journal of Abnormal Psychology*, 124, 764–769.

Clark, D.A., Beck, A.T. and Brown, G. (1989) Cognitive mediation in general psychiatric outpatients: A test of the content-specificity hypothesis. *Journal of Personality and Social Psychology*, 56, 958–964.

The Commission on Acute Adult Psychiatric Care (2015) Improving acute inpatient psychiatric care for adults in England. Interim report. London: The Commission on Acute Adult Psychiatric Care. Available at: www.caapc.info/ (accessed on 2 November 2015).

Coull, G. and Morriss, P.G. (2011) The clinical effectiveness of CBT-based guided self-help interventions for anxiety and depressive disorders: A systematic review. *Psychological Medicine*, 41, 2239–2252.

Craighead, W.E., Sheets, E.S., Brosse, A.L. and Ilardi, S.S. (2007) 'Psychosocial treatments for major depressive disorder', in *A Guide to Treatments That Work*. Eds. P.E. Nathan and J.M. Gorman. 3 Vol. New York: Oxford Press, pp. 289–308.

Cuijpers, P., Smit, F. and Bohlmeijer, E. (2010) Efficacy of cognitive-behavioural therapy and other psychological treatments for depression: Meta-analytic study of publication bias. *British Journal of Psychiatry*, 196, 173–178.

Cuijpers, P., Sijbrandij, M. and Foole, S.L. (2014) Adding psychotherapy to antidepressant medication in depression and anxiety disorders: A meta-analysis. *World Psychiatry*, 13, 56–67.

Database of Abstracts of Reviews of Effects (DARE) (2014) On 'Effectiveness of solution-focussed brief therapy by Gingerrich and Peterson (2013)' University of York Centre for Reviews and Dissemination.

Dell'Osso, B. and Altamura, A.C. (2010) Duration of untreated psychosis and duration of untreated illness: New vistas. *CNS Spectrum*, 15(4), 238–246.

Dell'Osso, B., Buoli, M. and Hollander, E. (2010) Duration of untreated illness as a predictor of treatment response and remission in obsessive-compulsive disorder. *World Journal of Biological Psychiatry*, 11(1), 59–65.

Dell'Osso, B., Glick, I.D. and Baldwin, D.S. (2013) Can long-term outcomes be improved by shortening the duration of untreated illness in psychiatric disorders: A conceptual framework. *Psychopathology*, 14, 14–21.

DiNardo, P.A., Brown, T.A. and Barlow, D.H. (1994) *Anxiety Disorders Interview Schedule for DSM-IV: Lifetime version (ADIS – IV – L)*. San Antonia, TX: Psychological Corporation.

Dormon, F. (2015) Is mental health care improving? London: The Health Foundation. Available at: www.health.org.uk/publication/mental-health-care-improving (accessed on 2 November 2015).

Drake, R.E., Mercer-McFadden, C., Mueser, K.T., McHugo, G.J. and Bond, G.R. (1998) Review of integrated mental health and substance abuse treatment for patients with dual disorders. *Schizophrenia Bulletin*, 24, 589–608.

References   159

Drew, D. (2014) *Little Stories of Life and Death@NHS Whistleblower*. Leicestershire: Troubador Publishing.

Ehlers, A., Grey, N. and Wild, J. (2013) Implementation of cognitive therapy for PTSD in routine clinical care: Effectiveness and moderators of outcome in a consecutive sample. *Behaviour Research and Therapy*, 51, 742–752.

Ewing, J.A. (1984) Detecting alcoholism: The CAGE Questionnaire. *JAMA*, 252, 1905–1907.

Eyberg, S.M., Nelson, M.M. and Boggs, S.R. (2008) Evidence-based psychosocial treatments for children and adolescents with disruptive behaviour. *Journal of Clinical Child and Adolescent Psychology*, 37, 215–237.

Eyberg, S.M. and Ross, A.W. (1978) Assessment of child behaviour problems: The validation of a new inventory. *Journal of Clinical Child Psychology*, 7, 113–116.

Fineberg, N.A., O'Doherty, C. and Rajagopal, S. (2003) How common is obsessive compulsive disorder in a dermatology outpatient clinic? *Journal of Clinical Psychiatry*, 64, 152–155.

First, M.B., Gibbon, M. and Spitzer, R.L. (1995) *Structured Clinical Interview for DSM IV Axis II Personality Disorders (SCID II version 2.0)*. New York: Biometrics Research Department, New York State Psychiatric Institute.

First, M.B., Spitzer, R.L., Gibbon, M. and Williams, J.B.W. (1997) *Structured Clinical Interview for DSM IV Axis 1 Disorders Clinician Version (SCID-CV)*. Washington, DC: American Psychiatric Press.

First, M., Spitzer, R.L., Gibbon, M. and Williams, J.B.W. (2002) *Structured Clinical Interview for DSM-IV – TR Axis I Disorders, Research Version, Patient ed. (SCID-I/P)*. New York: Biometrics Research, New York State Psychiatric Institute.

First, M., Williams, J.B.W., Karg, R.S. and Spitzer, R.L. (2015) *Structured Clinical Interview for DSM-5-CV, (SCID-5-CV)*. New York: Biometrics Research, New York State Psychiatric Institute.

Foa, E.B., Cashman, L., Jaycox, L. and Perry, K. (1997) The validation of a self-report measure of posttraumatic stress disorder: The Posttraumatic Diagnostic Scale. *Psychological Assessment*, 9, 445–451.

Foa, E.B. and Meadows, E.A. (1997) Psychosocial treatments for posttraumatic stress disorder: A critical review. *Annual Review of Psychology*, 48, 449–480.

Frances, A. (2013) *Saving Normal: An Insider's Revolt against Out-of-Control Psychiatric Diagnosis, DSM-5, Big Pharma, and the Medicalization of Ordinary Life*. New York: Harper Collins. Kindle Edition.

Fredrickson, B.L. and Losada, M.F. (2005) Positive affect and the complex dynamics of human flourishing. *American Psychologist*, 60(7), 678–686.

Freedman, R., Lewis, D.A. and Michels, R. (2013) The Initial field trials of DSM-5: New blooms old thorns. *American Journal of Psychiatry*, 170, 1–5.

Ghio, L., Gotelli, S. and Marcenaro, M. (2014) Duration of untreated illness and outcomes in unipolar depression: A systematic review and meta-analysis. *Journal of Affective Disorder*, 152–154: 45–51.

Gilbody, S., Littlewood, E. and Hewit, G. (2015) Computerised cognitive behaviour therapy (CCBT) as treatment for depression in primary care (REEACT) trial: Large scale pragmatic randomised controlled trial, *BMJ*, 351, h5627. DOI: 10.1136/bmj.h5627

Gingerich, W.J. and Peterson, L.T. (2013) Effectiveness of solution-focused brief therapy: A systematic qualitative review of controlled outcome studies. *Research on Social Work Practice*, 23, 266–283.

Goffman, E. (1961) *Asylums*. New York: Anchor.

160 References

Goldberg, J.F. and Ernst, C.L. (2002) Features associated with the delayed initiation of mood stabilizers at illness onset in bipolar disorder. *Journal of Clinical Psychiatry*, 63(11), 985–991.

Gould, R.A. and Clum, G.A. (1993) A meta-analysis of self-help treatment approaches. *Clinical Psychology Review*, 13, 169–186.

Grant, A., Townend, M., Mills, J. and Cockx, A. (2008) *Assessment and Case Formulation in Cognitive Behavioural Therapy*. London: Sage Publications.

Guo, T., Xiang, Y.-T. and Xiao, L. (2015) Measurement-based care versus standard care for major depression: A randomized controlled trial with blind raters. *American Journal of Psychiatry*, 172, 1004–1013.

Gyani, A., Shafran, R., Layard, R. and Clark, D.M. (2013) Enhancing recovery rates: Lessons from year one of IAPT. *Behaviour Research and Therapy*, 51, 597–606.

Health and Safety Executive (2016) Work related stress, anxiety and depression in Great Britain 2014/15. Website statistics February 14, 2016.

Health and Social Care Information Centre (2014) Psychological Therapies Annual Report on the use of IAPT services: England – 2013/2014 Experimental Statistics. www.hscic.gov.uk/pubs/psycther1314

Health and Social Care Information Centre (2015) *Psychological Therapies: Annual Report on the Use of IAPT Services; England 2014/15*. Leeds, UK: Community and Mental Health team, HSCIC.

Hofman, S.G. and Smits, J.A.J. (2008) Cognitive-behavioral therapy for adult anxiety disorders: A meta-analysis of randomised placebo-controlled trials. *Journal of Clinical Psychiatry*, 69, 621–632.

Hollon, S.D., DeRubeis, R.J. and Fawcett, J. (2014) Effect of cognitive therapy with antidepressant medications vs. antidepressants alone on the rate of recovery in major depressive disorder: A randomized clinical trial. *JAMA Psychiatry*, 73, 56–63.

Holman, J., Head, M.L., Lanfear, R. and Jennions, M.D. (2015) Evidence of experimental bias in the life sciences: Why we need blind data recording. *PLoS Biol*, 13(7), e1002190. DOI: 10.1371/journal.pbio.1002190

Hooley, J.M., Orley, J. and Teasdale, J.D. (1986) Levels of expressed emotion and relapse in depressed patients. *British Journal of Psychiatry*, 148, 642–647.

Howard, K.I., Kopta, S.M., Krause, M.S. and Orlinsky, D.E. (1986) The dose-effect relationship in psychotherapy. *American Psychologist*, 41, 159–164.

IAPT (2011) *Psychological Wellbeing Practitioners: Best Practice Guidelines*. London: IAPT.

IAPT Data Handbook Guidance on recording and monitoring outcomes to support local evidence-based practice (2011).

Insel, T. (2013) Quotation in "Mental health researchers reject psychiatry's new 'diagnostic bible'" by Maia Szalavitz, *Time Magazine* May 7th 2013.

Intention to treat analysis Cochrane. Available at: www.mrc-bsu.cam.ac.uk/cochrane/handbook/

Isaacs, D. and Fitzgerald, D. (1999) Seven alternatives to evidence-based medicine. *British Medical Journal*, 319, 1618.

Jacobson, N.S. and Gortner, E.T. (2000) Can depression be de-medicalised in the 21st century: Scientific revolutions, counter revolutions and the magnetic field of normal science. *Behaviour Research and Therapy*, 38, 103–117.

Jansen, S., White, R. and Hogwood, J. (2015) The 'treatment gap' in global mental health reconsidered: Sociotherapy for collective trauma in Rwanda. *European Journal of Psychotraumatology*, 6, 28706. http://dx.doi.org/10.3402/ejpt.v6.28706

References   161

Jauhar, S., McKenna, P.J. and Radua, J. (2014) Cognitive-behavioural therapy for the symptoms of schizophrenia: Systematic review and meta-analysis with examination of potential bias. *British Journal of Psychiatry*, 204, 20–29.

Joffres, M., Jaramillo, A., Dickinson, J., Lewin, G., Pottie, K., Shaw, E., Connor Gorber, S. and Tonelli, M. (2013) Canadian task force on preventive health care: Recommendations on screening for depression in adults. *CMAJ*, 185, 775–782.

Johnsen, T.J. and Friborg, O. (2015, May 11) The effects of cognitive behavioral therapy as an anti-depressive treatment is falling: A meta-analysis. *Psychological Bulletin*. Advance online publication. http://dx.doi.org/10.1037/bul0000015

Kahneman, D. (2011) *Thinking, Fast and Slow*, London: Allen Lane.

Kendler, K.S., Munoz, R.A. and Murphy, G. (2010) The development of the Feighner Criteria: A historical perspective. *American Journal of Psychiatry*, 167, 134–142.

Keyes, C.L.M. (2004) The nexus of cardiovascular disease and depression revisited: The complete mental health perspective and the moderating role of age and gender. *Aging and Mental Health*, 8, 266–274.

Keyes, C.L.M. (2005) Mental illness and/or mental health? Investigating axioms of the complete state model of health. *Journal of Consulting and Clinical Psychology*, 73, 539–548.

Khan, S. and Brabham, A. (2015) Preparing to implement the new access and waiting time standards for early intervention in psychosis. Presentation at the North East and Cumbria and Yorkshire and Humber EIP and IAPT Workshop, Leeds, 7 May. Available at: www.nescn.nhs.uk/wp-content/uploads/2015/04/Joint-North-Regional-Mental-Health-Event-Presentation-Final.pdf (accessed on 3 November 2015).

Kroenke, K., Spitzer, R.L. and Williams, J.B. (2001) The PHQ-9: Validity of a brief depression measure. *Journal of General Internal Medicine*, 16, 606–613.

Kroenke, K., Spitzer, R.L. and Williams, J.B. (2007) Anxiety disorders in primary care: Prevalence, impairment, comorbidity and detection. *Annals of Internal Medicine*, 146, 317–325.

Kuyken, W. (2006) 'Evidence-based case formulation: Is the emperor clothed?', in *Case Formulation in Cognitive Behaviour Therapy: The Treatment of Challenging and Complex Cases*. Ed. N. Tarrier. London: Routledge, pp. 12–35.

Kuyken, W., Fothergill, C.D., Musa, M. and Chadwick, P. (2005) The reliability and quality of cognitive case formulation. *Behaviour Research and Therapy*, 43, 1187–1201.

Kuyken, W. and Tsivrikos, D. (2009) Therapist competence, comorbidity and cognitive-behavioral therapy for depression. *Psychotherapy and Psychosomatics*, 78, 42–48.

Layard, R. (2015) Mental health: From rhetoric to reality? *Kings Fund* January 23rd 2015.

Layard, R. and Clark, D.M. (2014) *Thrive: The Power of Evidence-Based Psychological Therapies*. London: Penguin.

Leard, C.A., Mann, T.C. and Smith, B. (2009) Baseline self-reported functional health and vulnerability to post-traumatic stress disorder after combat deployment: Prospective US military combat study. *British Medical Journal*, 338, b1273.

Le Doux, J. (2015) *Anxious: The Modern Mind in the Age of Anxiety*. London: One World Publications.

Lees, J. (2016) *The Future of Psychological Therapy: From Managed Care to Transformational Practice* (p. 106). London: Taylor and Francis. Kindle Edition.

Leigh, S. and Flatt, S. (2015) App-based psychological interventions: Friend or foe? *Evidence Based Mental Health*, 18, 97–98.

Lewinsohn, P.M., Munoz, R.F., Youngren, M.A. and Zeiss, A.M. (2010) *Control Your Depression*. New York: Simon and Schuster.

162 *References*

Lewis, C.A., Simons, A.D. and Kim, H.K. (2012) The role of early symptom trajectories and pre-treatment variables in predicting treatment response to cognitive behavioural therapy. *Journal of Consulting and Clinical Psychology*, 80, 5525–5534.

Lieberman, J.A. (2015) *Shrinks: The Untold Story of Psychiatry*. London: Weidenfeld and Nicolson.

Linehan, M.M., Tutek, D.A., Heard, H.L. and Armstrong, H.E. (1994) Interpersonal outcome of cognitive behavioral treatment for chronically suicidal borderline patients. *American Journal of Psychiatry*, 151, 1771–1776.

Loucas, C.E., Fairburn, C.G. and Whittington, C. (2014) E-therapy in the in the treatment and prevention of eating disorders: A systematic review and meta-analysis. *Behaviour Research and Therapy*, 63, 122–131.

Maheswaran, H., Welch, S. and Powell, J. (2012) Evaluating the responsiveness of the Warwick Edinburgh Mental Well-being Scale (WEMWBS): Group and individual level analysis. Health and Quality of Life Outcomes, 10, n.p.

Maricutoiu, L.P., Sava, F.A. and Butta, O. (2016) The effectiveness of controlled interventions on employees' burnout: A meta-analysis. *Journal of Occupational and Organisational Psychology*, 89, 1–27.

Marsh, P. and Doel, M. (2005) *The Task-Centred Book*. London: Routledge.

Marshall, M., Lewis, S. and Lockwood, A. (2005) Association between duration of untreated psychosis and outcome in cohorts of first-episode patients: A systematic review. *Archives of General Psychiatry*, 62(9), 975–983.

Martinez, R., Whitfield, G., Dafters, R. and Williams, C. (2008) Can people read self-help manuals for depression? A challenge for the stepped care model and book prescription schemes. *Behavioural and Cognitive Psychotherapy*, 36, 89–97.

Maslach, C. (2003) Job burnout: New directions in research and intervention. *Current Directions in Psychological Science*, 12, 189–192.

Mausbach, B.T., Moore, R. and Roesch, S. (2010) The relationship between homework compliance and therapy outcomes: An updated meta-analysis. *Cognitive Therapy and Research*, 34, 429–438.

Mayo-Wilson, E. and Montgomery, P. (2013) Media-delivered cognitive behavioural therapy and behavioural therapy (self-help) for anxiety disorders in adults. *Cochrane Database of Systematic Reviews*, 9, n.p. Art. No.: CD005330. DOI: 10.1002/14651858. CD005330.pub4

McGrath, A. (2015) *Inventing the Universe: Why We Can't Stop Talking about Science, Faith and God*. London: Hodder & Stoughton. Kindle Edition.

McLellan, A.T., Luborsky, L., Woody, G.E., O'Brien, C.P. and Druley, K.A. (1983, June) Predicting response to alcohol and drug abuse treatments: Role of psychiatric severity. *Archives General Psychiatry*, 40(6), 620–605.

Mental Health Taskforce (2016) The Five Year Forward View for Mental Health: A Report from the Independent Mental Health Taskforce to the NHS in England February 2016.

MIND (2013) People with mental health problems still waiting over a year for talking treatments. Available at: www.mind.org.uk/news-campaigns/news/people-withmental-health-problems-still-waiting-over-a-year-for-talking-treatments/#.VaO36vlVikq4 (accessed on 13 May 2015).

MIND (2015) We need to talk. Getting the right therapy at the right time. Available at: www.mind.org.uk/media/280583/We-Need-to-Talk-getting-the-right-therapy-at-the-righttime.pdf (accessed on 15 May 2015).

Mojtabai, R. (2013) Clinician-identified depression in community settings: Concordance with structured-interview diagnoses. *Psychotherapy and Psychosomatics*, 82, 161–169.

References 163

Moran, P., Leese, M., Lee, T., Walters, P., Thornicroft, G. and Mann, A. (2003) Standardised assessment of personality abbreviated scale (SAPAS): Preliminary validation of a brief screen for personality disorder. *British Journal of Psychiatry*, 183, 228–232.

Morse, G., Salyers, M.P. and Rollins, A.L. (2012) Burnout in mental health services: A review of the problem and its remediation. *Administration and Policy in Mental Health*, 39, 1–12.

National Collaborating Center for Mental Health (NICE) (2005) *Depression in Children and Young People: Identification and Management*. London, UK: National Institute for Health and Clinical Excellence.

National Collaborating Center for Mental Health (2010) *The NICE Guideline on the Management and Treatment of Depression in Adults (Updated Edition)*. London, UK: National Institute for Health and Clinical Excellence.

National Confidential Inquiry into Suicide and Homicide by People with Mental Illness (NCISH) (2013) Patient suicide: The impact of service changes: A UK wide study. Manchester: University of Manchester. Available at: www.bbmh.manchester.ac.uk/cmhs/research/centreforsuicideprevention/nci/reports/patientsuicideimpactofservicechangesUKsummary/ (accessed on 27 October 2015).

National Institute for Health and Clinical Excellence (NICE) (2004) Eating disorders Core interventions in the treatment and management of anorexia nervosa, bulimia nervosa and related eating disorders.

National Institute for Health and Clinical Excellence (NICE) (2007) Chronic Fatigue Syndrome/Myalgic Encephalomyelitis (or Encephalopathy): Diagnosis and Management of CFS/ME in Adults and Children (Clinical Guideline CG53).

Newton-Howes, G., Tyrer, P. and Johnson, T. (2006) Personality disorder and the outcome of depression: Metaanalysis of published studies. *British Journal of Psychiatry*, 188, 13–20.

NICE (2011) Understanding NICE guidance: Information for people who use NHS services.

NICE (2015) 'Mental wellbeing and older people' and 'Promoting mental wellbeing at work overview'.

Nicholas, J., Larsen, M.E. and Proudfoot, J. (2015) Mobile apps for bipolar disorder: A systematic review of features and content quality. *Journal of Medical Internet Research*, 17(8), e198.

Norcross, J.C., Campbell, L.F. and Grohol, J.M. (2013) *Self-Help That Works*. Fourth Edition. Oxford: Oxford University Press.

Norcross, John C., Campbell, Linda F., Grohol, John M., Santrock, John W., Selagea, Florin and Sommer, Robert (2013–03–01) *Self-Help That Works: Resources to Improve Emotional Health and Strengthen Relationships (Kindle Locations 13549–13550)*. Oxford: Oxford University Press. Kindle Edition.

Norton, P.J. and Barrera, T.L. (2012) Transdiagnostic versus diagnosis-specific CBT for anxiety disorders: A preliminary randomized controlled non-inferiority trial. *Depression and Anxiety*, 29, 874–882.

Nuttall, J. (2016) 'Working in partnership with IAPT', in *The Future of Psychological Therapy: From Managed Care to Transformational Practice*. Ed. J. Lees. Taylor and Francis. Kindle Edition.

Oud, M., Mayo-Wilson, E. and Braidwood, R. (2016) Psychological interventions for adults with bipolar disorder: Systematic review and meta-analysis. *British Journal of Psychiatry*, 208, 213–222.

Ozer, E.J., Best, S.R. and Lipsey, T.L. (2003) Predictors of posttraumatic stress disorder and symptoms in adults: A meta-analysis. *Psychological Bulletin*, 129, 52–73.

164   *References*

Panagioti, M., Gooding, P.A. and Tarrier, N. (2012) A meta-analysis of the association between post-traumatic stress disorder and suicidality: The role of comorbid depression. *Comprehensive Psychiatry*, 53, 915–930.

Petty, R.E. and Cacioppo, J.T. (1986) The elaboration likelihood model of persuasion. *Advances in Experimental and Social Psychology*, 19, 123–205.

Poulsen, S., Lunn, S. and Daniel, S.I. (2014) A randomised controlled trial of psychoanalytic psychotherapy or cognitive-behavioral therapy for bulimia nervosa. *American Journal of Psychiatry*, 171, 109–116.

Power, M. (2015) *Understanding Happiness: A Critical Review of Positive Psychology*. London: Taylor and Francis. Kindle Edition.

Prins, A., Ouimette, P. and Kimerling, R. (2004) The primary care PTSD screen (PC-PTSD): Development and operating characteristics. *Primary Care Psychiatry*, 9, 9–14.

Prochaska, J.O., DiClemente, C.C. and Norcross, J.C. (1992) In search of how people change: Application to addictive behaviours. *American Psychologist*, 47, 1102–1114.

Rettew, D.C., Lynch, A.D. and Achenbach, T.M. (2009) Meta-analyses of agreement between diagnoses made from clinical evaluations and standardized diagnostic interviews. *International Journal of Methods in Psychiatric Research*, 18, 169–184.

Reynolds, W.M. (2010) The PHQ-9 works well as a screening but not diagnostic instrument for depressive disorder. *Evidence Based Mental Health*, 13, 96.

Ricci, B. and Dixon, L. (2015) What can we do about stigma. *Psychiatric Services*, 66, 1009.

Richards, D.A. and Borglin, G. (2011) Implementation of psychological therapies for anxiety and depression in routine practice: Two year prospective cohort study. *Journal of Affective Disorders*, 133, 51–60.

Rose, S., Bisson, J. and Wessely, S. (2001) A systematic review of brief psychological interventions ('debriefing') for the treatment of immediate trauma related symptoms and the prevention of post-traumatic stress disorder. *Cochrane Library*, 3. Oxford: Update Software, n.p.

Rounsaville, B.J., Dolinsky, Z.S., Babor, T.F. and Meyer, R.E. (1987) Psychopathology as a predictor of treatment outcome in alcoholics. *Archives of General Psychiatry*, June, 44(6), 505–513.

Royal College of Psychiatrists (2011) Do the right thing: How to judge a good ward: Ten standards for adult in-patient mental healthcare (Occasional Paper 79). London: Royal College of Psychiatry. Available at: www.rcpsych.ac.uk/usefulresources/publications/collegereports/op/op79.aspx (accessed on 2 November 2015).

Royal College of Psychiatrists (2014) Report of the second round of the National Audit of Schizophrenia (NAS) 2014. London: Healthcare Quality Improvement Partnership. Available at: www.rcpsych.ac.uk/workinpsychiatry/qualityimprovement/nationalclinicalaudits/schizophrenia/nationalschizophreniaaudit/reports.aspx (accessed on 2 November 2015).

Samuels, D.B. (2015) A review of the agreement between clinicians' personality disorder diagnoses and those from other methods and sources. *Clinical Psychology Science and Practice*, 22, 1–19.

Schildkrout, B. (2014) *Masquerading Symptoms: Uncovering Physical Illnesses That Present as Psychological Problems*. New York: John Wiley.

Scholte, W.F., Verduin, F. and Kamperman, A.M. (2015) The effect on mental health of a large scale psychosocial intervention for survivors of mass violence: A quasi-experimental study in Rwanda. *PLoS ONE*, 6(8), e21819.

Schumacher, E.F. (2011) *Small Is Beautiful: A Study of Economics as If People Mattered*. New York: Random House. Kindle Edition.

References   165

Scott, M.J. (1998) 'Stress and compensation: A critical analysis', in *Industrial Diseases Litigation*. Eds. A. Mc Donald and A. Georges. London: Sweet & Maxwell, pp. 393–403.

Scott, M.J. (2008) *Moving On After Trauma*. London: Routledge.

Scott, M.J. (2011) *Simply Effective Group Cognitive Behaviour Therapy: A Practitioners Guide*. London: Routledge.

Scott, M.J. (2014) *Simply Effective CBT Supervision*. London: Routledge.

Scott, M.J. (2015a) *A Cognitive Behavioural Approach to Client's Problems*. London: Routledge.

Scott, M.J. Ed. (2015b) *Traumatic Stress 4 Volume Work*. London: Sage Publications.

Scott, M.J. and Sembi, S. (2002) Unreliable assessment in civil litigation. *The Psychologist*, 15, 80–81.

Scott, M.J. and Stradling, S.G. (1987) The evaluation of a group parent training programme. *Behavioural Psychotherapy*, 15, 224–239.

Scott, M.J. and Stradling, S.G. (1990) Group cognitive therapy for depression produces clinically significant reliable change in community-based settings. *Behavioural Psychotherapy*, 18, 1–19.

Scott, M.J. and Stradling, S.G. (2001) Translating the psychobiology of post-traumatic stress disorder into clinically useful analogy. *British Journal of Medical Psychology*, 74, 249–254.

Seligman, M.E.P. (2011) *Flourish*. London: Nicholas Brealey Publishing. Kindle Edition.

Shapiro, F. (2001) *Eye Movement Desensitization and Reprocessing (EMDR): Basic Principles, Protocols and Procedures*. New York: Guilford Press.

Sharma, T., Guski, L.S. Freund, N. and Gotsche, P.C (2016) Suicidality and aggression during antidepressant treatment: Systematic review and meta-analyses based on clinical study reports. *BMJ*, 352, i65. http://dx.doi.org/10.1136/bmj.i65

Sharry, J., Davidson, R. and McLoughlin, O. (2013) A service-based evaluation of a therapist-supported online cognitive behavioural therapy programme for depression. *Medical Internet Research*, 15(6), E121.

Shaw, B.F., Elkin, I., Yamagughi, J., Olmsted, M., Vallis, T.M., Dobson, K.S., Lowery, A., Sotsky, S.M., Watkins, J.T. and Imber, S.D. (1999) Therapist competence ratings in relation to clinical outcome in cognitive therapy of depression. *Journal of Consulting and Clinical Psychology*, 67, 837–846.

Shear, M.K., Greeno, C., Kang, J., Ludewig, D., Frank, E., Swartz, H.A. and Hanekamp, M. (2000) Diagnosis of nonpsychotic patients in community clinics. *American Journal of Psychiatry*, 157, 581–587.

Sidley, G.L. (2015) *Tales from the Madhouse: An Insider Critique of Psychiatric Services*. Monmouth: PCCS books.

SIGN (2013) *Management of Chronic Pain: A National Clinical Guideline*. Edinburgh: Scottish Intercollegiates Guidelines Network.

So, M., Yamaguchi, S. and Hashimoto, S. (2013) Is computerised CBT really helpful for adult depression? A meta-analytic re-evaluation of CCBT for adult depression in terms of clinical implementation and methodological validity. *BMC Psychiatry*, 13, 113.

Spitzer, R.L. and Robins, E. (1978) Research diagnostic criteria: Rationale and reliability. *Archives of General Psychiatry*, 35, 773–782.

Spitzer, R.L., Williams, J.B., Gibbon, M. and First, M.B. (1992) The Structured Clinical Interview for DSM-III-R (SCID): I. History, rationale, and description. *Arch Gen Psychiatry*, 49, 624–629.

Steketee, G. and Frost, R.O. (2014) *Treatment for Hoarding Disorder Workbook*. New York: Oxford University Press.

166   *References*

Stewart-Brown, S.L. (2015) Public mental health: An interdisciplinary subject? *British Journal of Psychiatry*, 207, 192–194.

Stewart-Brown, S.L. (In Press) 'Population level: Wellbeing in the general population', in *Wellbeing Recovery and Mental Health*. Eds. M. Slade, L. Oades and A. Jarden. Cambridge: Cambridge University Press.

Stirman, S.W., DeRubeis, R.J., Crits-Christoph, P. and Rothman, A. (2005) Can the randomized controlled trial literature generalize to non-randomized patients? *Journal of Consulting and Clinical Psychology*, 73, 127–135.

Szasz, T.S. (2010) Kindle Edition the myth of mental illness. Foundation of a Theory of Personal Conduct.

Tennant, R., Hiller, L. and Fishwick, R. (2007) The Warwick-Edinburgh Mental Well-Being Scale (WEMWBS): Development and UK validation. *Health Quality of Life Outcomes* 5, 63.

Thase, M.E., Entsuah, A.R. and Rudolph, R.L. (2001) Remission rates during treatment with venlafaxine or selective serotonin reuptake inhibitors. *British Journal of Psychiatry*, 178, 234–241.

Tolin, D.F. (2014) Beating a dead dodo bird: Looking at signal vs. noise on cognitive-behavioral therapy for anxiety disorders. *Clinical Psychology and Practice*, 21, 351–362.

Tolin, D.F., McKay, D., Forman, E.M., Klonsky, E.D. and Thombs, B.D. (2015) Empirically supported treatment: Recommendations for a new model. *Clinical Psychology Science and Practice*, 22, 317–338.

Trepka, C. (1986) Attrition from an out-patient psychology clinic. *British Journal of Medical Psychology*, 59, 181–186.

Vittengl, J.R., Clark, L.A., Dunn, T.W. and Jarrett, R.B. (2007) Reducing relapse and recurrence in unipolar depression: A comparative meta-analysis of cognitive-behavioral therapy's effects. *Journal of Consulting and Clinical Psychology*, 75, 475–488.

Watts, J. (2016) 'IAPT and the ideal image', in *The Future of Psychological Therapies*. Ed. J. Lees. London: Routledge, n.p.

Weiss, R.L. and Margolin, G. (1977) 'Marital conflict and accord', in *Handbook for Behavioral Assessment*. Eds. A.R. Ciminero, K.S. Chalhoun and H.E. Adams. New York: Wiley, n.p.

Wertham, F. (1968) *A Sign for Cain: An Exploration of Human Violence*. London: Hale.

Westbrook, D. and Kirk, J. (2005) The clinical effectiveness of cognitive behaviour therapy: Outcome for a large sample of adults treated in routine practice. *Behaviour Research and Therapy*, 43, 1243–1261.

White, J., Keenan, M. and Brooks, N. (1992) Stress control: A controlled comparative investigation of large group therapy for generalised anxiety disorder. *Behavioural Psychotherapy*, 20, 97–114.

White, J., Keenan, M. and Brooks, N. (1995) Stress control: A controlled comparative investigation of large group therapy for generalized anxiety disorder. *Behavioural Psychotherapy*, 20, 97–114.

White, P.D., Chalder, T. and Sharpe, M. (2015) The planning, implementation and publication of a complex intervention trial for chronic fatigue syndrome: The PACE trial. *British Journal of Psychiatry Bulletin*, 39, 24–27. DOI: 10.1192/pb.bp.113.045005

Williams, C. (2014) *Overcoming Depression: A Five Areas Approach*. Florida: CRC Press.

Williams, C., Wilson, P. and Morrison, J. (2013) Guided self-help cognitive behavioural therapy for depression in primary care: A Randomised controlled trial. *PLoS ONE*, 8(1), e52735. DOI: 10.1371/journal.pone.0052735

Winerman, L. (2013) NIMH funding to shift away from DSM categories. American Psychological Association, July/August 2013. Available at: www.apa.org/monitor/2013/07–08/nimh.aspx (accessed on 25 March 2013).

References 167

Wittkampf, K., van Ravesteijen, H. and Baas, K. (2009) The accuracy of Patient Health Questionnaire-9 in detecting depression and measuring depression severity in high-risk groups in primary care. *General Hospital Psychiatry*, 31, 451–459.

Woody, G.E., McLellan, A.T., Luborsky, L. and O'Brien, C.P. (1985, November) Sociopathy and psychotherapy outcome. *Archives of General Psychiatry*, 42(11), 1081–1086.

World Health Organisation (2004) Promoting mental health: Concepts emerging evidence and practice. Summary report. Geneva.

World Health Organisation (2010) International statistical classification of diseases and related health problems 10th revision (ICD-10). Geneva.

Young, J. and Beck, A.T. (1980) *Cognitive Therapy Rating Scale: Rating Manual*. Unpublished Manuscript. Philadelphia: Centre for Cognitive Therapy, University of Pennsylvania.

Zimmerman, M. and Mattia, J.I. (1999) Psychiatric diagnosis in clinical practice: Is comorbidity being missed? *Comprehensive Psychiatry*, 40, 182–191.

Zimmerman, M. and Mattia, J.I. (2000) Principal and additional disorders for which outpatients seek treatment. *Psychiatric Services*, 51, 1299–1304.

Index

accomplishment, absence 131–2
achievement/pleasure, investment *142*
acute psychotic episode 90
addictions alcohol/drugs category 39
ADHD *see* attention deficit hyperactivity disorder
ADIS *see* Anxiety Disorders Interview Schedule
adolescents, mental health problems 74–5
adult attention deficit hyperactivity disorder 18
Advertising Standards Authority, criticism 57–8
agency, fuzzies (interaction) 80
AIDS, stigma 31
alcohol abuse 96
Alcoholics Anonymous (AA), impact 39–40
alcohol misuse services, commissioning 74
Alice's Adventures in Wonderland (Carroll) 51
American Declaration of Independence 15–16
American National Institute for Mental Health, research funding (cessation) 52–3
American Psychological Associations Division of Clinical Psychology, psychological therapies list 114
anger 69
Annual World Mental Health Day Festival 8
antidepressants: CBT, combination 101; prescribing 37–8, 99
anti-psychiatry/anti-medical model flavour, diagnostic interviews 109
anti-psychiatry movement 51; advocacy 52–3; development 71; exemplification 52
anxiety: client treatment, review 81; GHS intervention 65; IAPT programme,

attrition/recovery *82*; stand-alone test screen, operation 99; term, offering 12
anxiety disorders 18, 24–5, 56; diagnosable problem 74–5; self-help, Cochrane review 65
Anxiety Disorders Interview Schedule (ADIS) 49; testing 109
applications (apps): app-based self-delivered treatments 87; usage 59–60
Areas of Change Questionnaire (ACQ) 30
assessments: mental health assessments, demand 120; reliability, making (problems) 119–20
associated stigma 34–5
"Asylums" (Goffman) 71
attention deficit hyperactivity disorder (ADHD) 47–8, 50; diagnosable problem 74–5; diagnosis 18–19; label 19
attitude problem 149–51
attitudes *149*
autism 50
autism spectrum disorder 47–8
automatic negative thought, cross-examination 145
avoidance, decrease 62
avoidant personality disorder 95

BABCP *see* British Association of Behavioural and Cognitive Psychotherapy
BACP *see* British Association of Counseling and Psychotherapy
Beating the Blues 65, 93
Beck, Aaron 18, 106
Beck Depression Inventory Score: BDI-II score, reduction 77; requirement 77; ten-point reduction 59
Beck Depression Inventory, usage 55, 110
behavioural change 84

Berger, Luciana 70
"best practice" 89
best practice, assessment 118–19
Bethlehem Hospital 70
Big Pharma, product property 79–80
biological markers, absence 71
bipolar disorders 36, 50; psychological
therapies, access (increase) 73
blissful happiness 15–16
blood chemistry screening test, GP
arrangement 83
body dysmorphic disorder 95
bogus change 85–6
British Association for Behavioural and
Cognitive Psychotherapies (BABCP)
30–1, 76, 83
British Association of Counseling and
Psychotherapy (BACP), accredited
therapists list 76
British Psychological Society (BPS) 76,
83, 131; survey results 11
bulimia sufferer (case) 74

CAMHS See Child and Adolescent Mental
Health Services
Canadian Task Force on Preventative
Health Care, recommendations 99
cancer, stigma 31
Care Programme Approach 73
Care Quality Commission (CQC):
concerns 2; 24/7 crisis service 71–2
Carers UK (support group) 40–1
Carroll, Lewis 51
Case formulation 28
CBT Café 84
CCGs see Clinical Commissioning Groups
change, stages: basis 40; support groups,
impact 39–40
charities: impact 128; NHS, relationship 90
chats, examples 62–4
Child and Adolescent Mental Health Services
(CAMHS) 75; access standard 75
childhood depressive disorder, effect sizes 69
childhood somatic disorders, effect sizes 69
children: attention deficit hyperactivity
disorder (ADHD) 47–8; attention
deficit hyperactivity disorder (ADHD),
epidemic 18–19; autism spectrum
disorder 47–8; mental health problems
74–5; stigmatisation 18
Children and Young People's Improving
Access to Psychological Therapies
(CYPIAPT) programme, roll-out 75
chronic pain, effect sizes 69

Cinderella status 72
Clegg, Nick 30–1
clients: engagement/maintenance,
failure 81–2; recovery, absence 101;
satisfaction 97; self-referral proportion
80; telephone assessments 44; therapy,
fitting 100–1; treatment, review 81
"climate" change 43
Clinical Commissioning Groups (CCGs)
90, 101, 111; budget 70; concerns 2;
engagement 91; fidelity 123–4; impact
120; target, missing 69–70
clinical judgment: deleterious effects
19–20; diagnosis, relationship 20
clinical significance 117
Cochrane review 65
co-existing problems, addressing
(absence) 87
Cognitive Analytic Therapy 74
cognitive assessment, absence 100
*Cognitive Behavioural Approach to
Clients' Problems* 134
cognitive-behavioural therapy (CBT):
antidepressants, combination
101; Beating the Blues 93; C
recommendation 86–7; depressive
symptoms, resolution 56; evidence-
based psychotherapies 42; evidence-
based treatment 41; group CBT,
engagement 46; groups, evidence-based
treatment protocol 115; guided self-
help (GSH) intervention 65; meta-
analysis 88; positive response 83; RCTs
101; RCTs, contrast 77; relationship
therapy 30; skill training course, usage
6; studies 38; therapists, G4S 117;
therapists, importance 118; training
courses 20; trauma-focussed CBT,
usage 113; treatment 34; treatment,
psychoeducation component 55
cognitive behaviour therapy, treatment
promise 69
Cognitive Therapy Rating Scale (CTRS):
development 122; disagreements, usage
122–3; inter-rater reliability 122–3;
validity 125
"Coming Off Antidepressants,"
publication 38
Community Mental Health Teams
(CMHTs): 24/7 crisis service 71–2;
weekly visits 72
comorbidity: assessment 66; norm 45;
specialist NHS facilities, impact
(failure) 87

170 Index

compensation cases, study sample 92–3

competence: engine *124*, 124–5; three-dimensional view 124–5

compulsive self-reliance, developmental origins 36

computer-aided self-help therapy 89

computerised CBT (CCBT): direct access 65; usage 59

conduct disorders 50; diagnosable problem 74–5

confidence-based mental health practice 44

conflicts of interest, transparency 89

congenital scarring 95

consciousness, altered state 90

"Control Your Depression" (Lewinsohn, et al.) 60, 62

coper, being 32

counseling, psychodynamically flavour 58

Coyne, James 15

CQC *see* Care Quality Commission

Craiglockhart 52, 71

credible practitioners 83

crises 71–2; mental health services, in-patients (contact) 72; positive symptoms, impact 79; 24/7 crisis service 71–2

Crisis Intervention Services 85

CTRS *see* Cognitive Therapy Rating Scale

cut-offs, employment 98–9

CYPIAPT *See* Children and Young People's Improving Access to Psychological Therapies

Database of Abstracts of Reviews of Effects (DARE) 113

déjà vu, sense 53

demonstrated efficacy, PTSD 18

dependence, screen *56*

depression 36; analogy 145; ball and chain, relationship *146*; client treatment, review 81; continuation *140, 141*; CTRS validity 125; development, likelihood 129; development, process/continuation 140–1; diagnosable problem 75; diagnostic symptom 61; double depression 152; DSM diagnostic criteria 99; early warning signs 154; effect sizes 69; evidence-based treatment 96; GSH evaluation 77; IAPT programme, attrition/recovery *82*; kappa, usage 107; occurrence 147–8; older people, impact 78; overcoming 152; presentation 66; psychotherapy candidate 100; recovery, predictor 45; screening questions 57;

stand-alone test screen, operation 99; stepping stones *153*; suffering 95–6; survival manuals 56, 140; term, offering 12; treatment fidelity scales *123*

depression, CBT: RCTs, contrast 77; studies, meta-analysis 108; study (Beck) 107; superiority, detection (failure) 114

"Depression Survival Manual, The" 57

depressive disorders, GSH intervention 65

depressive symptoms, resolution 56

diagnosis: application 26; clinical judgment, relationship 20; concept 51–2; dangers 27–8; establishment 108; formulation 28; idea, jettisoning 52–3; interrater reliability *47*; language 18; meaning 26; problem, defining 25–26; recourse, absence 51; selection, decision 27; unreliability 88

diagnostic creep, overstatement 17

diagnostic criteria, refinement 17–18

diagnostic interview: anchor 98–9; anti-psychiatry/anti-medical model flavour 109; findings 110; time consumption 110–11; unreliability 105

difficulties, motivation (issues) 78–9

direct access 82–3

discharge, arbitrary criteria 97

disorders: combinations 91–2; fine-grained distinctions 119–20; mis-identification 99; motivation, issue 78–9; predictor, recovery 45; psychological disorders 46; recovery rate variation *98*; support groups 39; treatment, medical model 50–1

disruptive mood dysregulation disorder 18

Dodo verdict 51, 111; therapist belief 114

Donne, John 43

double depression 152

Drew, David 128

dropout, term usage (avoidance) 96

drug misuse 50

DSM-5: development 17; field trials, diagnoses (interrated reliability) *47*; "Other Conditions That May Be a Focus of Clinical Attention" category 29–30; problems 55; publication 58–9; reliability, distillation 106–7; symptom criteria 26

DSM-III, diagnostic criteria 58–9

DSM-IV, development 50–1

DSM-IV-TR: predecessor 59; stricture 19

DSM problems 18–19; impact 29–30

DSM reliability, assessment 49

duration of untreated illness (DUI) 36

Index 171

eating disorders, apps (usage) 59–60
ECBI *see* Eyberg Child Behavior Inventory
ECT, usage 100
effect size (ES) 14
Elaboration Likelihood Model of
  Persuasion 33
eloquence-based mental health practice 44
EMDR *See* Eye Movement Desensitisation
  Reprocessing
eminence-based mental health practice 44
eminence-based treatment 87, 89
emotional avoidance 152
emotion, intrapsychic/interpersonal
  determinants *42*
empirically supported psychological
  therapies, criteria 155
employee burnout, interventions
  (effectiveness) 131–2
enthusiasm, dangers 66
esteem, parity 69
ESTs *see* evidence-based treatments
evaluations, mirror image 88
evidence: documentary evidence 125;
  levels 86–7; question 134
evidence-based practice (EBP): model *112*;
  occurrence, doubt 43; re-examination
  112–14; research evidence, impact 112;
  term, usage 111
evidence-based psychological therapies:
  access, increase 70; delivery 92
evidence-based psychological treatment,
  provision 72
evidence-based psychotherapies 42, 91,
  96; NICE advocacy 120; provision 116
evidence-based treatments (EBTs) 2, 41;
  delivery 79; fidelity, ensuring 123–4;
  protocol 125; response, absence 121;
  translation (prevention), assessment
  unreliability (impact) 50–1
evidence-supported treatments (ESTs) 2,
  111; equivalence 155
excoriation disorder 95
expectation, experience (relationship)
  146–7, *147*
expediency, price payment 108
exposure therapy, effectiveness 112
Eyberg Child Behavior Inventory (ECBI)
  6; completion 26; list, impact 29–30
Eye Movement Desensitisation
  Reprocessing (EMDR) 19; switch 123

face-to-face assessment 41–2; session
  (IAPT) 95

face-to-face CBT 55
face-to-face contact 126
face-to-face support appointments 77–8
face-to-face therapy: impact 60; session 119
face-to-face treatment 65
false positives, production 56–7
fear factor 32
Feighner criteria 58–9
fidelity: elements 122–3; infidelity,
  countering 123–4
field studies (FS) 88
file drawer problem 38
findings, replication (funding) 89
flexibility, elements 122–3
Flourish (Seligman) 13
fluoxetine, usage 38
formulation 28
Frances, Allen 50–1
friends/family: questioning, enabling 43–4;
  socially significant change 42–3
full functioning, return 57–8
Functional Analysis Assessment 108
functioning, restoration 118
future, negative view *152*
fuzzies, agency (interaction) 80

GAD-7 95; assessment 93; depression/
  anxiety measures 95; measure 106;
  score 97, 100; usage 98–9
generalised anxiety disorder (GAD) 36;
  diagnostic symptom 61; effect sizes 69;
  referral source 37; two-item scale 57
general practitioners (GPs): appointment
  24; blood chemistry screening
  test, arrangement 83; concerns 2;
  consultation, absence 54; depression
  presentation 66; PHQ-9 administration
  85; practices, counsellor/psychologist
  employment 76; prescription 12; referral
  74; self-reference 20
general practitioners (GPs) records 92;
  details 31; review 41–2
Goffman, Erving 71
"gold standard" diagnostic interview 80
Google, usage 36–7
group intervention, effectiveness 115
group programme 131
guided self-help (GSH) 62, 65;
  attractiveness 66; CBT, usefulness
  66; evaluation 77; provision 76;
  psychological therapy, contrast 76–8;
  studies, improvement 77–8; usage,
  importance 77

172　*Index*

Hamilton Depression Rating Scale (HDRS) 106
Hamilton Depression score 86
Hamilton Rating Scale for Depression, administration 37
Hammond, Phillip 128
happiness, pursuit 15–16
hassles, encounter 145
HDRS *See* Hamilton Depression Rating Scale
Headway (support group) 40–1
Health and Safety Executive, stress definition 10–11
health mental programmes, evaluation (history) 58–9
high-intensity interventions 134
Hillsborough Football tragedy (1988) 45–6, 121

ICD 10 criteria, World Health Organisation usage 107
illness: burden 70; initial declaration 35
Improving Access to Psychological Therapy (IAPT) 2, 12; access 70; Annual Report (2013-2014) 80, 81; Annual Report (2014-2015) 96; care pathway 92–4; challenge 90; claim, recovery rate 86; clinicians, interaction 84; contact 92; disorders, mis-identification 99; documentation, anonymised example *94*; embarkation process, problems 94; exit 96–7; experience 93; face-to-face assessment session 95; focus 79; full recovery criteria 95; government funding 76, 105; interventions 86, 116; low-intensity worker 46; outcome *98*; overextension, danger 80; presentations 131; psychological therapy programme 86; quantitative evaluation 97; reach 92; referrals 83; service, positioning 126; service users, performance 91–2; sessions 95–6; success 105–6; success criteria 90; vision, restricted field 95; workers, confidence/competence (absence) 73; yardstick, problems 98–9
Improving Access to Psychological Therapy (IAPT) Programme (programme) 13; attrition/recovery *82*; reference 72
Improving Access to Psychological Therapy (IAPT) Service 82–3; funding 20
inappropriate treatment 105
ineffectiveness, sense 131–2

infidelity, countering 123–4
information processing biases *148*; usage 121–2
information-processing bias, usage (risk) 112
in-patient service, access 70
insecure attachment, developmental origins 36
Insel, Thomas 1
in-session written records 125–6
Institute of Psychiatry (IoP) 94
institutionalised discrimination 52
interest, loss 26
intermittent explosive disorder (IED), changes 99–100
internalized stigma 31–2
Internet-based self-help, effectiveness 65
Internet, usage 55
intervention: decision making 108–9; dissemination 134; effectiveness, reassurance (problem) 105–6; efficacy 85; group intervention, effectiveness 115; high-intensity interventions 134; large-group interventions 115–16; low-intensity intervention, offering 93; minimum 89; precipitous intervention 89–90; transdiagnostic intervention 115
interview: screen, usage 120; steps 136–8
investments, absence 142–3
I Will Listen program 35

Johnson, Alan 109
Judeo-Christian tradition, reflection 16

kappa 46–8; usage 107
Kings Fund, document 92

large groups, interventions 115–16
leprosy, stigma 31
liberal-progressive meta-narrative 51–2
Lieberman, Jeffrey 35
Life of Reason, The (Santayana) 106
local charities 45
London Institute of Psychiatry 70
long-term mental health problems 72
low-income families, children (risk) 75
low-intensity intervention, offering 93
low self-esteem, lifting *150*

marital distress 69
Masquerading Symptoms (Schildkrout) 83
media-delivered interventions, short-term/ long-term effectiveness 65
medico-legal examinations 91

mental health: assessments, demand
120; Cinderella status 72; depression
category 39; distribution *7*; eating
disorders category 39; effectiveness,
claims (interrogation process)
58; governance, inadequacy 111;
initiatives, problems 120–1; issues,
resolution 128; National Institute for
Health and Care Excellence, documents
8; practices, types 44; psychosis/
schizophrenia category 39; services,
in-patient contact 72; stepped care,
relationship 90–1; support groups
39; values, relationship 15–16; WHO
definition 5; workers, burnout rate
131–2
mental health problems: children/
adolescents 74–5; GP consultations,
proportion 76–7; onset 62; orientation,
relationship 24–5
mental health system 133; creation 105;
improvement 1
Mental Health Taskforce: formation
30–1; government appointment
70; psychological therapies access,
investment 73
mental illness: construing 52; idea,
jettisoning 52–3; perception 32;
problem/responsibility, identification
79–80; severe mental illness 72–3;
stigma 35
mental well-being (MWB): improvement,
NHS advice *6*; National Institute for
Health and Care Excellence, documents
8; stress, relationship 5; term, shift 11;
value, money (relationship) 6–7
mild neurocognitive disorder 18
MIND (charity) 75, 90
Mind (charity) 45
Mirtazepine, prescribing 99
"Mixed anxiety and depression," kappa
level 47–8
mobile-device applications, usage 59
mobile e-therapy programme 59
Mobile Mental Health (m-Health), usage 34
monitoring, care 89–90
MOOD chart *144*; usage 149–150
mood, management 62
Moody Gym 65
motivation, therapies (impact) 79
Moving On After Trauma (Scott) 34, 46,
57, 61, 62
multi-disciplinary teamwork, problems 126
"Myth of Mental Illness, The" 71

National Center for PTSD 46
national charities 45
National Health Service (NHS): advice
6; charities, relationship 90; practice
57; provision, shortcomings 76;
psychological therapy, conducting
107–8; specialist facilities, impact
87; trauma clinic, effectiveness
(evaluation) 118–19; working
conditions 128
National Institute for Health and
Care Excellence: documents 8;
recommendations 99
National Institute of Clinical Excellence
(NICE): Guidelines 38, 73–4;
guidelines 64–5, 71, 88; interventions
recommendation 72–3; NICE-
concordant services, delivery 73;
treatment guidelines 37, 50
Nazi Germany, stigmatisation 34
negative spin 147–8
negative support 43
NICE *see* National Institute for Health and
Care Excellence
non-academic therapists, usage 111
non-psychiatrists, therapeutic skills 73
normality, treatment 95

Obsessive Beliefs Questionnaire or Post-
traumatic Cognitions Inventory 100
Obsessive Compulsive Disorder
(OCD) 39
obsessive-compulsive disorder (OCD) 36,
99; telephone calls, usage 119
older people, depression (impact) 78
open-ended interviews 48; semi-structured
interviews, agreement (problem) 49;
usage 110
Open-ended interview, usage 28
open-ended psychiatric interview 48
Open Science Collaboration 88
operationalized diagnostic criteria,
systematic use 58–9
Oppositional Defiant Disorder (ODD),
DSM-5 criteria (meeting) 27–8
"Other Conditions That May Be a Focus of
Clinical Attention" category 29–30
other disorders, apps (usage) 60
outcome, self-report measures 65
*Overcoming Depression: A Five Areas
Approach* (Williams) 57, 77
overdiagnosis 99–100
overtreatment 99–100
Own, Wilfred 52

174 *Index*

pain-management programmes 74
panic attacks 54; management 116
panic disorder 36, 50, 119; effect sizes 69
panic, management 33
Paroxetine, usage 38
"Pathways to Mental Health" 133
PDS *see* Posttraumatic Diagnostic Scale
perceived expectations 129
perceived social support 41
perceived stigmatisation 32–3
perceived workload 129
personal injury 87
personality disorders 50; problem/
 responsibility, identification 79–80;
 psychological therapies, access
 (increase) 73
personality, standardised assessment
 (abbreviated scale) 139
PHQ-9 95; administration 85; depression/
 anxiety measures 95; metric 106;
 predictive value, reduction 105–6; score
 83, 86, 97, 100; self-report measure,
 usage 106; specificity, inadequacy 105;
 telephone assessment 93; usage 98–9
physiology, management 116
pick and mix, usage 29
pleasure, loss 26
political correctness 91
population, defining (problem) 88
positive psychology 13; advocacy
 13; psychological therapy, balance
 (achievement) 14–15; socially
 significant difference 14
positive, recollection 146–7
"Postcode Lottery for Mental Health
 Talking Therapies" 69–70
Posttraumatic Diagnostic Scale (PDS),
 administration 118–19
post-traumatic stress disorder (PTSD):
 agreement 107; autism, combination
 (treatment) 113; cardinal symptoms 48;
 CBT treatment 34; comorbid condition
 87; confines, extension 19; diagnosis
 33, 118; diagnostic symptom 61; effect
 sizes 69; exposure therapy, effectiveness
 112; management, social support
 predictor 62–3; onset, prevention 15;
 overrepresentation 91–2; prevention
 13, 14; psychobiology, translation 52;
 psychotherapy candidate 100; recovery
 79; recovery, predictor 45, 134; risk/
 protective factors, meta-analytical
 studies 41; screen *56*; screening question
 55; screening symptom questions 57;

selective serotonin reuptake inhibitors
 (SSRIs), comparison 37; sufferers,
 SCID identification 48; suffering 26, 80;
 survival manual 46
practitioners *see* general practitioners:
 credible practitioners 83; voice 84
precipitous intervention 89–90
presenteeism 131
preventative capacity, overstatement 17
primary care, impact 72
principles, set (adherence) 53
privacy, value 36–7
private practice 76
problem *149*; defining, psychometric tests
 (usage) 26–7; lists, modus operandi
 28–9; orientation, mental health
 (relationship) 24–5
problem solving 23; process 27
proof, burden 87
psychiatric disorders, agreement levels
 (DSM-5) 46–8
psychiatric outpatients, context 98–9
psychiatric social work, re-launching 29
psychiatric symptoms, elimination 53
psychiatrists, gatekeeper role 73
psychoanalysis, idiosyncratic
 formulations 108
psychoeducation 55–7; focus 62;
 introduction 116; usage 39
psychological assessment 84
psychological debriefing (PD), effects 25
psychological disorder 46, 51–3; absence
 10–11, 54–5; biological markers,
 absence 71; evidence-based treatments,
 diagnosis specificity 50; language 50;
 recovery, mechanics *53*, 53–5; social
 support 39
psychological practitioners, stress level 134
psychological records, vagueness 125
psychological sciences, laboratory
 findings 88
psychological services, provision 117
psychological therapists: British Psychological
 Society survey 127; communications,
 impact 125–6; face-to-face contact 126;
 goals, impossibility 131–2
psychological therapy 72; availability 66;
 criteria, summary 155; guided self-help,
 contrast 76–8; positive psychology,
 balance 14–15; programme 86;
 refusal 31; requirements 107–8; social
 significance 109–11; social significance,
 maintenance 117; trading standards,
 ensuring 121–2; usage, importance 77

Index   175

psychological therapy services: availability 69; consequence 99; quality 81

psychological treatment: example 25; initiation 119; questioning, friends/family (enabling) 43–4

Psychological Wellbeing Practitioners 84

psychological well-being practitioners (PWPs) 76, 93; training 94

psychometric tests: impact 27; selection, decision 27; usage 26–7, 122

Psychometric tests, usage 110

psychosis 50; psychological therapies, access (increase) 73; risk 17; services, early intervention 72

psychotropic medication, appropriateness 37–8

publication bias 89

public health intervention 115–16

PWPS *see* psychological well-being practitioners

quality control 85

questionnaire, steps 136–8

randomised controlled trials (RCTs) 29, 120; ambivalence 87–8; meta-analyses 69; protocols, testing 112

readability 61

Real diseases, belief 18

recovery: approach 53; mechanics *53, 53–5*; notion, operationalisation 110; predictor 45; rate, variation *98*; societal stigma, impact 54; term, usage 96

referral pathways, complexity 74

reflex, criticism 152

relapse, prevention 153–4

"Relationship Distress With Spouse or Intimate Partner" 30

relationships, management 62

reliability 46–8; increase 49

Research Diagnostic Criteria, development 107

research domain criteria 126

Research Domain Criteria (RDoC) 126

resources, demands (excess) 129–31, *130*

return, absence 142–3

Richmond Fellowship 90

Rose Hypothesis *7*

routine assessments, unreliability 48–9

routine practice, EBT translation prevention (assessment unreliability) 50–1

Santayana, George 106

"save normal," requirement 99

Saving Normal (Frances) 89

Schildkrout, Barbara 83

schizophrenia 36

SCID *see* Structured Clinical Interview for DSM-IV

science, values (relationship) 9–10

Scott, Michael J. 1

secondary care: access 70; evidence-based psychological treatments 73; non-psychiatrists, therapeutic skills 73; psychiatrists, gatekeeper role 73; specialists units, relationship 73–4

secondary mental health services, usage 73

selective serotonin reuptake inhibitors (SSRIs), comparison 37

self, attitude 150–2

self-efficacy, sense 36

self-harm, problem 70

self-help: computer-aided self-help therapy 89; delivery process 64–5; effectiveness 64–5; guided self-help 62; helping, guidance (paucity) 62–4; Internet-based self-help, effectiveness 65; materials, usage 34, 60, 62; scope 66; stand alone self-help 62; strengths/limits 59; usage, individual difficulties (impact) 61

self-help books: reading age 61; usage 60

self-labelling, presupposition 40–1

self-perception *151*

self-report 51; measures 59

Seligman, Martin 13

semi-structured diagnostic interview 91

semi-structured interviews, open-ended interviews (agreement problem) 49

sertraline, usage 38

service, therapists (bi-directional relationship) 113

service users, IAPT performance 91–2

severe mental illness 72–3

SFT *see* Solution-focussed Therapy

shell shock 52; suffering 70–1

Short Flourishing Scale 15

SIGN: evidence levels 87; grades, usage 86–7

Silverline 54

single-session PD, effects 25

skill acquisition, motivation 36

skin picking, disorder 95, 100

Skype, usage 55

Sleepio 59

sleep, management 116

socially significant change: demand 106; friends/family, arbiters 42–3

social phobia 99; effect sizes 69

176 *Index*

social services, impact 128
social significance, substitute tests (dangers) 117–18
social support 39; perceived social support 41; therapeutic neglect 41–2
societal stigma, impact 54
sociotherapy 7–8
Solution-focussed Therapy (SFT) 113
specialist unit: access 70; secondary care, relationship 73–4
stand alone self-help 62
Standardised Assessment of Personality Abbreviated Scale (SAPAS) 57
standardised diagnostic interviews 109
stepped care, mental health (relationship) 90–1
stigma 30–1; associated stigma 34–5; internalized stigma 31–2; reduction, efforts 33–4; societal creation 34; societal stigma, impact 54
stigmatisation: perception 32–3; treatment stigmatisation 33
stress 10–11; Health and Safety Executive definition 10–11; mental well-being, relationship 5; post-traumatic stress disorder (PTSD), prevention 13–15; term, offering 12
Stress Control Programme 115–16; appearance 86
stressor related disorders 11–12
Structured Clinical Interview for DSM-IV (SCID): conducting 118–19; diagnostic interview 99–100; diagnostic interview, post-treatment usage 119; gold standard 49; gold-standard diagnostic interview 105; initiation, open-ended interview (usage) 110; interview, usage 48; standardised semi structured interview 49; testing 109
subjective well-being, effect size 14
substance abuse/dependence, screen *56*
substance misuse services, commissioning 74
substitute tests, dangers 117–18
sufferers, treatment unavailability 69–70
suicidal behaviour 78; crisis teams, impact 78
suicidality, risk (increase) 38
suicide rates, increase 78
supervisors, therapists (agreement levels) 122–3
support groups: dimensionality, absence 45–6; strengths/weaknesses 40–1; umbrella, function 39–40
support, insufficiency 44
support providers, negative responses 43

survival fear 90
symptoms: assessment, psychometric tests (usage) 110; simultaneous presence, identification 49
Szasz, Thomas 71

Tales of the Madhouse (Sidley) 52
task-centered social work: movement 58; usage 28–9
Task-Centred Book (Marsh/Doel) 29
TAU 77–8
telephone assessment PHQ-9 93
telephone guided self-help 94–5
temper tantrums 18
therapeutic effectiveness, absence 66
therapeutic skill, measure (focus) 124
therapies: equality 111; historical problems 58
therapists: performance 85; service, bi-directional relationship 113; supervisors, agreement levels 122–3
therapy misconceptions, dispelling 33–4
Thrive (Layard/Clark) 13
time, healer role 24–5
toxic environment, goal 131
toxic negative thought, identification 145
transdiagnostic intervention 115
"Trauma and Stressor Related Disorders," DSM-5 category 11–12
trauma-focussed CBT, usage 113
trauma, management 33
treatment: adherence 77; ambivalence 23–4; delivery, mode (flexibility) 119; failure, mis-attribution 88; foundation reliability, absence 108–9; inappropriate treatment 105; minimalist approach, BABCP condemnation 84; mirror image 88; outcome 97; planning 108–9; response, failure 97; satisfaction 97; stigmatisation 33
"Treatment for Hoarding Disorder Workbook" 62
treatment gap (TG), presence 69–70

UK population, reading age 61
uncertainty 25
understandability 61
United States National Institute for Mental Health, focus 126

values: mental health, relationship 15–16; science, relationship 9–10
values, set (adherence) 53
vehemence-based mental health practice 44
vision, restricted field 95

"wait and see" policy 89
Warwick-Edinburgh Mental Well-being
Scale (WEMWBS): development
5; psychological disorder score 51;
statements 135
"Way Ahead for Adult Acute Mental
Healthcare Provision, The" (Royal
College of Psychiatrists) 71–2
web therapy programme 59

Wessely, Simon 70
whistleblowers, impact 128
Williams, Chris 57
Windows 10, usage 60
workplace bullying, experience 95–6
World Health Organization (WHO),
mental health definition 5
World Mental Health Day 109
wounded healers 127